SAT*II SUCCESS
Physics

Gary Graff

THOMSON
—— *——
PETERSON'S™

Australia • Canada • Mexico • Singapore • Spain • United Kingdom • United States

About The Thomson Corporation and Peterson's

With revenues approaching US$6 billion, The Thomson Corporation (www.thomson.com) is a leading global provider of integrated information solutions for business, education, and professional customers. Its Learning businesses and brands (www.thomsonlearning.com) serve the needs of individuals, learning institutions, and corporations with products and services for both traditional and distributed learning.

Peterson's, part of The Thomson Corporation, is one of the nation's most respected providers of lifelong learning online resources, software, reference guides, and books. The Education Supersite[SM] at www.petersons.com—the Internet's most heavily traveled education resource—has searchable databases and interactive tools for contacting U.S.-accredited institutions and programs. In addition, Peterson's serves more than 105 million education consumers annually.

Artwork by Timothy J. Finley

Editorial Development: Sonya Kapoor Turner

Special thanks to my wife, Faye, and Mrs. Cathy Walton.

For more information, contact Peterson's, 2000 Lenox Drive, Lawrenceville, NJ 08648; 800-338-3282; or find us on the World Wide Web at www.petersons.com/about.

ISBN 0-7689-0960-0

Printed in the United States of America

10 9 8 7 6 5 4 3 2 1   04 03 02

CONTENTS

Red Alert 1

About the Book 1

About the Physics Test 2
    Scoring 3
    Taking the Test 3

SAT II Physics Study Plans 4
    Preliminary Preparations 5
    The 18-week Plan 6
    The 9-Week Plan 8
    Panic Plan 9

Key Formulas and Equations 11

Units and Conversions 12

Diagnostic Test 13

Answers and Explanations 31

Chapter 1: Preliminary Concepts 45

Simple Equations and Algebra 47

Graphs 48

Right Triangles 52

Units and Conversions 56

Scalars and Vectors 57

Chapter Summary 67

Chapter 2: Mechanics 69

Statics 71

Torques 77

Kinematics 80

Motion in Two Dimensions.......................... 87

Newton's Laws of Motion 90

Work and Energy 96

Momentum.. 100

Circular and Rotary...................................... 103

Chapter Summary 109

Chapter 3: Waves 113

Wave Properties 115

Chapter Summary.. 135

Chapter 4: Heat and Thermodynamics 137

Temperature.. 139

Thermal Properties of Matter 140

Thermodynamics 149

Chapter Summary 160

Chapter 5: Electricity and Electromagnetism 161

Electrostatics 163

Electric Fields 166

Electric Circuits 168

Magnets and Magnetic Fields 179

Chapter Summary 191

CONTENTS

Chapter 6: Modern Physics 193

Particulate Theory of Light 195

Photoelectric Effect 198

Relativity 201

Chapter Summary 211

Chapter 7: The Atom 213

The Atom 215

Radioactivity 224

Particles 232

Chapter Summary 234

Practice Test 1 237

Practice Test 2 271

Practice Test 3 305

Practice Test 4 337

RED ALERT

ABOUT THE BOOK

Now that you have decided to tackle the SAT II Physics Test, you need to develop a plan to maximize your chances of achieving a high score. The reason you want a high score is simple. The higher your score, the better you look to the admissions officers at the college of your choice.

The SAT II Physics Test is designed to measure the knowledge and achievement of high school students who have completed a college preparatory physics class. This book will help you review for the SAT II Physics Test. If you have *not* taken a Physics class yet, it may be advisable to wait until after you complete one before you progress further.

This book is arranged in several sections, beginning with a diagnostic test. The purpose of this test is to identify your strengths and weaknesses. It will also help to familiarize you with the testing method used by the College Board. Do not skip the diagnostic test! Find a quiet, comfortable spot, turn off the TV, computer, and music, and try to take the *entire* diagnostic test within the time allotted. If you run out of time, mark on your answer sheet where you ran out of time. Then keep going until you complete the test.

After finishing the test, you deserve a break, so take one. But be sure to come back after no more than 15 minutes and check your answers. Then go back, reread the questions you missed, and try to figure out what went wrong. Did you jump to a conclusion, misread the question, stop at the first correct answer (sometimes there are multiple correct answers to one question), or just not know the material? None of these reasons is cause for serious concern right now, because every reason mentioned can be overcome. In fact, as you work through this book, each of these will be addressed.

Once the diagnostic test is done it's time to settle down to your preparation for the *real* SAT II Physics Test. Move on to the Physics review and study each section as if you had to learn the material all over again. Those sections you know well will go by smoothly and help you to build confidence, while your review of unfamiliar terms and concepts will allow you to learn it quickly and effectively.

When you have finished your review, take the practice tests. Once again, you should try to set up a test-like situation. Make sure all the electronic toys are out of the way (besides, the College Board doesn't allow them), time yourself, and do your best. After you check each test, read the explanations for those questions you missed, and for additional reinforcement, reread the Review Section that covers the material in the question.

ABOUT THE PHYSICS TEST

The SAT II Physics Test is a 75-question multiple-choice test. The test covers the following topics:

- Mechanics
- Heat/Kinetic Theory/Thermodynamics
- Waves
- Electricity and Magnetism
- Modern Physics
- Miscellaneous Topics (may include measurement, math, and history)

Nearly 40 percent of the SAT II Physics Test will test your knowledge of Mechanics. Electricity and Magnetism also make up a significant proportion of the material, accounting for about 25 percent of the questions. Approximately 20 percent of the questions deal with waves, and the remaining 15 percent covers the other topics listed above.

Because the material covered in high school physics courses can vary widely, you will probably find some questions on the test that cover topics with which you are unfamiliar. This may be impossible to avoid entirely; however, solid preparation and review of the concepts and information covered in this book will go a long way to helping you navigate unfamiliar territory.

The testing procedures for the SAT II Physics Test are similar to those you already know from your high school classroom. A few questions will be simple recall; about half of the questions will require you to be able to apply a physical concept for a given situation; and the more difficult questions will require that you be able to apply multiple concepts to multiple relationships.

In addition to a college preparatory physics course, you will also need a solid working knowledge of algebra and trigonometry, as well as laboratory experience. Familiarity with the metric system is critical.

You are not permitted to use a calculator during the test. The calculations focus on simple arithmetic and will not require a calculator.

SCORING

Your score on the SAT II Physics Test will be reported on a scale of 200–800. Each question you answer correctly counts as one point. Each incorrect answer counts as $\frac{1}{4}$ point against you. Unanswered questions do not count for or against you.

Clearly, the more incorrect answers you can eliminate from a set of choices, the better your chances of finding or guessing the correct answer.

TAKING THE TEST

You will be given one hour (60 minutes) to complete seventy-five questions. Because of the limited amount of time you have for each question, it is *vital* that you adopt a test-taking strategy and stick to it. There are several things that you can do to give yourself the best possible chance to score well on the test.

Set up a study program for yourself and faithfully follow it. Do not skip any part(s) of the program.

1. When you take the diagnostic and practice tests, make sure to familiarize yourself thoroughly with the test directions, as they are patterned after the actual directions on the SAT II Physics Test you will be taking. Becoming familiar with the directions saves you time in re-reading them on test day.
2. Quickly read the entire test question by question. Answer immediately the questions you know or can do as you read through the test the first time; skip those questions you can't answer right away.
3. Once you've gone through the entire test, go back to the beginning and work on the questions you skipped. Look for answers to eliminate. The more answers you can eliminate, the better your chances to recognize or guess the correct answer.
4. If you finish the test before time is up, go back and look over your answers. Only change an answer if you are *absolutely sure* you have the incorrect answer selected.
5. Get a good rest the night before the test. A primary reason for poor test performance is lack of sleep.

SAT II PHYSICS STUDY PLANS

You already know the importance of a study plan when preparing for this test. Needless to say, the amount of time you have before you're due to take the test has a lot to do with which of the following plans you'll select for your exam preparation.

Those of you who are not taking the SAT II Physics Test in the near future should follow our leisurely 18-week plan. This plan is favored because it gives you plenty of time to thoroughly prepare, review all required concepts, and restudy the material you find challenging.

The next option is the 9-week plan, which calls for a more concentrated effort on your part. You will have to pay more attention to your diagnostic and practice test results in this plan, as those questions you miss become indicators for the material to which you should pay extra attention.

Finally, the last method is the Panic Plan. This plan is for you if you've got hardly any time to prepare but still want to do your best, like when you find out your college of choice wants to see your SAT II Physics Test score and the next test administration is in just a few weeks! Using this plan you will spend as much time as you have available preparing for the SAT II Physics Test by using this book to line you up for the test.

PRELIMINARY PREPARATIONS

Browse through the book. Look at the chapter summaries. Take the *Diagnostic Test*. Follow the instructions for taking the test and then check your answers. After you have taken the test and graded it, be sure to read all the explanations for the answers. Pay particular attention to the explanations for the questions you missed. Try to identify the reasons why you answered a question incorrectly. Was it carelessness on your part? You would be surprised at the number of students who miss a question they knew by inadvertently marking the wrong choice. Perhaps you misread the question, or maybe you were hurrying too much.

Look through the answers and explanations for the questions you missed. Be sure you understand why the correct answer is correct. Write down the numbers of the questions you missed or would like to understand a little better. They are your benchmark questions. If you miss a lot of the questions about magnetism or thermodynamics, for example, this tells you where to concentrate your efforts. Identifying these weak areas is especially important if you are following the Panic Plan and will be helpful no matter how long you have to prepare.

Sometimes students say the test questions are tricky, but the students who know the material are difficult to fool and quickly eliminate the "tricky" answers. This is not to say that they don't have to think about what they are doing. Some of the questions are truly challenging and will require your best effort, so prepare yourself well.

Start each chapter by reading the summary at the end, which lists everything in the chapter. As you read through a chapter, work out the problems on your own when you come to them. When you reach the end of a chapter, read the summary again. **Repetition is a powerful learning tool.**

THE 18-WEEK PLAN

Week 1   ***Diagnostic Test***
Review the answers to the *Diagnostic Test.*
Review *Chapter 1: Preliminary Concepts*

Week 2   ***Chapter 2*: Mechanics**
Statics
Kinematics
Dynamics

Week 3   ***Chapter 2*: Mechanics**
Work and Energy
Momentum
Circular and Rotary Motion

Week 4   ***Chapter 3*: Waves**
Wave Properties
Reflection
Refraction

Week 5   ***Chapter 3*: Waves**
Polarization of Light
Interference
Diffraction

Week 6   ***Chapter 4*: Heat and Thermodynamics**
Thermal Properties of Matter
Kinetic Molecular Theory
Gases

Week 7   ***Chapter 4*: Heat and Thermodynamics**
Laws of Thermodynamics
Heat Engines
Calorimetry

Week 8   ***Chapter 5*: Electricity and Electromagnetism**
Coulombs Law
Electric Fields and Potential
DC Circuits

Week 9   ***Chapter 5*: Electricity and Electromagnetism**
Magnets and Magnetic Fields

Week 10   *Chapter 6*: **Modern Physics**
                Quantum Mechanics
                Work Function

Week 11   *Chapter 6*: **Modern Physics**
                Relativity
                Heisenberg
                Compton
                deBroglia

Week 12   *Chapter 7*: **The Atom**
                The Nucleus
                Atomic Spectra
                Bohr's Atom

Week 13   *Chapter 7*: **The Atom**
                Nuclear Reactions, Equations, and Radiation
                Fission and Fusion
                Binding Energy and Mass Defect

Week 14   *Practice Test 1 and Practice Test 2*
                Review Answers and Explanations
                Reread all the chapter summaries

Week 15
                Review the material from the questions you missed on
                    Practice Test 1 and Practice Test 2
                Reread the chapter summaries

Week 16   *Practice Test 3 and Practice Test 4*
                Review Answers and Explanations
                Reread all the chapter summaries

Week 17
                Review the material from the questions you missed on
                    Practice Test 3 and Practice Test 4
                Reread the chapter summaries

Week 18
                Start the week by reading all of the chapter summaries.
                Go over all of the test questions you missed on the
                Diagnostic Test and the four practice tests. Review the material
                you are not sure you have mastered! *Think positive. You are
                ready!*

THE 9-WEEK PLAN

Week 1	***Diagnostic Test*** ***Chapter 1***: Preliminary Concepts
Week 2	***Chapter 2***: Mechanics
Week 3	***Chapter 3***: Waves
Week 4	***Chapter 4***: Heat and Thermodynamics
Week 5	***Chapter 5***: Electricity and Electromagnetism
Week 6	***Chapter 6***: Modern Physics
Week 7	***Chapter 7***: The Atom
Week 8	***Practice Tests 1 and 2*** Review the answers to the questions you missed
Week 9	***Practice Tests 3 and 4*** Review the answers to the questions you missed. Reread the chapter summaries, paying particular attention to any material you missed previously

PANIC PLAN

This last plan is for the group of students (and I hope it is small) who for whatever reason don't have much time to prepare for the SAT II Physics Test. Perhaps you have just completed a physics class and you don't think you need to spend much time in preparation, or maybe you have just decided to take the test. Only you know how much study time you have and how much energy you are willing to devote to preparation. Try to use both your time and energy wisely.

The list below will help you to prepare for the test in whatever time you have available. By all means try to do everything on the list. If that is not a possibility, the most important items are first. Do them! In fact do as much as you can.

- Read the chapter summaries, which will help you renew your basic physics knowledge.
- Take the *Diagnostic Test*, and review the questions you miss. This gives you an idea of your needs.
- Take *Practice Test 1*, and go over any questions you miss.
- Take *Practice Test 2*, and go over the questions you miss.
- Take *Practice Test 3*, and go over the questions you miss.
- Take *Practice Test 4*, and go over the questions you miss.
- Reread the chapter summaries

Good luck!

KEY FORMULAS AND EQUATIONS

$\text{Slope} = \dfrac{\Delta y}{\Delta x}$

$r^2 = y^2 + x^2$

$\sin\theta = \dfrac{y}{r}$

$\cos\theta = \dfrac{x}{r}$

$\tan\theta = \dfrac{y}{x}$

$\sum F = 0$

$\sum F_x = 0$

$\sum F_y = 0$

$\sum F_z = 0$

$T = F \geq$

$\sum T = 0$

$\sum +T = \sum -T$

$\text{Speed (U)} \dfrac{\text{distance}}{\text{time}} = \dfrac{d}{t}$

$V = \dfrac{S}{t}$

$V = \dfrac{V_f + V_0}{2}$

$\Delta V = V_f - V_0$

$\Delta t = t_f - t_o$

$a = \dfrac{\Delta V}{\Delta t}$

$a = \dfrac{V_f - V_0}{t_f - t_0}$

$V_f = V_0 + at$

$V_f^2 = V_o^2 + 2as$

$S = V_o t + \dfrac{1}{2} at^2$

$S = \dfrac{1}{2} gt^2$

$F = ma$

$W_t = mg$

$\text{Work} = F \bullet S \bullet \cos\theta$

$PE = mgh$

$KE = 1/2\ mv^2$

$\text{Power} = \dfrac{\text{work}}{\text{time}}$

$P = mv$

$Ft = m\Delta V$

$F_c = \dfrac{mV^2}{r}$

$F = G\dfrac{(m_1)(m_2)}{r^2}$

$\theta_{\text{radians}} = \dfrac{\text{arclength}}{\text{radius}} = \dfrac{s}{r}$

$s_{tan} = \theta r$

$V_{tan} = Wr$

$a_{tan} = \alpha r$

$V = \lambda f$

$f = \dfrac{1}{T}$

$\dfrac{h_i}{h_0} = \dfrac{q}{p}$

$\dfrac{1}{f} = \dfrac{1}{p} + \dfrac{1}{q}$

$n_1 \sin\theta_1 = n_2 \sin\theta_2$ (Snell's Law)

$n\lambda = d\sin\theta$

$PV = nrt$

$P_1 V_1 = P_2 V_2$

$\dfrac{V_1}{T_1} = \dfrac{V_2}{T_2}$

$\dfrac{P_1}{T_1} = \dfrac{P_2}{T_2}$

$\dfrac{(P_1)(V_1)}{T_1} = \dfrac{(P_2)(V_2)}{T_2}$

$\Delta Q = \Delta U + \Delta W$

$Q = cm\Delta T$

$F = K\dfrac{(q_1)(q_2)}{r^2}$

$F = EQ$

$V = IR$

$R_t = R_1 + R_2 + R_3 + R_{...}$

$\dfrac{1}{R_t} = \dfrac{1}{R_1} + \dfrac{1}{R_2} + \dfrac{1}{R_3}$

$P = VI$

$F = B_\perp IL$

$F = B_\perp qV$

$EMF = BLV$

$\dfrac{V_s}{V_p} = \dfrac{N_s}{N_p}$

$E = hf$

$\phi = hf$

$\Delta E = E_2 - E_1$

Relativistic Factor

$$\left[\dfrac{1}{\sqrt{1 - (\frac{v}{c})^2}} \right]$$

$E = mc^2$

$\text{Activity} = \dfrac{\Delta N}{\Delta t}$

$T_{1/2} = \dfrac{.693}{\lambda}$

$\dfrac{\Delta N}{\Delta t} = \lambda N_o$

UNITS AND CONVERSIONS

SI Units

length	meter	m
mass	kilogram	kg
time	second	s
electric current	ampere	A
temperature	Kelvin	K

Metric Prefixes

T	tera	1×10^{12}	10^{12}
G	giga	1×10^{9}	10^{9}
M	mega	1×10^{6}	10^{6}
hK	hectokilo	1×10^{5}	10^{5}
ma	myria	1×10^{4}	10^{4}
K	kilo	1×10^{3}	10^{3}
h	hecto	1×10^{2}	10^{2}
d	deka	1×10^{1}	10^{1}

Basic Unit   1 meter - 1 gram - 1 liter

d	deci	1×10^{-1}	10^{-1}
c	centi	1×10^{-2}	10^{-2}
m	milli	1×10^{-3}	10^{-3}
dm	decimilli	1×10^{-4}	10^{-4}
cm	centimilli	1×10^{-5}	10^{-5}
u	micro	1×10^{-6}	10^{-6}
n	nano	1×10^{-9}	10^{-9}
p	pico	1×10^{-12}	10^{-12}

Diagnostic Test

PHYSICS TEST

Pure

OK.

DIAGNOSTIC TEST

PHYSICS TEST

While you have taken many standardized tests and know to blacken completely the ovals on the answer sheets and to erase completely any errors, the instructions for the SAT II Physics Test differ in an important way from the directions for other standardized tests. You need to indicate on the answer key which test you are taking. The instructions on the answer sheet will tell you to fill out the top portion of the answer sheet exactly as shown.

1. Print PHYSICS on the line under the words *Subject Test (print)*.
2. In the shaded box labeled *Test Code* fill in four ovals:

    —Fill in oval 1 in the row labeled V.
    —Fill in oval 6 in the row labeled W.
    —Fill in oval 3 in the row labeled X.
    —Fill in oval C in the row labeled Y.
    —Leave the ovals in row Q blank.

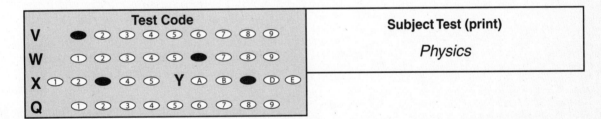

There are two additional questions that you will be asked to answer. One is "How many semesters of physics have you taken in high school?" The other question lists courses and asks you to mark those that you have taken. You will be told which ovals to fill in for each question. The College Board is collecting statistical information. If you choose to answer, you will use the key that is provided and blacken the appropriate ovals in row Q. You may also choose not to answer, and that will not affect your grade.

When everyone has completed filling in this portion of the answer sheet, the supervisor will tell you to turn the page and begin. The answer sheet has 100 numbered ovals, but there are only approximately 75 multiple-choice questions on the test, so be sure to use only ovals 1 to 75 (or however many questions there are) to record your answers.

PHYSICS TEST

Part A

> <u>Directions:</u> Each of the sets of lettered choices below refers to the questions and/or statements that follow. Select the lettered choice that is the best answer to each question and fill in the corresponding oval on the answer sheet. <u>In each set, each choice may be used once, more than once, or not at all.</u>

<u>Questions 1-3</u> relate to the following chart, which is a partial energy level diagram for the hydrogen electron.

$-.54eV$ _____ $n = 5$

$-.85eV$ _____ $n = 4$

$-1.51eV$ _____ $n = 3$

$-3.4eV$ _____ $n = 2$

$-13.6eV$ _____ $n = 1$

Use the choices below to answer the questions that follow. The questions relate to a hydrogen electron located at E-3.

A) $\pm.66eV$
B) $\pm.966eV$
C) $\pm1.89eV$
D) $\pm10.2eV$
E) $\pm12.09eV$

1. What is the emission energy when the electron falls to E-2 from E-3?

2. What is the absorbed energy when the electron jumps to E-5 from E-3?

3. What is the emission energy when the electron falls to E-1 from E-3?

PHYSICS TEST—*Continued*

Questions 4-6 relate to the changes that could be made in the following scenario and the results such changes would produce.

A pendulum swings at a rate of .75 vibrations/second.

A) Mass of the bob was increased
B) Length of the pendulum was increased
C) Mass of the bob was decreased
D) Length of the pendulum was decreased
E) Displacement from zero was increased

4. The period of the vibrations would increase because…

5. The frequency of the vibrations would decrease because…

6. The velocity of the pendulum would increase because…

Questions 7-9 relate to the following scenario.

A dog walks 120 m due east before turning and running 45 m west. He then turns and trots 40 m due north. After completing his journey, he is 85 m northeast of his home. When he hears his master call him, he runs directly home.

A) The eastward leg
B) The westward leg
C) The northward leg
D) The distance from home
E) The distance to home

7. Which part of the trip is a negative vector?

8. Which part of the trip is an equilibrant?

9. Which part of the trip is the longest vector?

GO ON TO THE NEXT PAGE

PHYSICS TEST—*Continued*

Questions 10–12 relate to the following.

A) Frequency
B) Amplitude
C) Wavelength
D) Velocity
E) Period

The choices below give a description of the quantities listed above. Match the statement below with the quantity it describes above.

10. The number of wave crests passing a given point per unit of time.

11. The distance between two points or two consecutive waves.

12. The product of the frequency and the wavelength.

Part B

> Directions: Each question or statement below is followed by five possible answers. In each case, select the best possible answer and fill in the corresponding oval on the answer sheet.

13. A wooden crate is pushed across a concrete floor at 5 m/s and released. It slides to a stop after moving a short distance. The same crate is filled until it weighs twice as much as it did previously and again slid across the floor at 5 m/s and released. The stopping distance for the crate will be

   (A) $\frac{1}{4}$ as far.

   (B) $\frac{1}{2}$ as far.

   (C) the same distance.

   (D) twice as far.

   (E) four times as far.

14. A team of skydivers jumps from a plane and holds hands to form a flower-like design. As the skydivers begin their free fall, their velocity increases and their

   (A) acceleration increases.

   (B) acceleration decreases.

   (C) acceleration is constant.

   (D) acceleration is zero.

   (E) air resistance is reduced.

15. A professional golfer drives a golf ball 230 meters down the fairway. When the club head strikes the golf ball
    (A) the impact force on the golf ball is greatest
    (B) the impact force on the club head is greatest
    (C) the impact force is the same for both.
    (D) the impact force has no effect on the club
    (E) the impact force has no effect on the ball

16. When a woman pushes on her grocery cart, the woman moves because of
    (A) the force the woman exerts on the grocery cart.
    (B) the force the grocery cart exerts on the woman.
    (C) the force the woman exerts on the ground.
    (D) the force the ground exerts on the woman.
    (E) the force the grocery cart exerts on the ground.

17. During a company picnic, 6 accounting department workers participate in a tug of war with 6 sales force personnel. Each team pulls on the rope with 1200N of force. What is the tension in the rope?
    (A) 2400N
    (B) 1200N
    (C) 600N
    (D) 200N
    (E) 100N

18. The catcher prepares to receive a pitch from the pitcher. As the ball reaches and makes contact with his glove, the catcher pulls his hand backward. This action reduces the impact of the ball on the catcher's hand because
    (A) the energy absorbed by his hand is reduced.
    (B) the momentum of the pitch is reduced.
    (C) the time of impact is increased.
    (D) the time of impact is reduced.
    (E) the force exerted on his hand remains the same.

19. A 12,500 kg boxcar rolling through a freight yard has a velocity of 1 m/s when it strikes another boxcar of the same mass that is at rest. Both cars stick together and continue to roll down the track with a momentum of
    (A) 0 kg • m/s
    (B) 3125 kg • m/s
    (C) 6250 kg • m/s
    (D) 12,500 kg • m/s
    (E) 25,000 kg • m/s

20. A 750 g peregrine falcon dives straight down towards a 400 g pigeon, which is flying level to the ground. Just before the falcon makes impact its velocity is 35 m/s. The velocity of the falcon and the pigeon in its talons immediately after impact is most nearly
    (A) 35 m/s
    (B) 31.95 m/s
    (C) 28.9 m/s
    (D) 25.85 m/s
    (E) 22.8 m/s

GO ON TO THE NEXT PAGE

PHYSICS TEST—*Continued*

21. A father holds his child on his shoulders during a parade. The father does no work during the parade because
    (A) no force acts on the child.
    (B) the momentum of the child is constant.
    (C) the potential energy of the child is gravitational.
    (D) the child's kinetic energy is constant.
    (E) the child's distance from the ground remains the same.

22. Golden Glove boxers, who are amateurs, use larger, more padded gloves than professional boxers use. The amateur boxers are more protected from injury because
    (A) the larger glove exerts a larger impulse on the boxer.
    (B) the larger glove exerts a larger force on the boxer.
    (C) the larger glove exerts more energy on the boxer.
    (D) the larger glove increases time of impact on the boxer.
    (E) the larger glove increases the power exerted on the boxer.

23. The driver of an automobile traveling at 80 km/hr locks his brakes and skids to a stop in order to avoid hitting a deer in the road. If the driver had been traveling at 40 km/hr, how much faster would he have stopped?
    (A) 4 times the distance
    (B) 2 times the distance
    (C) $\frac{1}{2}$ the distance
    (D) $\frac{1}{4}$ the distance
    (E) Not enough information to tell

24. During a laboratory experiment, a 19.6N pile driver is dropped 2 m on to the head of a nail, which is driven 2.45 cm into a wood board. The frictional force exerted by the wood on the nail is
    (A) 96.04N
    (B) 165N
    (C) 1600N
    (D) 1960N
    (E) 3200N

25. For question 24 above, what is the magnitude of the acceleration of the pile driver while it drives the nail into the board?
    (A) -165 m/s^2
    (B) -800 m/s^2
    (C) -1600 m/s^2
    (D) -2000 m/s^2
    (E) -3200 m/s^2

26. A child is swinging on a swing set. As the child reaches the lowest point in her swing
    (A) the tension in the rope is equal to her weight.
    (B) the tension in the rope supplies a centrifugal force.
    (C) her kinetic energy is at maximum.
    (D) her tangential acceleration equals gravity.
    (E) her angular velocity is minimum.

27. A bicycle wheel spins on its axis at a constant rate but has not yet made a complete rotation. Which of the following statements is correct?
    (A) The angular displacement is zero.
    (B) The linear displacement is zero.
    (C) The angular acceleration is zero.
    (D) The angular velocity is zero.
    (E) None of these is zero.

PHYSICS TEST—*Continued*

28. An Olympic diver performs a $3\frac{1}{2}$ somersault. During his dive he uses the tuck position so that he will have
    (A) larger angular momentum.
    (B) smaller angular momentum.
    (C) larger rotational rate.
    (D) smaller rotational rate.
    (E) longer time in the air.

29. While riding on a merry-go-round, you decide to move from a position close to the center to a position on the outside rim of the merry-go-round. After you have changed position, which of the following has remained the same?
    (A) Tangential acceleration
    (B) Centripetal force
    (C) Angular displacement
    (D) Tangential velocity
    (E) Tangential displacement

30. The International Space Station is currently under construction. Eventually, simulated earth gravity may become a reality on the space station. What would the gravitational field through the central axis be like under these conditions?
    (A) zero

    (B) $\frac{1}{4}$ g

    (C) $\frac{1}{2}$ g

    (D) $\frac{3}{4}$ g

    (E) 1 g

31. A person who normally weighs 900N at sea level climbs to the top of Mt. Everest. While on top of Mt. Everest that person will weigh
    (A) zero.
    (B) approximately 900N.
    (C) considerably less than 900N but more than zero.
    (D) considerably more than 900N.
    (E) Need more information.

32. If a shaft were drilled through the center of the earth and all you had to do was step into the shaft to "fall" to the other side, and a 800N person took the trip, her weight at the exact time she passed through the exact center of the earth would be
    (A) zero.
    (B) 800N.
    (C) less than 800N but more than zero.
    (D) more than 800N.
    (E) Need more information.

33. A 750N person stands on a scale while holding a briefcase inside a freely falling elevator. Which of the following is true?

    (A) If the briefcase were released it would rise to the ceiling.
    (B) The person's acceleration is zero.
    (C) The person's attraction toward the earth is zero.
    (D) The person's apparent weight is zero.
    (E) If the briefcase were released it would fall to the floor.

GO ON TO THE NEXT PAGE

PHYSICS TEST—*Continued*

34. The time it takes a satellite to make one orbit around the earth depends on the satellite's
    - (A) acceleration.
    - (B) weight.
    - (C) direction of rotation.
    - (D) distance from earth.
    - (E) launch speed.

35. Geosynchronous satellites remain over the same spot on the earth's surface because they
    - (A) orbit the earth every 24 hours.
    - (B) are in polar orbits.
    - (C) rotate opposite the earth's rotational direction.
    - (D) have a varying orbital height.
    - (E) use terrain reading technology to remain on station.

36. Rutherford's results in his famous gold foil experiment proved that atoms
    - (A) are mostly space.
    - (B) are in continuous motion.
    - (C) have negative orbitals.
    - (D) have diffuse charge distribution.
    - (E) have dense crystalline structure.

37. A hanging weight stretches a spring 8 cm. If the weight is doubled and the spring constant is not exceeded, how much will the spring stretch?
    - (A) 4 cm
    - (B) 8 cm
    - (C) 12 cm
    - (D) 16 cm
    - (E) 20 cm

38. The volume of an ideal gas is reduced to half its original volume. The density of the gas
    - (A) remains the same.
    - (B) is halved.
    - (C) is doubled.
    - (D) is tripled.
    - (E) is quadrupled.

39. Refrigerators and freezers perform their functions by
    - (A) converting hot air to cold air.
    - (B) keeping hot air out with cold air pressure.
    - (C) removing heat from inside themselves.
    - (D) blowing cold inside them.
    - (E) producing cold air.

40. An empty soda can with a few ml of water inside is heated to steaming and quickly inverted into an ice water bath. The can is instantly crushed because
    - (A) energy in the can is lost.
    - (B) water vapor condenses leaving a vacuum, which sucks the can in.
    - (C) water vapor condenses and outside air pressure crushes the can.
    - (D) the cold water shrinks the hot can.
    - (E) water pressure in the ice bath crushes. the can

41. The first law of thermodynamics is a restatement of
    - (A) Guy-Lassac's Law.
    - (B) the principle of entropy.
    - (C) the principle of enthalpy.
    - (D) conservation of energy.
    - (E) Avogadro's hypothesis.

PHYSICS TEST—*Continued*

42. If 360 g of water at 95°C is mixed with 275 g of water at 10°C, what is the resulting temperature of the water?
    (A) 37°C
    (B) 49°C
    (C) 58°C
    (D) 70°C
    (E) 82°C

43. While anchored at sea, a captain notices the wave peaks are separated by 16 m and occur at a rate of 1 wave every 2 seconds. What is the velocity of these waves?
    (A) 4 m/s
    (B) 8 m/s
    (C) 16 m/s
    (D) 32 m/s
    (E) 64 m/s

44. Some opera singers are able to use their voice to shatter a crystal glass. They can do this because of
    (A) acoustic reflection.
    (B) multiple echoes.
    (C) interference.
    (D) resonance.
    (E) beats.

Questions 45–47 refer to the waves shown below. Each wave is moving in the direction shown by the arrow.

Select the graph that answers the questions below.

45. Which set of pulses will soon show constructive interference?

46. Which set of pulses has already been through interference?

47. Which set of pulses will soon show destructive interference?

48. A rider on a subway train hears the engineer blow the train whistle. A moment later she hears an answering whistle from an approaching train. Why does the whistle she hears from the approaching train change pitch?
    (A) The frequency of the waves of the approaching train's whistle is decreasing.
    (B) The frequency of the waves of the approaching train's whistle is increasing.
    (C) The loudness of the waves of the approaching train is decreasing.
    (D) The loudness of the waves of the approaching train is increasing.
    (E) The echoes of the two trains' whistles are combining.

GO ON TO THE NEXT PAGE

PHYSICS TEST—*Continued*

49. Two charged objects are moved 50% closer to one another. Which statement about the electric force between the objects is true?
    (A) The force between them doubles.
    (B) The force between them halves.
    (C) The force between them remains the same.
    (D) The force between them reverses.
    (E) The force between them operates in the same direction.

50. The distribution of the charge density on the surface of a conducting solid depends upon
    (A) the density of the conductor.
    (B) the shape of the conductor.
    (C) the size of the conductor.
    (D) the age of the conductor.
    (E) the substance of the conductor.

51. A pair of point charges, which have charges of -3 *micro coulombs* and -4 *micro coulombs*, is separated by 2 cm. What is the value of the force between them?
    (A) 600N
    (B) 300N
    (C) 540N
    (D) 270N
    (E) 400N

52. At what point between a pair of charged parallel plates will the electric field be strongest?
    (A) It is strongest between the plates.
    (B) It is strongest near the positive plate.
    (C) It is strongest near the negative plate.
    (D) The field is constant between the plates.
    (E) The field is variable, therefore the strong point also varies.

53. Which of the following best describes the electric field about a positive point charge?
    (A) The field strengthens as the distance from the point charge increases.
    (B) The field is a constant throughout space.
    (C) The field weakens as the distance from the point change increases.
    (D) The field is oriented toward the point charge.
    (E) The field cannot be determined.

54. A 6 volt battery is connected across a resistor, and a current of 1.5 *A* flows in the resistor. What is the value of the resistor?
    (A) 2Ω
    (B) 4Ω
    (C) 6Ω
    (D) 8Ω
    (E) 10Ω

55. As a battery ages, its internal resistance increases. This causes the current in the external circuit to
    (A) remain the same.
    (B) polarize.
    (C) reverse direction.
    (D) increase.
    (E) decrease.

Questions 56–58 refer to the circuit below.

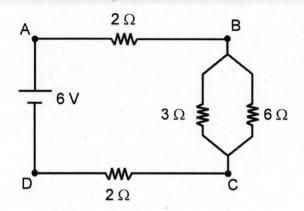

56. What is the resistance in the parallel circuit above between points *B* and *C*?

    (A) 2Ω

    (B) 4Ω

    (C) 6Ω

    (D) 8Ω

    (E) 10Ω

57. The current in the circuit is

    (A) 1 *A*

    (B) 2 *A*

    (C) 3 *A*

    (D) 9 *A*

    (E) 18 *A*

58. What is the voltage change between point *B* and point *C*?

    (A) 1 *V*

    (B) 2 *V*

    (C) 3 *V*

    (D) 9 *V*

    (E) 18 *V*

59. A charged particle moving through a magnetic field will experience the largest force when

    (A) moving with the field.

    (B) moving against the field.

    (C) moving at a 45° angle to the field.

    (D) moving at a 90° angle to the field.

    (E) the particle will not be affected.

60. Which of the following is caused completely or in some part by magnetic lines of force?

    (A) The picture on a computer screen

    (B) Radio reception interference

    (C) Aurora Borealis

    (D) V.H.S. films

    (E) All of these

61. Electrical energy is converted into mechanical energy by which of the following?

    (A) Magnet

    (B) Transformer

    (C) Motor

    (D) Generator

    (E) Battery

62. A transformer contains 4000 turns on its primary side and 500 turns on the secondary side. If the input voltage is 240 *V*, calculate the voltage output of the secondary side.

    (A) 15 *V*

    (B) 30 *V*

    (C) 60 *V*

    (D) 120 *V*

    (E) 240 *V*

GO ON TO THE NEXT PAGE

PHYSICS TEST—*Continued*

63. While standing in front of a plane flat mirror and looking at yourself, you raise your right hand. Which is the best description of the image you see?
    (A) Erect and enlarged
    (B) Erect and reduced
    (C) Erect and reversed
    (D) Inverted and reversed
    (E) Inverted and reduced

64. Which of the following occurs when light passes into a clear glass cube?
    (A) The light's wavelength changes.
    (B) The light's frequency changes.
    (C) The light's speed changes.
    (D) The light is polarized.
    (E) Both A and C

65. A light ray is moving parallel to the principal axis of a concave mirror, which it strikes. How will the light ray be reflected?
    (A) Back upon itself
    (B) Through the focal point
    (C) Through the radius of curvature
    (D) Through a point equal to $\frac{1}{2}f$
    (E) Through a point equal to $2r$

Questions 66 and 67 refer to the drawing below. The drawing represents the results in a Young's double slit interference pattern experiment.

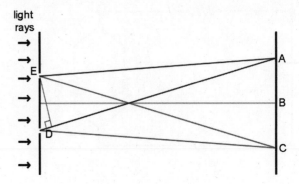

66. Which letter represents the wavelength of the light?

67. Which letter represents the zero*th* order fringe?

68. What does the photoelectric effect demonstrate?
    (A) The particulate nature of light
    (B) The wave nature of light
    (C) The diffuse reflection of light
    (D) The total internal reflection of light
    (E) The polarization of light

69. An electric current is applied to a gas discharge tube, causing it to glow. When the discharge is viewed through a spectroscope, which type of spectrum is seen?
    (A) Monochromatic
    (B) Continuous
    (C) Line absorption
    (D) Line spectra
    (E) Polarimeter

PHYSICS TEST—*Continued*

70. Einstein based his theory of relativity on the postulate that
    (A) photoelectrons absorb and emit photons.
    (B) the velocity of light is the same for all observers.
    (C) mass and energy are intra-convertible.
    (D) the universe is an entropic system.
    (E) energy and momentum are conserved.

71. DeBroglie theorized that all moving objects emit waves (matter waves) based on their momentum $\left(\lambda = \dfrac{h}{mv} \right)$. Accordingly, as your team's defensive end, it is your job to stop the other team's 250 pound fullback. If you could hear the fullback's matter waves and you listened as the opposing fullback received the ball and accelerated toward you, what sound would you hear?
    (A) An increase in loudness and an increase in frequency
    (B) An increase in loudness and a decrease in frequency
    (C) A decreasing loudness and an increasing frequency
    (D) A decreasing loudness and a decreasing frequency
    (E) Just a loud thump! thump! thump!

72. An atom that has lost an electron is considered to be a(n)
    (A) positron.
    (B) negatron.
    (C) baryon.
    (D) hadron.
    (E) ion.

73. What is the major product of the fission reaction of 235 *U*? The basic fission reaction is

$$ {}^{235}_{92}U + {}^{1}_{0}p = {}^{141}_{56}Ba + 3\,{}^{1}_{0}p + ? $$

    (A) Protons
    (B) Neutrons
    (C) Radiation
    (D) Heat
    (E) Light

74. A radioactive isotope of iodine has a half-life of 8 hours and causes a counter to register 180 counts/min. Find the count rate for this sample of iodine two days later.
    (A) 1.4/min
    (B) 2.8/min
    (C) 5.6/min
    (D) 11.2/min
    (E) 22.4/min

75. The three natural radiations, in order from most penetrating to least penetrating, are
    (A) alpha, beta, and gamma.
    (B) beta, gamma, and alpha.
    (C) gamma, alpha, and beta.
    (D) gamma, beta, and alpha.
    (E) beta, alpha, and gamma.

STOP
IF YOU FINISH BEFORE THE TEST SESSION ENDS, YOU MAY REVIEW YOUR WORK ON THIS TEST ONLY. YOU MAY NOT TURN TO ANY OTHER TEST IN THIS BOOK.

ANSWER SHEET

Leave any unused answer spaces blank.

	Test Code										Subject Test (print)					
V	①	②	③	④	⑤	⑥	⑦	⑧	⑨							
W	①	②	③	④	⑤	⑥	⑦	⑧	⑨							
X ①	②	③	④	⑤	**Y** Ⓐ	Ⓑ	Ⓒ	Ⓓ	Ⓔ		FOR ETS USE ONLY	R/C	W/S1	FS/S2	CS/S3	WS
Q	①	②	③	④	⑤	⑥	⑦	⑧	⑨							

1 Ⓐ Ⓑ Ⓒ Ⓓ Ⓔ		21 Ⓐ Ⓑ Ⓒ Ⓓ Ⓔ		41 Ⓐ Ⓑ Ⓒ Ⓓ Ⓔ		61 Ⓐ Ⓑ Ⓒ Ⓓ Ⓔ		81 Ⓐ Ⓑ Ⓒ Ⓓ Ⓔ
2 Ⓐ Ⓑ Ⓒ Ⓓ Ⓔ		22 Ⓐ Ⓑ Ⓒ Ⓓ Ⓔ		42 Ⓐ Ⓑ Ⓒ Ⓓ Ⓔ		62 Ⓐ Ⓑ Ⓒ Ⓓ Ⓔ		82 Ⓐ Ⓑ Ⓒ Ⓓ Ⓔ
3 Ⓐ Ⓑ Ⓒ Ⓓ Ⓔ		23 Ⓐ Ⓑ Ⓒ Ⓓ Ⓔ		43 Ⓐ Ⓑ Ⓒ Ⓓ Ⓔ		63 Ⓐ Ⓑ Ⓒ Ⓓ Ⓔ		83 Ⓐ Ⓑ Ⓒ Ⓓ Ⓔ
4 Ⓐ Ⓑ Ⓒ Ⓓ Ⓔ		24 Ⓐ Ⓑ Ⓒ Ⓓ Ⓔ		44 Ⓐ Ⓑ Ⓒ Ⓓ Ⓔ		64 Ⓐ Ⓑ Ⓒ Ⓓ Ⓔ		84 Ⓐ Ⓑ Ⓒ Ⓓ Ⓔ
5 Ⓐ Ⓑ Ⓒ Ⓓ Ⓔ		25 Ⓐ Ⓑ Ⓒ Ⓓ Ⓔ		45 Ⓐ Ⓑ Ⓒ Ⓓ Ⓔ		65 Ⓐ Ⓑ Ⓒ Ⓓ Ⓔ		85 Ⓐ Ⓑ Ⓒ Ⓓ Ⓔ
6 Ⓐ Ⓑ Ⓒ Ⓓ Ⓔ		26 Ⓐ Ⓑ Ⓒ Ⓓ Ⓔ		46 Ⓐ Ⓑ Ⓒ Ⓓ Ⓔ		66 Ⓐ Ⓑ Ⓒ Ⓓ Ⓔ		86 Ⓐ Ⓑ Ⓒ Ⓓ Ⓔ
7 Ⓐ Ⓑ Ⓒ Ⓓ Ⓔ		27 Ⓐ Ⓑ Ⓒ Ⓓ Ⓔ		47 Ⓐ Ⓑ Ⓒ Ⓓ Ⓔ		67 Ⓐ Ⓑ Ⓒ Ⓓ Ⓔ		87 Ⓐ Ⓑ Ⓒ Ⓓ Ⓔ
8 Ⓐ Ⓑ Ⓒ Ⓓ Ⓔ		28 Ⓐ Ⓑ Ⓒ Ⓓ Ⓔ		48 Ⓐ Ⓑ Ⓒ Ⓓ Ⓔ		68 Ⓐ Ⓑ Ⓒ Ⓓ Ⓔ		88 Ⓐ Ⓑ Ⓒ Ⓓ Ⓔ
9 Ⓐ Ⓑ Ⓒ Ⓓ Ⓔ		29 Ⓐ Ⓑ Ⓒ Ⓓ Ⓔ		49 Ⓐ Ⓑ Ⓒ Ⓓ Ⓔ		69 Ⓐ Ⓑ Ⓒ Ⓓ Ⓔ		89 Ⓐ Ⓑ Ⓒ Ⓓ Ⓔ
10 Ⓐ Ⓑ Ⓒ Ⓓ Ⓔ		30 Ⓐ Ⓑ Ⓒ Ⓓ Ⓔ		50 Ⓐ Ⓑ Ⓒ Ⓓ Ⓔ		70 Ⓐ Ⓑ Ⓒ Ⓓ Ⓔ		90 Ⓐ Ⓑ Ⓒ Ⓓ Ⓔ
11 Ⓐ Ⓑ Ⓒ Ⓓ Ⓔ		31 Ⓐ Ⓑ Ⓒ Ⓓ Ⓔ		51 Ⓐ Ⓑ Ⓒ Ⓓ Ⓔ		71 Ⓐ Ⓑ Ⓒ Ⓓ Ⓔ		91 Ⓐ Ⓑ Ⓒ Ⓓ Ⓔ
12 Ⓐ Ⓑ Ⓒ Ⓓ Ⓔ		32 Ⓐ Ⓑ Ⓒ Ⓓ Ⓔ		52 Ⓐ Ⓑ Ⓒ Ⓓ Ⓔ		72 Ⓐ Ⓑ Ⓒ Ⓓ Ⓔ		92 Ⓐ Ⓑ Ⓒ Ⓓ Ⓔ
13 Ⓐ Ⓑ Ⓒ Ⓓ Ⓔ		33 Ⓐ Ⓑ Ⓒ Ⓓ Ⓔ		53 Ⓐ Ⓑ Ⓒ Ⓓ Ⓔ		73 Ⓐ Ⓑ Ⓒ Ⓓ Ⓔ		93 Ⓐ Ⓑ Ⓒ Ⓓ Ⓔ
14 Ⓐ Ⓑ Ⓒ Ⓓ Ⓔ		34 Ⓐ Ⓑ Ⓒ Ⓓ Ⓔ		54 Ⓐ Ⓑ Ⓒ Ⓓ Ⓔ		74 Ⓐ Ⓑ Ⓒ Ⓓ Ⓔ		94 Ⓐ Ⓑ Ⓒ Ⓓ Ⓔ
15 Ⓐ Ⓑ Ⓒ Ⓓ Ⓔ		35 Ⓐ Ⓑ Ⓒ Ⓓ Ⓔ		55 Ⓐ Ⓑ Ⓒ Ⓓ Ⓔ		75 Ⓐ Ⓑ Ⓒ Ⓓ Ⓔ		95 Ⓐ Ⓑ Ⓒ Ⓓ Ⓔ
16 Ⓐ Ⓑ Ⓒ Ⓓ Ⓔ		36 Ⓐ Ⓑ Ⓒ Ⓓ Ⓔ		56 Ⓐ Ⓑ Ⓒ Ⓓ Ⓔ		76 Ⓐ Ⓑ Ⓒ Ⓓ Ⓔ		96 Ⓐ Ⓑ Ⓒ Ⓓ Ⓔ
17 Ⓐ Ⓑ Ⓒ Ⓓ Ⓔ		37 Ⓐ Ⓑ Ⓒ Ⓓ Ⓔ		57 Ⓐ Ⓑ Ⓒ Ⓓ Ⓔ		77 Ⓐ Ⓑ Ⓒ Ⓓ Ⓔ		97 Ⓐ Ⓑ Ⓒ Ⓓ Ⓔ
18 Ⓐ Ⓑ Ⓒ Ⓓ Ⓔ		38 Ⓐ Ⓑ Ⓒ Ⓓ Ⓔ		58 Ⓐ Ⓑ Ⓒ Ⓓ Ⓔ		78 Ⓐ Ⓑ Ⓒ Ⓓ Ⓔ		98 Ⓐ Ⓑ Ⓒ Ⓓ Ⓔ
19 Ⓐ Ⓑ Ⓒ Ⓓ Ⓔ		39 Ⓐ Ⓑ Ⓒ Ⓓ Ⓔ		59 Ⓐ Ⓑ Ⓒ Ⓓ Ⓔ		79 Ⓐ Ⓑ Ⓒ Ⓓ Ⓔ		99 Ⓐ Ⓑ Ⓒ Ⓓ Ⓔ
20 Ⓐ Ⓑ Ⓒ Ⓓ Ⓔ		40 Ⓐ Ⓑ Ⓒ Ⓓ Ⓔ		60 Ⓐ Ⓑ Ⓒ Ⓓ Ⓔ		80 Ⓐ Ⓑ Ⓒ Ⓓ Ⓔ		100 Ⓐ Ⓑ Ⓒ Ⓓ Ⓔ

Diagnostic Test

ANSWERS AND EXPLANATIONS

Quick-Score Answers

1. C	14. B	27. C	40. C	52. D	64. E
2. B	15. C	28. C	41. D	53. C	65. B
3. E	16. D	29. C	42. C	54. B	66. D
4. B	17. B	30. A	43. B	55. E	67. B
5. B	18. C	31. B	44. D	56. A	68. A
6. E	19. D	32. A	45. D	57. A	69. D
7. B	20. E	33. D	46. A	58. B	70. B
8. E	21. E	34. D	47. E	59. D	71. A
9. A	22. D	35. A	48. B	60. E	72. E
10. A	23. D	36. A	49. E	61. C	73. D
11. C	24. C	37. D	50. B	62. B	74. B
12. D	25. B	38. C	51. D	63. C	75. D
13. C	26. C	39. C			

ANSWERS AND EXPLANATIONS

ANSWERS TO PART A
QUESTIONS 1-12

1. **The correct answer is (C).** The solution to the problem is found by $\Delta E = E_3 - E_2$. The calculation yields $+1.89\ eV$. The positive sign tells us the electron releases energy as it falls to a lower energy level.

2. **The correct answer is (B).** The solution is found again by using Bohr's equation, $\Delta E = E_3 - E_5$. The calculation yields $-.966\ eV$. The negative sign tells us the electron absorbs energy as it moves further from the nucleus.

3. **The correct answer is (E).** Also using Bohr's equation we have $\Delta E = E_3 - E_1$. The answer is $+12.09\ eV$, therefore the electron releases energy.

4. **The correct answer is (B).** The period of the pendulum is

$$T = 2\pi\sqrt{\frac{\ell}{g}}$$. We can see from the equation that the shorter the

length of the pendulum, the shorter is the period of the pendulum.

5. **The correct answer is (B).** The frequency is the inverse of the period. Lengthening the pendulum increases the length of the period, which means the frequency decreases.

6. **The correct answer is (E).** An increase in the displacement of the pendulum raises the pendulum bob to a greater height, which gives it more potential energy. When the bob passes through the zero point, the potential energy will be transformed into greater kinetic energy, which means a greater velocity.

7. **The correct answer is (B).** When you set the problem into the x, y coordinate system, the negative y axis is the westward direction. Any vector in the western direction is negative.

8. **The correct answer is (E).** The resultant vector is the distance the dog is from home. The opposite of the resultant vector is the equilibrant vector.

9. **The correct answer is (A).** The numerical value is the magnitude of the vector. The one with the largest numerical value is the longest vector.

10. **The correct answer is (A).** The definition of the frequency of a wave is correctly stated in A

11. **The correct answer is (C).** This is the correct definition for wavelength.

12. **The correct answer is (D).** The product of the frequency and the wavelength can be obtained by the dimensional analysis. $V = \lambda f$, which yields

$$V = \left(\frac{m}{\text{wave}} \right) \left(\frac{\text{wave}}{\text{sec}} \right) = \frac{m}{s}, \text{ a velocity unit.}$$

ANSWERS TO PART B
Questions 13-75

13. **The correct answer is (C).** The coefficient of friction remains the same so the frictional force doubles, but the net force also doubles. Thus the crate is brought to a stop in the same distance.

14. **The correct answer is (B).** The acceleration of the skydivers continues to decrease until the terminal velocity of the group is reached. When the air resistance reaches the point where it exactly balances the force exerted on the divers by the earth's gravitational attraction, their acceleration becomes zero.

15. **The correct answer is (C).** The contact between the golf club and the ball constitutes an equal and opposite force pair.

16. **The correct answer is (D).** The woman pushing on the ground is one part of a force pair. The second part of the pair is the ground pushing on the woman. The force the woman exerts cannot move the ground, but the force the ground exerts does move the woman.

17. **The correct answer is (B).** The tension in a rope is the same throughout. Both teams must pull with a force of 1200N to maintain static equilibrium, so the total tension is 2400N.

18. **The correct answer is (C).** The momentum of the pitched ball is changed by the impulse *Ft*. The catcher reduces the magnitude of the force on his hand by increasing the time required to change the momentum of the ball.

19. **The correct answer is (D).** This is a conservation of momentum question. Since the momentum before an event must equal the momentum after an event, the momentum must be 12,500 kg • m/s.

20. **The correct answer is (E).** Use conservation of momentum for the problem.

$P_{before} = P_{after}$ which is $(mV_f + mV_p)_{before} = (m_f + m_p)V_{after}$.

The pigeon has no downward velocity before the collision, leading to:

$(m_fV_f)_{before} = (m_f + m_p)\ V_{after}$

Rearrange, substitute, and solve:

$$\frac{m_f V_f}{m_f + m_p} = V$$

$$\frac{750g \bullet 35m/s}{750g + 400g} = 22.8 \text{ m/s.}$$

21. **The correct answer is (E).** The father holds the child at the same distance from the ground. If there is displacement, there is no work done.

22. **The correct answer is (D).** The larger amount of padding in the amateur gloves causes the time of impact to be increased, which results in less force being exerted.

23. **The correct answer is (D).** The same car traveling at twice the velocity has four times the energy. Constant frictional force from the tires will therefore require four times the stopping distance. The car moving at the lower rate only requires $\frac{1}{4}$ the stopping distance.

24. **The correct answer is (C).** This is a work-energy problem.

    PE = Work → $mgh = F \bullet D$.
    Rearrange, substitute, and solve (remember $m \bullet g = $ wt):

    $$\frac{mgh}{D} = F \therefore \frac{19.6N \bullet 2m}{.0245m} = 1600N$$

25. **The correct answer is (B).** The velocity of the pile driver at the time it first contacts the head of the nail is $V_f^2 = 2gs$. Since, by conservation of energy, $\frac{1}{2}mVp^2 = mgd$. V is also the original velocity as the nail is driven into the wood for a distance of .0245m.

    Stating the equations:
    $$V_f^2 = 2gd$$
    and $V_0^2 = 2 - ad$
    but $V_f^2 = V_0^2$
    and $\dfrac{2 \bullet 9.8m/s^2 \bullet 2m}{2 \bullet -.0245m} = -800m/s^2$

26. **The correct answer is (C).** All the gravitational potential energy at the top of the child's swing pathway is converted into kinetic energy at the bottom of her swing pathway.

27. **The correct answer is (C).** The wheel is moving at a constant rate (angular velocity). There is no angular acceleration because $\Delta\omega$ is zero.

28. The correct answer is (C). The diver needs to complete the rotations as quickly as possible. The tuck position reduces the moment of inertia of the diver's body, allowing the diver to spin at a higher rate.

29. The correct answer is (C). Regardless of where on the merry-go-round you are located during the ride, your angular displacement is the same for the whole ride.

30. The correct answer is (A). The central axis would have a gravitational force of zero because there is no radial distance to provide a centripetal acceleration or centripetal force.

31. The correct answer is (B). Although the person has moved further from the center of the earth, that person now has the additional mass of Mt. Everest under him.

32. The correct answer is (A). Since $F = G\dfrac{m_1 \bullet m_2}{r^2}$, the person will be weightless at the center of the earth because $r = 0$, and all the mass of the earth is attracting the person from outside the center.

33. The correct answer is (D). The apparent weight is zero. The person is in free fall. No forces are acting on the person except gravity.

34. The correct answer is (D). The centripetal force required to keep a satellite in orbit remains constant. That means the closer to earth a satellite is, the faster it must travel in its orbit $F_c = \dfrac{mV^2}{r}$. The farther the satellite is located from the earth, the slower it travels in orbit.

35. The correct answer is (A). The geosynchronous satellite circles the earth at the same rate as the earth turns beneath it. Thus the satellite stays in the same position relative the earth.

36. The correct answer is (A). Most of the alpha particles passed through the gold foil, leading Rutherford to conclude that atoms were composed mostly of space with a dense core.

37. **The correct answer is (D).** Based on Hooke's Law, $F = kx$ where F is mg and x is the elongation. Solving for $x = \dfrac{mg}{k}$, so if m is doubled, x is doubled as well.

38. **The correct answer is (C).** The same number of gas particles now occupies half the volume. The formula for density is $d = \dfrac{m}{v}$ where mass can be restated as the mass of the *gas = (mol. Mass) (Avogadro's Number)*. Thus the mass is directly related to the number of particles in the space. More particles in less space yield greater density.

39. **The correct answer is (C).** Refrigerators and freezers operate in a reversed direction from a heat engine. Instead of using a hot source to produce work, work is done on a warm source and heat is removed, producing the cooling effect.

40. **The correct answer is (C).** The water vapor in the can is hot and at atmospheric pressure. Cooling the can quickly condenses the water vapor, which also reduces the pressure inside the can. The outside atmospheric pressure is greater, thus crushing the can.

41. **The correct answer is (D).** The first law of thermodynamics can be stated as:

$$\begin{bmatrix} \text{the heat added} \\ \text{to a system} \end{bmatrix} - \begin{bmatrix} \text{the work done} \\ \text{by the system} \end{bmatrix} = \begin{bmatrix} \text{the increase in} \\ \text{system energy} \end{bmatrix}$$

or

$$\Delta Q - \Delta W = \Delta U$$

42. **The correct answer is (C).** This is a calorimetric problem. Since the ratio of $C°$ to K is 1 to 1, we will not change temperature scales.

Our working equation is $Cm_1\Delta \, T_{hot} + Cm_2\Delta \, T_{cold} = 0$

$$Cm_1(t_f - t_0)_{hot} + Cm_2(t_f - t_0)_{cold} = 0$$

factor out the C's $\quad m(t_f - t_0) + m(t_f - t_o) = 0$

$$360g(t_f - 95°C) + 275g(t_f - 10°C) = 0$$

$$360gt_f - 34200gC° + 275gt_f - 2750gC° = 0$$

$$635gt_f - 36950gC° = 0$$

$$t_f = \frac{36950gC°}{635g} = 58°C$$

43. **The correct answer is (B).** The velocity of a wave is $v = \lambda \bullet f$. Substitute into the equation and solve.

$$v = \lambda \bullet f$$

$$= \left(16\,\frac{meters}{wave}\right)\left(.5\,\frac{waves}{second}\right)$$

$$= 8\,\frac{meters}{second}$$

44. **The correct answer is (D).** If the input frequency of a wave system is equal to its vibrating frequency, the resonant system acts to amplify the waves, thus transferring their energy into the delicate crystal and breaking it.

45. **The correct answer is (D).** When the two impulses are located at the same point they will algebraically add the two positive peaks, yielding a larger wave, which is equal to both of their magnitudes.

46. **The correct answer is (A).** The two waves are moving away from one another.

47. **The correct answer is (E).** When the two pulses are located at the same point they will algebraically add the positive peak to the negative peak yielding no wave or disturbance. They have destroyed one another at that spot.

48. **The correct answer is (B).** The sound waves from the approaching whistle strike the listener's ears at an increasing rate, producing the increasing pitch.

49. **The correct answer is (E).** The charge on the two does not change, so the force between them MUST operate in the same direction. The magnitude of the force increases by 4.

50. **The correct answer is (B).** Charge will distribute itself equally over the surface of a body because of the repulsion the electrons have for one another.

51. **The correct answer is (D).** Coulombs Law is $F = k\dfrac{q_1 q_2}{r^2}$.

    The solution is $F = \left(9 \times 10^9 \, \mathrm{N}\dfrac{m^2}{C^2}\right)\dfrac{(-3 \times 10^{-6}\,f)(-4 \times 10^{-6}\,f)}{(.02m)^2} = 270\mathrm{N}$

52. **The correct answer is (D).** The electric field between two parallel plates is constant throughout. The value of the field is defined as $E = \dfrac{F}{q}$ where E is the electric field, F is force, and q is charge.

53. **The correct answer is (C).** The value of the electric field about a point source is $E = k\dfrac{q}{r^2}$. The distance from the point in question determines the strength of the electric field in this case.

54. **The correct answer is (B).** This is a problem that requires an Ohm's Law calculation to find resistance. Rearrange the equation to find resistance.

$$V = IR$$

$$R = \frac{V}{I} = \frac{6V}{1.5A} = 4\Omega$$

55. **The correct answer is (E).** The higher internal resistance in the battery leads to a reduction in the terminal potential of the battery. The lower terminal potential can produce less current in the circuit.

56. **The correct answer is (A).** The total resistance is found by using the reciprocal method.

$$R_t = \cfrac{1}{\cfrac{1}{R_1} + \cfrac{1}{R_2}} = \cfrac{1}{\cfrac{1}{3\Omega} + \cfrac{1}{6\Omega}} = \cfrac{1}{\cfrac{1}{2}} = 2\Omega$$

57. **The correct answer is (A).** $V = IR$, rearrange and $I = \dfrac{V}{R_t}$

$$I = \frac{6V}{2\Omega + 2\Omega + 2\Omega} = \frac{6V}{6\Omega} = 1A$$

58. **The correct answer is (B).** Use Ohm's Law to solve the problem.

$$V = IR$$
$$(1A)(2\Omega) = 2V$$

59. **The correct answer is (D).** The more magnetic field lines a charged particle crosses, the stronger the force exerted on the particle. Moving through the magnetic field in a perpendicular path (90°) will cause the particle to cross the most field lines.

60. **The correct answer is (E).** Your computer picture is caused by manipulating a magnetic yoke to produce a picture. The interference with radio is caused by magnetic lines and radio waves interacting. VHS films are produced by magnetic pulses, and the Aurora Borealis is the visual show produced when cosmic particles enter the earth's magnetic field.

61. **The correct answer is (C).** Motors are used in a variety of mechanical devices such as saws, sanders, drills, and pumps. The electric energy is converted to mechanical energy by the rotation of a loop of wire in a magnetic field.

62. **The correct answer is (B).** The transformer equation is

$$\frac{V_p}{V_s} = \frac{\text{\# of primary turns}}{\text{\#of secondary turns}}$$

$$V_s = \frac{(V_p)(\text{\#of secondary turns})}{\text{\# of primary turns}}$$

$$V_s = \frac{(240V)(500 \text{ turns})}{4000 \text{ turns}} = 30V$$

63. **The correct answer is (C).** Your image is standing upright. Your feet and the image of your feet are down, and your head and the image of your head are up. When you raise your right hand, the left hand of the image is raised. This is a reversal of left and right.

64. **The correct answer is (E).** Light slows down when it enters a material that is more optically dense. Since the velocity is related to both the frequency and the wavelength by $V = \lambda f$ it follows that one of these quantities will change, too. Since the distance between the waves changes at the optical boundary, the wavelength also changes. The frequency remains unchanged.

65. **The correct answer is (B).** A ray parallel to the central radius is reflected through the focal point.

66. **The correct answer is (D).** The relative retardation of the light wave (the letter D in the diagram) is also its wavelength. The bright spots produced on the screen represent $n = 1, 2, 3$, etc., whole number values of wavelengths.

67. **The correct answer is (B).** The zero*th* fringe is the central bright spot where both waves from the two slits have traveled the same distance.

68. **The correct answer is (A).** The wave nature of light does not satisfactorily explain why low frequency light cannot energize electrons from the surface of metals, which high frequency light does. The intensity of the light doesn't matter. This is explained by the particle theory in which photons carry energy, which is transferred to electrons in the metal.

69. **The correct answer is (D).** The energized atoms of the gas emit energy in specific regions of the visible spectrum called line spectra.

70. **The correct answer is (B).** One of two postulates of Einstein's theory of special relativity is that the speed of light in a vacuum is the same for all observers.

71. **The correct answer is (A).** A combination of Doppler effect and matter waves. The waves being emitted by the moving fullback reach you at a rate greater than they are produced. Additionally the approaching fullback is getting louder, too.

72. **The correct answer is (E).** All charged particles are called ions.

73. **The correct answer is (D).** The reactors produce heat, which in turn changes water to steam, which is used to turn the turbines to generate electricity.

74. **The correct answer is (B).** Half-life means that half of the substance decays away during that time. Over 48 hours there are 6 half-lives.

$$\frac{48 \text{ hours}/8 \text{ hours}}{\text{halflife}} = 6 \text{ half lives}$$

$$\left(\frac{1}{2}\right)^6 (180 \text{ counts/min}) = 2.8 \text{ counts/min}$$

75. **The correct answer is (D).** The penetrating capability of radiation is based upon its energy. Gamma radiation is most energetic followed by beta then alpha.

Chapter 1

PRELIMINARY CONCEPTS

CHAPTER 1
PRELIMINARY CONCEPTS

SIMPLE EQUATIONS AND ALGEBRA

Physics is the branch of science that studies physical phenomena. Why does the sound of a starter's pistol reach an observer standing at the race finish line *after* the puff of smoke is seen when the gun is fired? Why do some objects float in water, while other objects sink? What causes a ball to roll downhill?

These questions and more are the stuff of physics. Sometimes the study of physical phenomena involves observation, experimentation, and calculation. The calculations used in this review are accomplished by using a little algebra, a little geometry, and a little trigonometry.

Many relationships in physics can be expressed as equations. For example:

$$F = ma$$
$$s = vt$$

Sometimes the value to be found is not by itself (isolated) in the equation. Take, for example, the linear motion equation:

$$V_f^2 = V_0^2 + 2as$$

Let's suppose the acceleration *a* is the only unknown quantity in the equation. We must perform a little algebraic manipulation to isolate *a* so that it is the only quantity on its side of the equal sign. Before starting the process, remember one simple rule: whatever operation you perform on one side of the equal sign, you must also perform on the other side of the equal sign.

Let's begin by isolating *a* in the equation below:

$$V_f^2 = V_0^2 + 2as$$

We then subtract V_o^2 from both sides:

$$V_f^2 - V_o^2 = V_o^2 - V_o^2 + 2as$$

This leads to:

$$V_f^2 - V_o^2 = 2as$$

Then we divide both sides by $2s$:

$$\frac{V_f^2 - V_0^2}{2s} = \frac{2as}{2s}$$

Clearing fractions gives:

$$\frac{V_{f^2} - V_0^2}{2s} = a$$

If you find this algebra to be difficult, you might need to stop here and review your math skills before proceeding.

GRAPHS

Some relationships studied in physics exist between experimental values. The relationships between these quantities can be shown using a technique called **graphing**. With this technique, one quantity (the independent variable) is carefully controlled, while the other quantity (the dependent variable) is measured at each value of the independent variable.

The independent variable is plotted along the x axis of the graph, and the dependent variable is plotted along the y axis of the graph.

The slope for the graph is calculated by dividing the ΔY by the ΔX.

$$Slope = \frac{\Delta y}{\Delta x}$$

A graph is a picture of the relationship between two or more quantities. A *direct* relationship is one in which both quantities increase (or decrease) in the same manner. In an *inverse* relationship, one quantity increases and the other decreases. A *parabolic* relationship exists when one quantity varies as the square of the other.

DIRECT RELATIONSHIP

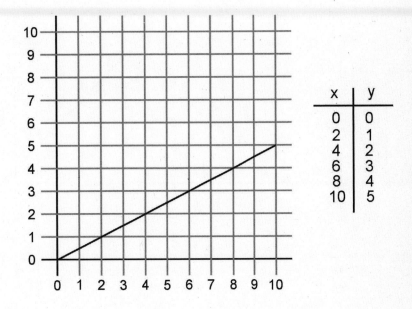

x	y
0	0
2	1
4	2
6	3
8	4
10	5

GRAPH A

Graph A shows a linear relationship between x and y. For every 2 units' increase in variable x, variable y increases by 1 unit. The slope of the graph is calculated as rise over run.

INVERSE RELATIONSHIP

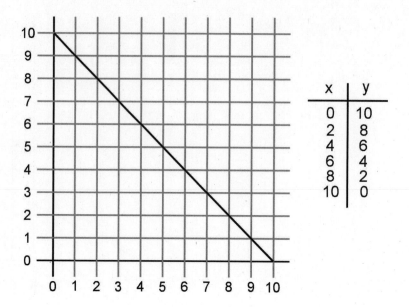

x	y
0	10
2	8
4	6
6	4
8	2
10	0

GRAPH B

Graph B shows an indirect linear relationship between x and y.

Peterson's SAT II Success: Physics

PARABOLIC RELATIONSHIP

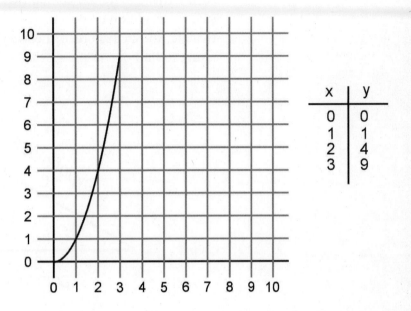

x	y
0	0
1	1
2	4
3	9

GRAPH C

Graph C shows a parabolic relationship between *x* and *y*.

The ability to read a graph is crucial. They are used to display and compare physical concepts. *Be sure you can read and evaluate graphs.*

RIGHT TRIANGLES

Any triangle with a 90° internal angle is defined as a right triangle. In such a triangle, the remaining two internal angles of the right triangle sum to an additional 90°. If you are sure you are dealing with a right triangle, the **Pythagorean theorem** becomes a useful tool when trying to find one of the sides.

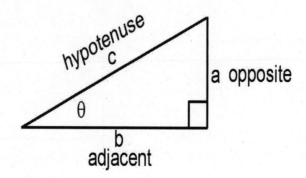

The right triangle above is labeled according to convention. The side opposite the 90° angle is called the hypotenuse and is labeled c. The side beside the smaller of the remaining two angles is called the adjacent side b, and the side across from the smaller angle is called the opposite side a.

The Pythagorean theorem is stated mathematically as $c^2 = a^2 + b^2$. Thus, should we know the size of any two sides, we can find the missing side.

$$\text{Side } c = \sqrt{a^2 + b^2}$$
$$\text{Side } a = \sqrt{c^2 - b^2}$$
$$\text{Side } b = \sqrt{c^2 - a^2}$$

Right triangles have special relationships not only with their sides but also with their internal angles. For every right triangle, the sides of that triangle and the internal angles of that triangle form a ratio.

These are given as:

$$\text{sine } \theta = \frac{opposite}{hypotenuse} \quad \text{or } \sin \theta = \frac{a}{c}$$

$$\text{cosine } \theta = \frac{adjacent}{hypotenuse} \quad \text{or } \cos \theta = \frac{b}{c}$$

$$\text{tangent } \theta = \frac{opposite}{adjacent} \quad \text{or } \tan \theta = \frac{a}{b}$$

Further, no matter how long the sides of the triangle may be, the ratio between the three sides remains the same as long as the internal angle remains the same.

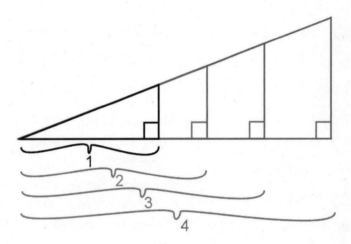

Triangles 1, 2, 3, and 4 above all have an internal angle of 30°. Thus the sine, cosine, and tangent values are the same in all four triangles.

CARTESIAN COORDINATES

The construction and use of right triangles is a valuable tool in solving physics problems. Unfortunately, not all measures and quantities begin neatly at zero. Rather than allow this to complicate matters, we simplify by using the **Cartesian Coordinate System** in conjunction with triangles. You may also recognize this as the four quadrant *x* and *y* system.

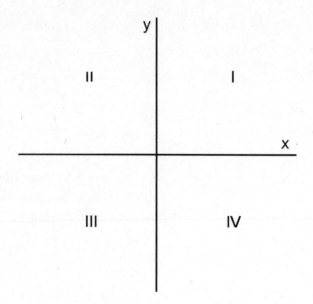

- The region between the x and y coordinates on the upper right is called the first quadrant. All x and y quantities in the first quadrant are positive.

- The region between the x and y coordinates on the upper left is called the second quadrant. All x quantities in the second quadrant are negative, and all y quantities in the second quadrant are positive.

- The region between the x and y coordinates on the lower left is called the third quadrant. All x and y quantities in the third quadrant are negative.

- The region between the x and y coordinates on the lower right is called the fourth quadrant. All x quantities in the fourth quadrant are positive and all y quantities in the fourth quadrant are negative.

Quadrant	X coordinate	Y coordinate
I	$+x$	$+y$
II	$-x$	$+y$
III	$-x$	$-y$
IV	$+x$	$-y$

Situations where the Cartesian Coordinate System is used conventionally follow the *x, y* system for labeling purposes. When a right triangle is placed within the coordinate system, its sides can be renamed as follows:

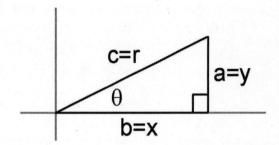

Thus, we could look at the trigonometry functions for a right triangle that has been placed into the coordinate system as:

$$\sin \theta = \frac{a}{c} \quad \text{changes to} \rightarrow \quad \sin \theta = \frac{y}{r}$$

$$\cos \theta = \frac{b}{c} \quad \text{changes to} \rightarrow \quad \cos \theta = \frac{x}{r}$$

$$\tan \theta = \frac{a}{b} \quad \text{changes to} \rightarrow \quad \cos \theta = \frac{y}{x}$$

The conventional *a, b, c* labeling is changed to represent the physics application, thus becoming *x, y, r*, where *r* is the hypotenuse. The Pythagorean Theorem now looks like this:

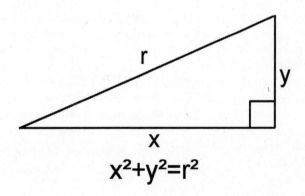

$$x^2 + y^2 = r^2$$

Conventional labeling becomes coordinate system labeling.

UNITS AND CONVERSIONS

Oftentimes students will be given a value for a physical quantity such as 50 km/hr and asked to perform operations that require them to convert to m/sec. Finding the correct units in this situation means that you must be able to change kilometers to meters and to change hours to seconds. Experience has shown most students to be very capable at performing the mathematic operation. The problem seems to be one of setting up the conversions between the differing units.

50 km/hr = ? m/sec

One factor that can cause difficulty with conversions is that many students lack some basic information. You should know instantly that there are 60 seconds in one minute and 3600 seconds in one hour. The metric units you should know are:

1000 meters = 1 kilometer
100 centimeters = 1 meter
1000 millimeters = 1 meter

Then there are the equivalent values for volume (liters) and mass (grams) as well. There is a list of constants, equivalents, and physics formulas on page 15. Be sure you are very familiar with this information.

Returning to the conversion mentioned, we begin:

50 km/hr = ? m/sec

There are 1000 meters in a kilometer, thus we multiply 50 km by 1000 m/km, yielding 50,000 meters.

Now we have:

50,000 m/hr = ? m/sec

There are 3600 seconds per hour, thus we multiply one hour by 3600 sec/hr, yielding 3600 seconds.

Divide distance by time for the final value.

$$\frac{50,000m}{3600sec} = 13.88m/sec$$

The whole conversion can be made into a one-step calculation by writing each part and solving.

$$(50 \text{ km/hr})(1{,}000 \text{ m/km})\left(\dfrac{1}{\dfrac{3600 \text{ sec}}{\text{hr}}}\right) = 13.88 \text{ m/sec}$$

During the conversion process it is absolutely essential that you state and complete your dimensional analysis.

SCALARS AND VECTORS

SCALARS

The treatment of physical quantities is based upon the kind of quantity in question. Two important physical quantities we will study are scalars and vectors.

Quantities defined strictly by their magnitude are called scalar quantities. Scalars are easy to recognize: a dozen eggs, a gross of paper clips, half a dozen apples, a kilogram of cheese. All the stated quantities denote a number (12, 144, 6, 1) of the item listed, nothing more.

Therefore, a Sunday drive could easily be described by the number of miles traveled: "We drove 80 km today." Should we wish to add more information, such as *where* we traveled, then another physical quantity is used.

VECTORS

Quantities defined both by their magnitude and direction are called vector quantities. Vectors are also easily recognized, as they *must* include *both* magnitude and direction: four steps to the right, 50 meters south, 9N @ 45°. Taking another look at the Sunday drive above, we can define it as a vector by saying "We drove 80 km to the museum and back today." Vectors are always stated in respect to a reference point.

Solving Scalar and Vector Problems

Numerical operations with scalars are simply a matter of adding or subtracting the numbers.

Example
We have 9 marbles and find 5 marbles. How many do we now have?

Solution

$$9 \text{ marbles}$$
$$\underline{(+) \, 5 \text{ marbles}}$$
$$14 \text{ marbles}$$

As you can see, simply add to perform the operation.

The same operation with vector quantities requires a bit more thought, as both the magnitude and direction must be included.

We'll start with a straightforward addition problem.

Example
A student walks 4 blocks east and stops at an ice cream truck. After purchasing a snow cone, he walks another 10 blocks east. Where is the student in respect to his starting point?

Solution

$$4 \text{ blocks @ east}$$
$$\underline{(+)10 \text{ blocks @ east}}$$
$$14 \text{ blocks @ east}$$

The student has walked a total of 14 blocks due east.

As in this example, when two vectors are added together, the result is conveniently called the *resultant vector.* The original vectors, which were added together, are the *component vectors.*

The problem above shows the nature of vectors. *Both* magnitude and direction must be included in operations with vectors.

Peterson's SAT II Success: Physics

The next problem requires the use of the Pythagorean Theorem when we add a pair of vectors. We will also use the Cartesian Coordinate System (*x* and *y* axis).

Example

A bird is perched in the tree where it has its nest. The bird flies 500 m due east and lands on the ground in a field where it finds a worm. When the bird takes off, it is chased by a hawk, so the bird flies 300 m due north before landing in a tree.

What direction must the bird fly to find its nest, and how far away is the nest?

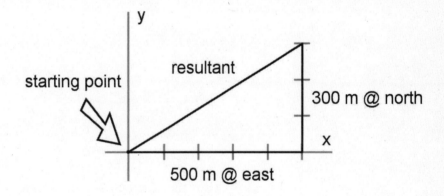

Solution

When solving physics problems, always use a convenient method with which you are comfortable. This is how you should approach any problem you are solving. A method is suggested below.

1. Draw a diagram (above)
2. Isolate and label the parts of the problem
3. Identify both *x* and *y* components
4. Write the equation
5. Solve for the unknown

Let's place the bird's starting point at the *x, y* juncture, which is also its starting point at the nest. The bird is presently located at the head of the 300 m north vector.

Before solving the problem, convert the compass values to the *x, y* coordinate system. The due east vector is located directly along the *x* coordinate, which is 0°. The due north vector is located directly along the *x* coordinate, which is 90°.

As we inspect the problem it becomes clear that the Pythagorean Theorem is the best way to solve the problem.

$$c^2 = a^2 + b^2$$ Change to the x, y coordinates and
$$c^2 = y^2 + x^2$$ identify c (the hypotenuse) as the resultant
$$r^2 = y^2 + x^2$$ vector.

$$r = \sqrt{(300m)^2 + (500m)}$$
$$r = 583m$$

This is the magnitude value of the resultant vector. The direction for the resultant can be found with a little right triangle trigonometry.

$$\tan\theta = \frac{y}{x}$$
$$\tan\theta = \frac{300m}{500m}$$
$$\tan\theta = .6$$
$$\theta = 31°$$

Thus the resultant vector (where the bird is located in respect to its starting point) is

583m @ 31°

Recall that the bird wanted to fly back to its nest. It can't fly at 31° from its current position because that path takes the bird farther from its nest. The direction we have found must be reversed for the bird to return to its nest.

The resulting direction is exactly 180° opposite the direction the bird must fly. Take the resultant vector and add (or subtract) 180° to or from the vector's direction.

180° + 31° = 211°

The bird must fly 583 m @ 211° from its present position to reach its nest. When this is done, the bird will effectively cancel out the resultant vector. That's why its flight will be the equilibrant.

An equilibrant vector is a vector that is exactly equal in magnitude and opposite in direction from the resultant vector.

Example

Let us look at one more vector problem.

Suppose 4 ropes were used to pull on a stationary object.

- Rope *a* pulls in a direction of 15° with a force of 25N.

- Rope *b* pulls in a direction of 215° with a force of 16N.

- Rope *c* pulls in a direction of 75° with a force of 20N.

- Rope *d* pulls in a direction of 300° with a force of 30N.

If a single rope were to replace the four ropes, with what force and in what direction must the rope pull?

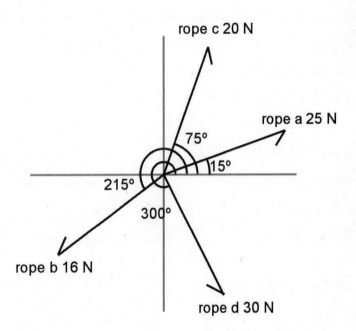

Solution

The diagram above allows us to see each vector in relation to all the other vectors.

We will isolate each vector in its turn and break each one into its *x* and *y* components. Then we can combine all the individual *x* and *y* components to find the resultant vector.

First, check and make sure that when you construct your triangles, the *y* side of the triangle is the opposite side of the triangle, and the *x* side is the adjacent side of the triangle.

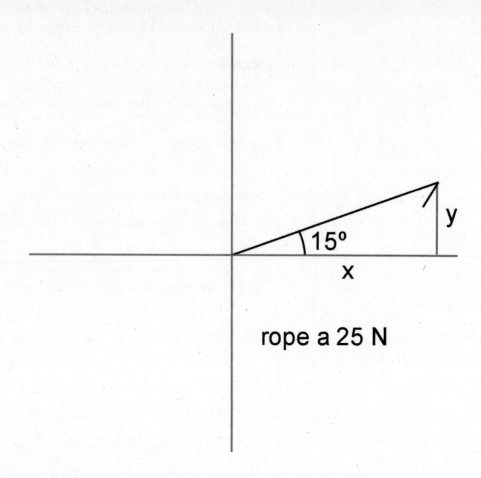

rope a 25 N

Rope *a* extends 15° into the first quadrant.

Side y = Side r (sin 15°) = (30N) (.26) =   7.8N
Side x = Side r (cos 15°) = (30N) (.97) = 29.1N

Both components of rope *a* are located in the first quadrant.

y = positive $\therefore$ +7.8N

x = positive $\therefore$ +29.1N

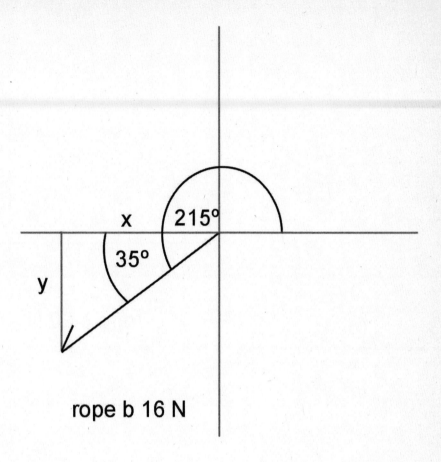

rope b 16 N

Rope *b* extends 35° into the third quadrant .

Side *y* = (side *r*) (sin 35°)   =   (16N) (.57) =   9.1N
Side *x* = (side *r*) (cos 35°)   =   (16N) (.82) = 13.1N

Both components of rope *b* are located in the third quadrant.

y = negative ∴ −9.1N

x = negative ∴ −13.1N

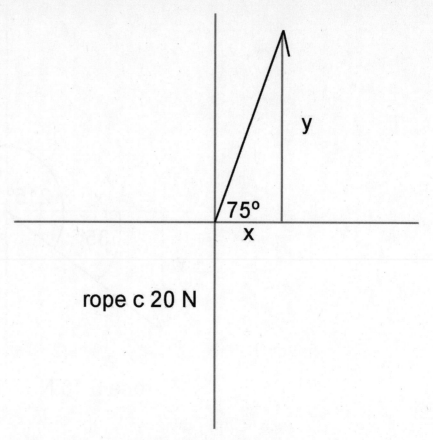

Rope *c* extends 75° into the first quadrant.

Side y = (side *r*) (sin 75°) = (20N) (.97) = 19.4N
Side x = (side *r*) (cos 75°) = (20N) (.26) = 5.2N

Both components of rope *c* are located in the first quadrant.

y = positive ∴ +19.4N

x = positive ∴ +5.2N

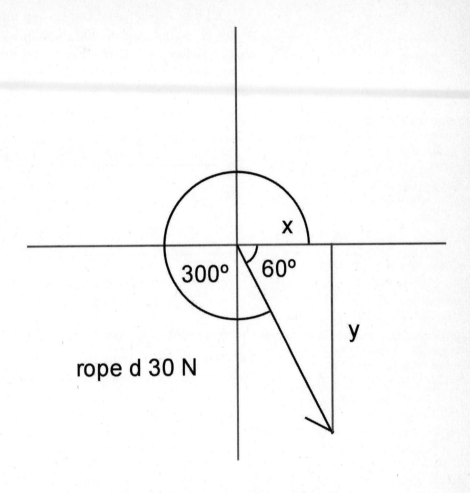

Rope *d* extends 30° into the third quadrant.

Side *y* = (side *r*) (sin 60°)   = (30N) (.87) = 26.1
Side *x* = (side *r*) (cos 60°) = (30N) (.5)   = 15.0N

Both components of rope *d* are located in the fourth quadrant.

y = negative ∴ −26.1N

x = positive ∴ +15.0N

All four ropes have been broken into their component vectors at this point. It is time to add them up. We can accomplish this by using a simple *x, y* chart. The chart is filled in with the individual components we have just found. Having done that, we then algebraically combine all the *y* components and do the same with the *x* components

ROPE	Y axis	X axis
Rope *a*	+ 7.8N	+29.1N
Rope *b*	− 9.1N	−13.1N
Rope *c*	+19.4N	+ 5.2N
Rope *d*	−26.1N	+15.0N

–8N in *x* direction
+36.2N in *y* direction

After combining the *x* components and the *y* components, the values are the two components of the new *resultant* vector. Apply the Pythagorean Theorem to find its magnitude.

$$r = \sqrt{x^2 + y^2}$$
$$r = \sqrt{(-8N)^2 + (+36.2N)^2}$$
$$r = 37N$$

Now that we know the magnitude of the resultant, we'll use the tangent function to find the direction of the resultant vector.

Using the tangent function yields:

$$\tan\theta = \frac{y}{x} = \frac{-8N}{+36.2N} = -.22 = -1°$$

This number tells us that the direction of the resultant vector is –1°. That means that to find the value of the resultant vector, we simply subtract 1° from 360° to find the direction a single rope must pull to equal the pull from the original four ropes.

The resultant vector is 37N @ 359°

Simply stated: One rope pulling with a force of 37N in a direction of 359° accomplishes the exact same thing as the other four ropes.

CHAPTER SUMMARY

- Scalar quantities are defined by their magnitude only. They are treated simply as numbers in the mathematics operations involving them.

- Vector quantities are defined by both their magnitude and direction. Mathematics operations involving vectors require both the magnitude and the direction to be included.

- The direction of a vector may be implied, given as compass headings, or given as Cartesian Coordinates

- A resultant vector is the vector formed when two or more other vectors are combined.

- Every vector may be broken into its x and y components.

- An equilibrant vector is a vector whose magnitude is exactly equal to and opposite in direction of a given vector.

Chapter 2

MECHANICS

CHAPTER 2

MECHANICS

STATICS

Objects that are not free to move are said to be in equilibrium. For an object to be in equilibrium, the following two conditions must be met:

1. All the applied forces must equal zero.
2. All the applied torques must equal zero.

Let's stop a moment to give a quick definition for force. A force is a push or a pull.

That's all there is to it, a push or a pull.

All forces occur in pairs, and the force pairs act on different bodies. When a force is directed toward a point of contact, the force is called a *compression*. When a force is directed away from a point of contact, the force is called a *tension*.

Using what we know about vectors, we can see that every set of forces can be resolved into just three lines of action: along the x axis, the y axis, and the z axis. We can restate the above (called the First Condition of Equilibrium) in the following manner:

$$\Sigma F = 0$$

This can be broken down to address the three axes individually.

$$\Sigma F_x = 0$$
$$\Sigma F_y = 0$$
$$\Sigma F_z = 0$$

The symbol "Σ" is read as "the sum of." We'll use it to state the conditions of equilibrium mathematically.

The x axis is horizontal (side to side), the y axis is vertical (up and down), and the z axis is altitude (in and out).

Example

One illustration of the first condition of equilibrium is a book resting on a flat surface as shown above. The book rests on the surface with a force equal to its weight, say 10 N. The surface doesn't collapse or push the book away from itself, which means that the surface is pushing back on the book with a force *equal* to the force the book exerts on it. The book is in equilibrium. This statement can be shown as an equation.

$$\Sigma F = 0 \quad \therefore$$

$$\Sigma F_x = 0$$

$$\Sigma F_y = 0$$

$$\Sigma F_z = 0$$

Solution

Looking at the individual axes:

$$\Sigma F_x = 0 \quad \text{(there are no } x \text{ forces)}$$

$$\Sigma F_z = 0 \quad \text{(there are no } z \text{ forces)}$$

$$\Sigma F_y = 0 = F_{book} - F_{surface} = 0$$

$$F_{book} = F_{surface}$$

Example

A problem involving an object hanging by a wire is solved in a similar manner.

A 25N mercury vapor light is hung from the ceiling by a wire. What is the tension (T_1) in the wire?

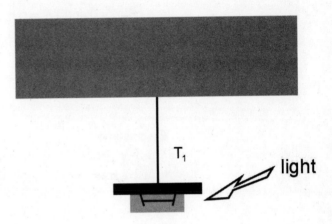

Don't forget the force pairs:

- The light pulls on the cable.

- The cable pulls on the light.

- They are equal in magnitude and opposite in direction to one another.

Solution

$$\Sigma F = 0$$

$$\Sigma F_x = 0$$

$$\Sigma F_y = 0$$

$$\Sigma F_z = 0$$

$\Sigma F_x = 0$ and $\Sigma F_z = 0$ because no forces are applied
on either of the x or z axes

$$\Sigma F_y = T_1 - 25\text{N} = 0$$

$$T_1 = 25\text{N}$$

Example

Another problem involving objects constrained by cables requires us to use some trigonometry to find a solution.

A 100N traffic light is suspended in the middle of an intersection by three different cables. The three cables meet at point A. Find the tensions in T_1, T_2, and T_3.

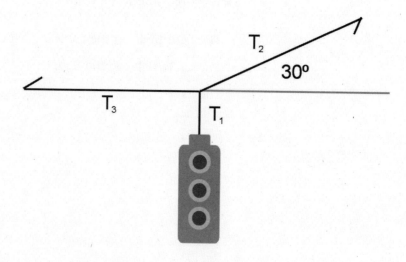

Solution

There is no movement of point A, so point A must be in equilibrium. Summing forces about point A:

$$\Sigma F = 0$$

$$\Sigma F_z = 0 \text{ (there are \textit{no} forces on the } z \text{ axis)}$$

$$\Sigma F_x = 0 \text{ (there \textit{are} forces on the } x \text{ axis)}$$

$$\Sigma F_y = 0 \text{ (there \textit{are} forces on the } y \text{ axis)}$$

We can solve the $y = $ axis tension first

$$\Sigma F_y = T_1 - 100\text{N} = 0$$

$$T_1 = 100\text{N}$$

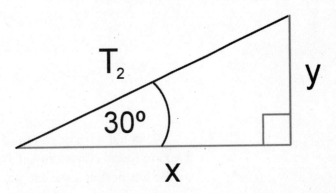

- T_2 is a resultant vector with components located along the x and y axis.

- T_2 is an unknown value, but it does pull upward toward the $+x$ direction.

- If T_2 is both pulling up and to the right against point A, then something must be pulling down and left against point A.

- Pulling down is T_1 and pulling left is T_3.

Having identified the equilibrant pulls as T_1 and T_3, we can set T_{2y} against the upward pull of T_2, which is T_{2y}. This meets the condition of equilibrium on the y axis, which is stated in the equation below.

$$\Sigma F_y = T_1 - T_{2y} = 0$$

$$T_1 = T_{2y}$$

$$T_1 = 100\text{N}$$

$$100\text{ N} = T_{2y}$$

T_2 is found by substituting and solving

$$100\text{N} = T_2(\sin 30°)$$

$$\frac{100\text{N}}{.5} = T_2$$

$$200\text{N} = T_2$$

T_3 could have been found before T_2, but the order in which these two are found is not critical. Looking at point A again, T_3 is identified as the left pull, and we can set T_3 against the right pull of T_2, which is T_{2x}. This meets the condition of equilibrium on the x axis, which we state in the following equation.

$$\Sigma F_x = T_3 - T_{2x} = 0$$

$$T_3 = T_{2x}$$

$$T_{3x} = \frac{T_{2y}}{\tan 30°}$$

Substitute for T_{2x}

$$T_3 = \frac{100\text{N}}{.58}$$

$$T_3 = 172\text{N}$$

Alternate method

$$\Sigma F_x = T_3 - T_{2x} = 0$$

$$T_3 = T_{2x}$$

$$T_3 = T_2(\cos 30°)$$

Substitute for T_{2x}

$$T_3 = 200\text{N}(.86)$$

$$T_3 = 172\text{N}$$

The solution to the problem is

$T_1 = $ 100N

$T_2 = $ 200N

$T_3 = $ 300N

TORQUES

When all the forces acting on an object along the three axes sum to zero, there can be no up and down, side to side, or in and out motion. However the object *can* still spin or rotate. The First Condition of Equilibrium addresses straight line or concurrent forces, which do not cause objects to rotate. The Second Condition of Equilibrium relates to the turning effects that act upon an object. These turning effects are called *torques*. The Second Condition of Equilibrium states that the sum of all the applied torques must equal zero.

$$\Sigma T = 0$$

Having written the second condition of equilibrium, we can restate it as:

$$\Sigma (+ T) = \Sigma (- T)$$

This tells us that the turning effects in one direction about a point must equal the turning effects in the other direction about the point (pivot point). These effects can be labeled clockwise/counter-clockwise, left/right, or up/down. My preference is to use the (+) and (–) signs. This way one direction can always be set opposite the other without worrying about additional perspectives.

Torques are further defined as $T = F_\ell$, where F is an applied force and ℓ is the distance from the applied force to the point of rotation (pivot point).

When working with torques we must also consider the weight of the object involved. Gravity pulls on each and every part of an object. These parts cause torques about the central point in the object. If all the individual torques were set against one another and canceled out, then one point, a point about which all the other points rotate, would remain. All the weight of the object could be considered to operate from this point too. That point is called the *Center of Gravity* (CG).

A force whose action line passes through the pivot point exerts no torque. The ℓ is the "lever arm," which is defined as the perpendicular distance from the applied force to the pivot point.

When an object is supported at its center of gravity, the point of rotation for torques is also located at the CG. Therefore, the weight of the object is not a factor in the identification of the applied torques. This occurs because of the definition of the lever arm. The object is supported at the CG, so the force exerted by the object's weight does *not* have a lever arm; there is no distance from the applied force to the pivot point.

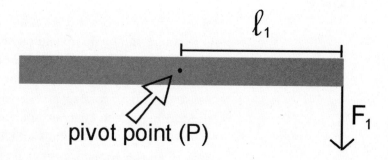

The uniform rod above weighs 2N and is 1m long. The force F_1 is applied at the end of the rod, as shown. The lever arm ℓ_1 is the distance from the force F_1 to the pivot point P. Should values of 10N be added for the force and a length of .5m for ℓ, the calculation of the torques becomes:

$$T = F_\ell$$

$$T = (10N)(.5m)$$

$$T = 5N \bullet m$$

Note: The units of torque are a force unit multiplied by a length unit.

The situation above can change drastically by simply allowing the rod to rotate at a different point.

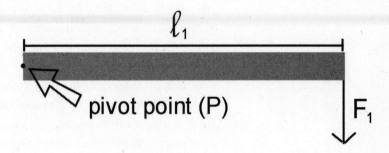

The new situation above requires that we remember the weight of the object in addition to the already known F_1. The calculation of the torques is:

$$T = (F_1 \ell_1) + (F_{wt} \ell_{wt})$$

There are two torque-producing entities.

$$T = (10\text{N} \bullet 1\text{m}) + (2\text{N} \bullet .5\text{m})$$

$$T = 10\text{N} \bullet \text{m} + 1\text{N} \bullet \text{m}$$

$$T = 11\text{N} \bullet \text{m}$$

Should we pick the other end of the rod as the pivot point, F_1 completely cancels out of the problem and the applied torque becomes 1N • m.

KINEMATICS
MOTION IN A STRAIGHT LINE

An object that changes its position as time passes is in motion. Straight line motion deals with objects that begin, continue, or complete their motion along a straight line.

The quantities *speed* and *velocity* are often used interchangeably. Speed is a scalar quantity and velocity is a vector quantity. Although they are different physical quantities, they can be used together as long as the motion involved is an absolutely straight line. We simply accept that there is an inferred direction.

Speed is defined as the distance an object travels per unit of time taken.

$$\text{Speed }(U) = \frac{\text{distance}}{\text{time}} = \frac{d}{t}$$

The units of speed are m/s.

The distance shown has no direction, so it makes no difference if the motion is a straight line or not.

Velocity is defined as the displacement of an object per unit of time taken.

$$\text{Velocity}(v) = \frac{\text{displacement}}{\text{time}} = \frac{s}{t}$$

The units of velocity are m/s.

The use of the term "displacement," which is a vector and reads *displacement vector,* confirms that velocity is also a vector quantity.

When the displacement is the total displacement of an object and the time is the total time taken, the velocity of the object is its average velocity.

$$v = \frac{s}{t}$$

Sometimes it is necessary to know the velocity of an object exactly at a specific instant in time. This is called *instantaneous velocity.* Instantaneous velocity is found by restricting the passage of time to as close to zero as possible. The exact velocity of an object at a specific time is called its instantaneous velocity (v_{ins}). An instantaneous velocity is used to monitor the velocity of an object before it starts moving, at any time while it is moving, or just as it stops moving. These are called the original velocity (v_o) and the final velocity (v_f), respectively. Both the original velocity and the final velocity together can be used to find the average velocity.

$$v = \frac{v_f + v_o}{2}$$

The quantity Δv means change in velocity and can be found by $\Delta v = v_f - v_o$.

This is important because when an object undergoes a Δv (change in velocity) it is considered to be *accelerated*. An acceleration is defined as a time rate change in velocity.

$$a = \frac{\Delta v}{\Delta t} \quad \text{or} \quad a = \frac{v_f - v_o}{t_f - t_o}$$

The units for acceleration are m/s^2. Acceleration is a vector quantity.

The basic linear equations are:

$$v = \frac{s}{t} \qquad \Delta v = v_f - v_o$$

$$\Delta t = t_f - t_o \qquad v = \frac{v_f + v_o}{2}$$

$$a = \frac{\Delta v}{\Delta t} \qquad a = \frac{v_f - v_o}{t_f - t_o}$$

The equations above are used to derive three more useful linear motion equations, which are shown below.

$$v_f = v_o + at$$

$$v_f^{\,2} = v_o^{\,2} + 2as$$

$$s = v_o t + \frac{1}{2}at^2$$

In general, students do well solving linear motion problems, so we'll only try one here.

Example

A subway train starts from rest at the station and accelerates at a rate of 1.25 m/s² for 14 seconds, then coasts at a velocity for 50 seconds. The conductor then applies the brakes to slow the train at a rate of 1.2 m/s² to bring it to a complete stop at the next station. How far apart are the two train stations?

Solution

Upon analysis of the situation we find there are three parts to the problem:

1. The train speeds up (acceleration).
2. The train coasts (constant velocity).
3. The train slows down (negative acceleration).

The operation $s = v_o t + \frac{1}{2}at^2$ is suitable for part one. Remember that the train started from rest, so the $(v_o t)$ term is zero. The working equation is:

$$s = \frac{1}{2}at^2$$

$$s = \frac{1}{2}(1.25\text{m/s}^2)(14\sec)^2$$

$$s = 122\text{m}$$

Peterson's SAT II Success: Physics

The train coasts at velocity for the second part of the problem. Once we find the velocity, we will be able to determine how far the train coasts in 50 seconds. We must start at the station with the train at rest in order to find the velocity of the train when the acceleration stops. The equation ($v_f = v_o + at$) works, but remember, the train is initially at rest, making $v_o = 0$, which drops the term from the equation to yield

$v_f = at$.

Substituting and solving gives the final velocity of the train when acceleration stops. Remember that this is also the average velocity while the train is coasting.

$$v_f = at$$

$$v_f = (1.25 \text{m/s}^2)(14\text{s})$$

$$v_f = 17.5 \text{m/s}$$

Now we find the displacement while the train coasts, using:

$s = v\,t$
$s = (17.5 \text{ m/s})(50\text{s})$
$s = 875 \text{ m}$

The equation that best fits the third part of the problem is ($v_f^2 = v_o^2 + 2as$). Again we can drop a term from the equation. The final velocity of the train is zero, which allows us to eliminate it. Before writing the equation think about the situation. What is happening? The train is slowing down. This is a negative acceleration, which *must* be entered as such in the equation. The average velocity the train has had for the past 50 seconds now becomes the original velocity at the start of the negative acceleration (deceleration).

$$v_f^{\,2} = 0$$

$$0 = v_o^{\,2} + 2(-a)s$$

$$-\frac{(v_o^{\,2})}{2(-a)} = s$$

$$\frac{-(17.5\text{m/s})^2}{2(-1.25\text{m/s})^2} = s$$

$$s = 127.6\text{m}$$

Before completing the problem, let's take a look at the solution above. Correct signs are critical! When v_o^2 was subtracted from both sides of the equation, we were manipulating a negative squared quantity. When the v_o quantity is squared, the negative sign *does not* become positive. Likewise the acceleration is negative. When the $-a$ is divided into both sides of the equation, we are left with a negative again. Carrying out the solution gave *a* positive displacement when both negative signs cancelled out, an expected result since the train continued in the *same* direction as it slowed to a stop.

Calculating the final answer to the problem requires the addition of the displacement of the train during each of the three parts. They are:

122 m	Part 1 (acceleration)
875 m	Part 2 (constant velocity)
+ 127.6 m	Part 3 (negative acceleration)
1124.6 m	

The total distance between the two subway stations is 1124.6 meters.

FREE FALL

When an object is released near the earth and nothing except the earth affects the object, the object is in free fall. We notice that as soon as any object is placed into free fall, the object moves toward the earth at an increasing rate. That being the case, the object must be accelerating. In the absence of air, all objects fall toward the earth at a constant rate of 9.8 m/s^2. The acceleration due to the earth's gravitational attraction is commonly referred to as "g."

Several interesting situations occur when an object is thrown straight up. Since we will be discussing vector quantities, the direction of the vector will be mentioned first. The direction toward the earth (down) will be considered positive. The direction away from the earth (up) will be considered negative.

Restating: An object is thrown straight up.

While the object is rising:
• The displacement of the object is up (negative).

• The velocity of the object is up (negative).

• The acceleration of the object is *down* (positive).

The instant the object reaches its maximum height:
- The displacement of the object is zero.

- The velocity of the object is zero.

- The acceleration of the object is *down* (positive).

While the object is falling:
- The displacement of the object is down (positive).

- The velocity of the object is down (positive).

- The acceleration of the object is *down* (positive).

All objects in free fall near the earth are accelerated toward the earth (down) at a rate of 9.8 m/s².

Other interesting facts about objects that are thrown straight up near the earth and return to the same spot are:
- Time up = time down.

- Displacement up = displacement down.

- Velocity up = velocity down.

Example

Imagine that we drop a rock from the top of a watchtower. Since all objects fall at the same rate (ignoring air resistance), the mass and size of the object do not matter. The rock is found to hit the ground below in 4.25 seconds. How high is the tower?

Solution

At first you might think that we need more information, but we don't. This is really a linear motion problem with constant acceleration (g). We know the object starts from rest, accelerates at 9.8 m/s², and takes 4.25 seconds to hit the ground. The displacement can be found with the following equation:

$$s = v_o t + \frac{1}{2} g t^2$$

Notice the g instead of a. The object starts from rest, which allows us to eliminate the ($v_o t$) term, leaving the working equation:

$$s = \frac{1}{2}gt^2$$

$$s = \frac{1}{2}(9.8\text{m/s}^2)(4.25\text{sec})^2$$

$$s = 88.5\text{m}$$

Example

Let's look at a problem where an object is thrown into the air and returns.

A girl throws a baseball straight up and catches the ball at the same height 2.6 seconds later. How fast did the girl throw the ball into the air?

Solution

Again, we can use the equation $s = v_o t + \frac{1}{2}gt^2$. Displacement is a vector quantity, so when the ball returns to the girl's hand, there is no displacement (the ball started in her hand and has therefore not gone anywhere). The equation becomes:

$$0 = v_o t + \frac{1}{2}gt^2$$

$$-v_o = \frac{gt^2}{2t}$$

$$-v_o = \frac{(9.8\text{m/s}^2)(2.6\text{s})^2}{2(2.6\text{s})}$$

$$-v_o = 12.74\text{m/s}^2$$

Note: The negative v_o lets us know that the girl is throwing the ball upward.

MOTION IN TWO DIMENSIONS

CURVILINEAR MOTION

The motion of a football observed when a quarterback throws a long pass or when a baseball is hit into the air are examples of *curvilinear motion*. Curvilinear motion is the flight of an object as it first rises into the air and then falls to the ground while at the same time moving from one point to another in a straight line along the x axis.

Let's look at an example of curvilinear motion.

A boy is playing with some marbles on the kitchen table. As he rolls the marbles around, one of them rolls off the edge of the table. Does the marble fall directly to the floor? No it doesn't. Why not? The answer is because once the marble is in free fall, the only force acting on it is the earth's gravitational attraction.

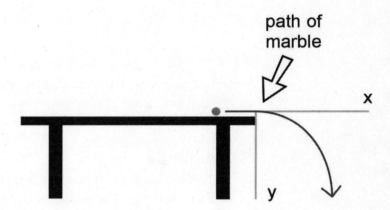

Nothing slows the marble in its movement along the x axis. The marble would continue moving along the x axis permanently if it didn't strike the floor. When the marble clears the tabletop it is in free fall. Its velocity with respect to the y axis is zero, but in free fall, the marble is accelerated toward the earth at a rate of 9.8 m/s^2. The time it takes the marble to fall to the floor is also the time the marble can continue to move along the x axis. That is why the marble does not hit the floor directly under the edge of the table.

The same condition applies to the motion of an object that is hit or released at an angle above the horizontal (also called projectile motion).

Example

Consider a fisherman making a long cast. His lure is released as the rod moves forward on the cast. The lure rises into the air while at the same time moving forward across the water. The lure then falls to the water as it reaches the fisherman's target.

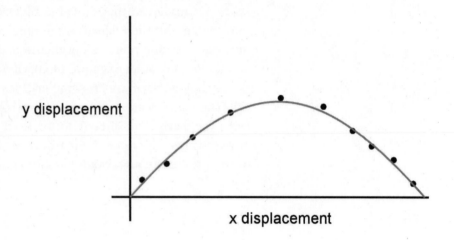

After careful observation, one can state the following information about the fisherman's cast (above): The lure always leaves the rod tip (considered ground level) at an angle of 30° and a velocity of 22 m/s. How far does the fisherman cast his lure?

Solution

This is another two-axis problem. The x-axis solution requires that we know the time. The y-axis information is sufficient to find the total time the lure is in free fall, thus providing the time to complete the x-axis solution.

We'll begin with the y axis. The actual straight up velocity v_y is not known. The velocity the lure has as it leaves the tip of the fisherman's rod is v_L and can be considered to be the hypotenuse of a right triangle in which v_y is the opposite side.

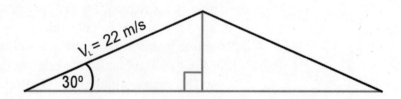

After finding v_y, apply the appropriate free fall equation to find the time.

$$v_y = v_L \ (\cos 30°)$$
$$v_y = (22 \text{ m/s})(.5) = 11 \text{ m/s}$$

The equation that yields the time is $v_{fy} = v_{oy} + at$ (using the subscript "y" to denote the vertical axis).

$$v_{fy} = v_{oy} + at$$

$$\frac{v_{fy} - v_{oy}}{a} = t$$

$$\frac{(11\text{m/s}) - (-11\text{m/s})}{9.8\text{m/s}^2} = t = 2.24s$$

The total time the lure is in the air (free fall) is 2.24 seconds.

The x component of the lure's velocity (v_x) must also be calculated with the trigonometry.

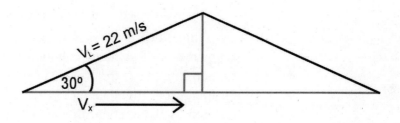

$$v_x = v_L \ (\cos 30°)$$
$$v_x = (22 \text{ m/s})(.866)$$
$$v_x = 19 \text{ m/s}$$

With both the time and x velocity known, the distance the lure travels can be found using:

$$s = v \, t$$
$$s = (19 \text{ m/s}^2) \ (2.24 \text{ sec})$$
$$s = 42.56 \text{ m}$$

NEWTON'S LAWS OF MOTION

Unbalanced forces are the cause of motion. This can be seen by taking a walk and watching any objects that are not moving. A stone on the ground, a flowerpot on a window ledge, or a hat on someone's head all remain where they rest unless something happens. What exactly must happen? Sir Isaac Newton applied his attention to that same question almost 400 years ago. The result was Newton's Laws of Motion. The first Law of Motion as expressed by Sir Isaac has come to be known as the Law of Inertia.

Newton's First Law of Motion:

> An object that is at rest will remain at rest, and an object in motion will remain in motion unless a nonzero force acts upon the object.

This means that *all objects have a tendency to remain as they are.* They do not easily change their state of rest or motion. Should you push on an object such as a chair, the chair pushes back on you. That same chair with someone sitting in it becomes much more difficult to push. This is because the chair is now an object with more mass. The greater difficulty in pushing the chair happens because of the larger mass of the chair with a person sitting in it, and therefore the chair has a larger inertia.

Newton's Third Law of Motion:

> For every action there is an equal and opposite reaction.

This is called the *action-reaction* law. A good example of the action-reaction is when a balloon has been blown up and released. The balloon flies about the room. The action in this case is pressurized gas escaping from the opening in the balloon. The balloon provides the reaction by flying about the room. The action-reaction statement is what leads us to the following statement:

> All forces occur in pairs.

Force pairs are always equal in magnitude and opposite in their direction. This means they act upon different objects. They do not act on the same object.

Newton's Second Law of Motion:

> Newton's Second Law of Motion is the one from which we derive the famous equation $F = ma$. This tells us that an unbalanced force accelerates an object in the same direction as the applied force. By rearranging the equation, we get $\frac{F}{m} = a$. We can see that the acceleration is directly related to the applied force and indirectly related to the mass of the body involved.

When a force is applied to a body, the body is accelerated in the direction of the force at a rate that is indirectly related to the mass of the body and directly related to the force applied.

The unit for force is kg • m/s^2, which is more commonly called the Newton (N). Force is a vector quantity.

The mass of an object is not the same as the weight of an object. Mass is an inertial measure of matter, while weight is the measure of the earth's gravitational attraction to an object. From this statement, we can see that weight and force are two quantities that are really the same:

$$F = ma \qquad\qquad wt = mg$$

$$F = kg \bullet m/s^2 \quad = \quad wt = kg \bullet m/s^2$$

An example of the force required to initially move an object resting on a surface is shown on the following diagram. It is a typical representation for the force required to overcome the frictional force between two surfaces.

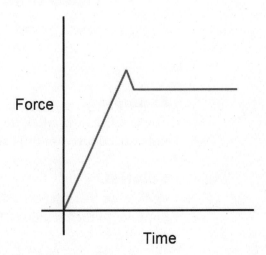

As we see in the graph above, more force is required to start an object in motion than is required to keep the object in motion.

APPLICATION OF NEWTON'S SECOND LAW

Newton's Second Law makes it clear that an object will not change its state of motion or non-motion unless a force is applied to it. Objects on earth that have forces applied to them will move once frictional forces are overcome.

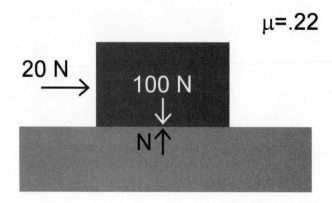

Example

The coefficient of friction between the surfaces above is .22. Find the unbalanced force and the acceleration of the block.

Solution

Remember that frictional force resists motion and will always be opposite to the direction of the applied force.

F_A is the applied force, and F_f is the frictional force.

$$F = ma \quad \text{The applied force is 20N}$$

$$F_A - F_f = ma \quad \text{The frictional force is } \mu \bullet n.$$

$$F_A - (.22)(100\text{N}) = ma$$

$$20\text{N} - 22\text{N} = ma$$

We can stop here. The block will not move! This is because the applied force is not large enough to overcome friction.

Let's change the applied force to 62.8N and find the acceleration with the new conditions. Once again F_A is the applied force, and F_f is the frictional force.

$$F = ma \quad \text{The applied force is 62.8N.}$$

$$F_A - F_f = ma \quad \text{The frictional force is } u \bullet n.$$

$$F_A - (.22)(100\text{N}) = ma$$

$$62.8\text{N} - 22\text{N} = ma \quad F_A \text{ is larger than } F_f.$$

The block will move.

$$\text{mass of the block } = \frac{100\text{N}}{9.8 \text{ m/s}^2} = 10.2 \text{ kg}$$

$$\frac{62.8\text{N} - 22\text{N}}{10.2 \text{ kg}} = a$$

$$4 \text{ m/s}^2 = a$$

The block accelerates in the direction of the unbalanced force.

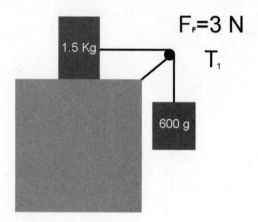

Example

The frictional force between the surface above and the mass resting on it is 3N. The hanging object has a mass of 600 *g*. Find the acceleration of the system. (The string is massless and the pulley is frictionless). The applied force is from the hanging mass (m • *g* = wt) minus the frictional force.

Solution

Start the problem by writing the Second Law Equation, and then insert all the values into the equation step by step.

$$F = ma$$
$$F_A - F_f = ma$$

We are looking for *a*, so we rearrange and insert values.

$$a = \frac{(.6 \text{ kg})(9.8 \text{ m/s}^2) - (3\text{N})}{.6 \text{ kg} + 1.5 \text{ kg}}$$

$$a = 1.37 \text{ m/s}^2$$

The 600 *g* (.6 kg) hanging mass is the cause of the applied force in the system. Multiply this mass by *g* (9.8 m/s²) to convert it into weight. Friction is subtracted because friction always opposes motion. *Both* masses will be accelerated (if motion does occur), so we add them together.

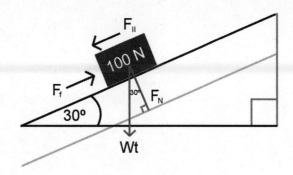

The diagram above shows a block sliding down a raised plane at a constant rate. The force parallel ($F_{||}$) is the applied force, the weight (wt) of the object acts directly toward the earth, the normal force (F_N) acts directly out of the surface, and the frictional force (F_f) opposes the motion of the block.

The (F_N) is the result of a part of the weight being directed down the plane. [F_N = (wt sin 30°)]. The (F_N) is also called the perpendicular force ($F_\perp$) and is directed from the plane into the block.

[$F_N = F_\perp$ = (wt cos 30°)]. The block slides down the plane at a constant rate, meaning no acceleration; thus no unbalanced forces are in operation down the plane. Under these conditions, the force of friction equals the force parallel ($F_{||} = F_f$). The coefficient of friction is:

$$\frac{F_{||}}{F_\perp} = \frac{\text{wt } \sin\theta}{\text{wt } \cos\theta} = \frac{\sin\theta}{\cos\theta} = \tan\theta$$

WORK AND ENERGY

WORK

Work is defined as the product of a displacement and a force in the direction of the displacement. This translates to:

$$\text{Work} = F \bullet s \bullet \cos\theta$$

When the direction of the force applied is the same as the displacement and is in the same direction as the proposed work, the $\cos\theta$ is cos 90°, which is 1, and may be dropped from the equation. The force unit is the *Newton* (N), and displacement is in meters (m). The unit of work is N • m, or *Joule* (J). Work is not a vector quantity.

Work is done by carrying, pushing, or pulling an object some distance, or it may be done in lifting an object to a height against gravity. In these cases work is accomplished and is a positive quantity. Should the applied force not move the object in question, no work is done, or worse, negative work is done (imagine pushing forward against a car that is rolling backwards).

The act of holding an object does not constitute the performance of work. *A displacement is always required for work to be done.* When a moving automobile skids along a road, the road does frictional work against the tires. That is what brings the car to a stop.

Work is usually mentioned with energy because the two quantities are interchangeable.

ENERGY

Energy is defined as the ability to do work. There are two types of energy: kinetic energy (KE) and potential energy (PE). The interrelationship of work, potential energy, and kinetic energy can be seen through the manipulation of the equations representing them.

$$\text{Work} = F \bullet s$$
$$= \text{N} \bullet \text{m}$$
$$= Joule$$

$$\text{PE} = mgh$$
$$= \text{kg} \bullet \text{m/s}^2 \bullet \text{m}$$
$$= \text{N} \bullet \text{m}$$
$$= Joule$$

$$\text{KE} = \frac{1}{2}mv^2$$
$$= \text{kg} \bullet \frac{\text{m}^2}{\text{s}^2}$$
$$= \text{N} \bullet \text{m}$$
$$= Joule$$

It should be pointed out that the Work and PE equations are essentially the same. The mg in the PE equation is the weight of the object, while the h (height) is a displacement yielding an alternate for PE as Wt $\bullet$ s, which is essentially the same as $F \bullet s$.

Clearly the three entities are really one and the same. That's why they are interchangeable. The Law of Conservation of Energy is stated, *"energy can not be created or destroyed,"* leading to the following equation for work and energy.

$$(\text{Work} + \text{KE} + \text{PE})_{\text{before an event}} = (\text{Work} + \text{KE} + \text{PE})_{\text{after an event}}$$

When an object possesses 50 *J* of potential energy, the object has the ability to do 50 *J* of work or to gain 50 *J* of kinetic energy.

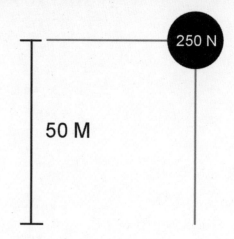

50 M

The 250N boulder shown in the diagram above possesses PE, which can be stated in equation form below.

$$PE \quad = \quad mgh \quad = \quad wt\ h$$
$$= \quad (250N)(50m)$$
$$= \quad 12,500\ J$$

If the boulder fell to the ground, all of the PE would transform into KE just before the boulder struck the ground. Thus its KE would be 12,500 J. When the boulder came to rest after striking the ground, the ground would have done 12,500 J of frictional work to bring the boulder to a halt.

Should we know that the boulder penetrates 6 cm into the ground, then the work/energy theorem can be used to find the frictional force exerted by the ground on the boulder.

$$(Work + PE + KE)_{before} = (Work + PE + KE)_{after}$$

At the top of the cliff the boulder only has PE, so the work and KE disappear from the equation, leaving

$$PE_{before} = (Work + PE + KE\ )_{after}$$

At the bottom of the cliff, all of the PE is transformed into KE, which promptly changes to the work done on the ground. Conveniently, the work done by the boulder on the ground is exactly the work done by the ground on the boulder, leaving:

$$PE_{before} = Work_{after}$$
$$mgh = F \cdot s \cdot \cos \theta$$

Cos θ is 1 in the problem because all motion is in the direction of the proposed work. Therefore, it may be dropped.

$$\frac{mgh}{s} = F_f \qquad \text{Remember to change cm to m.}$$

$$\frac{12,500J}{6cm\big/100cm/m} = 208333.3 \text{ N}$$

A *pendulum* is a device that shows the interchange of potential energy and kinetic energy. When the pendulum bob is raised above the zero point, it gains potential energy. Releasing the bob and allowing it to swing freely allows the PE to convert to KE. The bob falls and swings through its zero or resting point, where the PE has been changed to KE. As the bob swings to and fro, the PE and KE continue to transform into one another.

A *spring* is another device that shows the transformation of potential energy into kinetic energy. Stretching and compression of the spring provide the PE interchange with the KE, which is maximized in between the two extremes of the stretching and compression of the spring. Both the pendulum and the spring also undergo "simple harmonic motion" when they vibrate. That concept will be discussed in Chapter Three.

POWER

Power is defined as the rate at which work is done or energy is produced.

$$\text{Power} = \frac{work}{time} = \frac{Joule}{s}$$

The unit for power is the $\frac{Joule}{s}$ or the Watt.

Variations of the power equation are either of the energy units divided by time.

$$\frac{PE}{time} \quad \text{or} \quad \frac{KE}{time}$$

When a person climbs a flight of stairs, his or her body weight is lifted a distance against gravity. The work performed to move up the stairs is the same as the PE required when moving any object away from the surface of the earth (*mgh*). Walking up the stairs slowly takes longer than running up them, but the work performed in either case is the same. The difference is the *time*. Power output when walking up the stairs is definitely less than when running up the stairs.

MOMENTUM

Momentum is the product of the mass of an object multiplied by the velocity of the object. Momentum is represented by *P.*

$$P = mv$$
$$= \text{kg} \bullet \text{m/s}$$

The unit for momentum is the kg • m/s. Momentum is a vector quantity.

Objects resist changes in their state of motion. Remember Newton's First Law of Motion, which states that an object has inertia whether it is at rest or in motion. This statement is *not* true for the momentum of an object. A physics book at rest on a desk has inertia, but it has zero momentum. Anyone could move the book simply by picking it up, yet how many of us would like to try to catch that same book as it fell from the top of the Empire State Building? Not me, for sure! Nor you either, I suspect.

The falling book not only has inertia, it also has the momentum it gained in falling from the top of the building. As you can tell from looking at the momentum equation, the greater the velocity of an object, the more momentum it will possess. In fact that is one momentous physics book!

Whenever an object moves it has momentum. A change in the velocity of an object produces a change in the momentum of that object. Manipulation of Newton's Second Law equation gives:

$$F = ma$$

$$F = m\frac{\Delta v}{t}$$

$$\frac{\Delta v}{t} = a$$

The $m\Delta$ is a change in momentum. An equivalent term, *Ft*, is called impulse. A change in the momentum of an object only occurs when an impulse is applied to the object. Thus, an impulse produces a change in momentum.

Let's investigate an example of momentum (*mv*), a Δ momentum ($m\Delta v$), and an impulse (*Ft*) event.

The space shuttle takes off from Cape Canaveral on its way to the International Space Station (ISS). As the shuttle approaches the space station, it is moving with a larger velocity than the space station, so the pilot fires the shuttle's retro-rockets to slow down and match speeds with the ISS. Before the retro-rockets fire, the shuttle has a velocity (v_o) that, when combined with the mass of the shuttle, give it a momentum of mv_o.

The retro-rockets fire, thereby exerting a force (*F*) on the shuttle for the time the rockets are fired. This produces an impulse (*Ft*), which acts on the shuttle. After the retro-rockets have finished the burn, the shuttle has a new momentum of (mv_f).

$$F = ma$$

$$F = m\frac{\Delta v}{t}$$

$$Ft = m\Delta v$$

This is the impulse that caused the change in momentum we expected and required for the shuttle to dock with the ISS.

COLLISIONS

When objects collide, the collisions are called *perfectly elastic, inelastic*, or *perfectly inelastic*. A perfectly elastic collision is one in which no kinetic energy is lost from the system. A perfectly inelastic collision is one in which all kinetic energy is lost from the system. An inelastic collision is any collision in between the two perfect conditions and is how collisions really occur in the real world. The lost energy (from the system in discussion) appears elsewhere, so the law of conservation of energy is not disobeyed.

If two pool balls of equal mass collide head on under perfect conditions, no kinetic energy would be lost. Leading to the following situation:

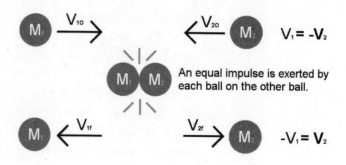

After the collision v_{1o} equals v_{1f} and v_{2o} equals v_{2f}. The momentum of each pool ball before the collision is the same as their momentum after the collision. Momentum is conserved, leading to the statement of the Law of Conservation of Momentum.

The Law of Conservation of Momentum states that the momentum of an isolated system remains constant.

Example

Here is an interesting example of an inelastic collision.

A freight train is being assembled in the freight yard. An empty car (A) with a mass of 4000 kg is moving along the track with a velocity of 1.5 m/s. Another car (B) is completely loaded, has a mass of 16,000 kg, and is moving in the opposite direction at 10 m/s. The boxcars collide, couple together, and move off. What is the velocity and direction of movement of the two boxcars?

Solution

The combined momentum of the two boxcars before the collision must equal their combined momentum after the collision. Thus:

$$(m_A v_A)_{BEFORE} + (m_B v_B)_{BEFORE} = (m_A v_A)_{AFTER} + (m_B v_B)_{AFTER}$$

$$\frac{(m_A)(-v_A) + (m_B v_B)}{m_A + m_B} = v_{AFTER} \qquad \text{choosing } v_A \text{ as negative}$$

$$\frac{(4000\text{kg})(-1.5\text{m/s}) + (1600\text{kg})(10\text{m/s})}{4000\text{kg} + 1600\text{kg}} = v_{AFTER}$$

$$= 7.7\text{m/s}$$

Notice the velocity is positive. Both boxcars are moving in the same direction as boxcar B was moving at the start.

CIRCULAR AND ROTARY

CIRCULAR MOTION

A body moving in a circular path is said to have uniform circular motion. Amusement park rides such as the Ferris wheel and the carousel are common examples of bodies moving with uniform circular motion. A student watching the slow constant motion of the second hand around the face of the clock is another example, as is the boy who twirls a rubber stopper on a string around his head at a constant rate. The rate is constant, but the direction is not. This constitutes a change in velocity, which is an acceleration.

According to Newton, acceleration is caused by an unbalanced force, so where is the force in this case? In investigating the case of the string and stopper, it's clear the stopper will fly off in a straight line if the string is cut. The string attached to the stopper provides the force that keeps the stopper turning in a circle. That force is called *centripetal force* and is directed inward toward the center of the circle.

The equation for centripetal force is:

$$F_c = \frac{mv^2}{r}$$

And by substituting *ma* for F_c we have:

$$ma = \frac{mv^2}{r}$$

Which leads us to the equation for centripetal acceleration by factoring (canceling) the masses out of the equation.

$$a_c = \frac{v^2}{r}$$

Planets and satellites stay in their orbits due to the gravitational force exerted on them by the body they circle. Newton stated his explanation of satellite motion in his law of universal gravitation. Essentially, it says that all matter in the universe attracts all other matter based upon the mass of the bodies and the inverse of the square of the distance between them. The gravitational constant is:

$$(G = 6.67e^{-11}\text{N} \bullet \frac{m^2}{\text{kg}^2})$$

The centripetal force that keeps the planetary bodies in their proper places around the sun and the sun in its place in the galaxy can be explained by using the equations below.

$$F = G\frac{(m_1)(m_2)}{r^2}$$

Recognizing *F* as a centripetal force and substituting the two equations for the equivalent forces yields

$$F_G = F_c$$

$$\Downarrow$$

$$G\frac{(m_1)(m_2)}{r^2} = \frac{mv^2}{r}$$

Newton's law of gravitation was a summary of the work done by Copernicus, Galileo, and Kepler.

KEPLER'S LAWS

Johannes Kepler derived the following three laws of planetary motion:

1. Planets move in ellipses. The sun is at one focus.
2. A line joining any planet to the sun sweeps out equal areas in equal times.
3. For all the planets in the solar system, the cube of the average distance from the sun divided by the square of its period of revolution is a constant $k = \dfrac{r^3}{T^2}$

Example

Try the following problem involving the Laws of Gravitation.

A newly discovered planet in another solar system was determined to have a mass .85 that of the earth, and its diameter was 1.25 that of earth. How would your weight on the planet compare to your weight on the earth?

Solution

The earth's attraction for your body and the new planet's attraction for your body can be found by using the gravitation equation for both planets and setting the two equal to one another.

$$F = G\frac{(m_e)(m_2)}{r_e^2} \quad \text{and}$$

$$F = G\frac{(m_p)(m_2)}{r_p^2} \quad \text{Factor out the G's, and your mass, too.}$$

$$\frac{m_e}{r_e^2} = \frac{m_p}{r_p^2}$$

Letting the earth values equal unity we have:

$$\frac{1}{1^2} = \frac{.85}{(1.25)^2} = .544$$

This tells us that your weight on the new planet would be a little more than half your weight on the earth.

Example

Let's go back to the International Space Station (ISS), which has a period of 98.2 minutes and is at an average height of 380 km above the earth's surface. Find the orbital velocity of the ISS (the radius of Earth is 6400 km and its mass is 6×10^{24} kg).

Solution

$$F_c = \frac{mv^2}{r} \text{ and } F = G\frac{(m_1)(m_2)}{r^2}$$

$$v = \sqrt{\frac{Gm}{r}}$$

Setting the equations equal to each other and rearranging yields:

$$v = \sqrt{\frac{\left(6.67 \times 10^{-11} \text{N} \frac{\text{m}^2}{\text{kg}^2}\right)(6 \times 10^{24} \text{kg})}{6.4 \times 10^6 \text{m} + 3.81 \times 10^5 \text{m}}}$$

$$v = 5.9 \times 10^6 \text{m/s}$$

WEIGHTLESSNESS

The strength of the earth's gravitational field decreases as the distance from the earth's center increases. A person stands on a scale on the earth and reads his weight as 800N. If the scale worked at 300 km, 900 km, and 2000 km above the earth's surface, the person's weight would be 727N @ 300 km, 613N @ 900 km, and 462N @ 2000 km. Remember the force with which the earth attracts is based on the inverse of the square of the distance $\frac{1}{r^2}$.

The apparent weightlessness of a body orbiting the earth is the result of the object freely falling toward the earth's surface at all times. The body never reaches the earth because the earth's surface curves out from under it at the same rate at which the object falls.

ROTARY MOTION

Objects that roll along a surface exhibit two kinds of motion: linear motion as the object moves from point A to point B, and rotary motion as the edge of the object rotates about a central point or axis. An example of these types of motion is a bicycle wheel rolling along the ground. The rotation of the wheel is measured by the number of circular turns the wheel makes and is measured in rotations per minute (rpm), revolutions per minute (rev), or the number of degrees turned by the wheel. The radian is another convenient and frequently used method for measuring angular values.

The radian measure is a ratio between the arc length of a circular path and the radius of the circle. Angular displacement θ is also the ratio of the arc length to the radius of the circle.

$$\theta_{RADIANS} = \frac{\text{arc length}}{\text{radius}} = \frac{s}{r}$$

Remember: 1 rev = 1 rotation = 360° = 2 radians

- The rotational analog of linear velocity (*v*) is angular velocity ω.

- The rotational analog of linear acceleration (*a*) is angular acceleration α.

- The rotational analog of linear displacement (*s*) is angular displacement θ.

Each of these quantities is the rotational analog of its linear counterpart, so all the linear velocity equations work in the same way simply by substituting the angular quantity for the linear quantity.

Let's return to the bicycle wheel to discuss a quantity that is both rotational and linear (tangential quantities). While the wheel rolls along the ground, it moves a linear distance as it simultaneously moves an angular distance.

$$s_{tan} = r\theta$$

The linear distance traveled by the wheel is a direct result of the angle through which the wheel turns and the radius of the wheel. The constant linear rate at which the bicycle wheel moves from point A to B can be expressed tangentially as:

$$v_{tan} = \omega r$$

Should the bicycle wheel be changing velocity, then a linear and an angular acceleration occurs.

$$a_{tan} = \alpha r$$

The radian measure must be used in solving tangential quantities.

Example

A bicyclist coasts a distance of 180 m in 30 seconds. How many revolutions do the wheels make in that time? The bicycle wheels are 80 cm in diameter.

Solution

The information given is linear, while the requested quantity is rotational (angular displacement θ).

$$s_{tan} = r\theta$$

$$\theta = \frac{s_{tan}}{r}$$

$$\theta = \frac{180m}{.4m/radian}$$

$$\theta = 450 \text{ radians}$$

Change radians to revolutions (see previous)

$$\frac{450 \text{ radians}}{2\pi \text{ radians/revolutions}} = 71.6 \text{ revolutions}$$

The angular velocity of the wheels can be found easily enough, too.

$$v_{tan} = \omega r$$

$$\omega = \frac{v_{tan}}{r}$$

$$\omega = \frac{180m/30s}{.4 \text{ m/radian}}$$

$$\omega = 15 \text{ radians/s}$$

CHAPTER SUMMARY

STATICS AND TORQUES

- Statics is the study of objects that are not free to move.

- Objects that are not free to move are in equilibrium.

- The two conditions of equilibrium are:

    —The sum of all applied forces is equal to zero.

    —The sum of all applied torques is equal to zero.

- A torque is defined as the product of a force multiplied by its lever arm.

- A lever arm is defined as the perpendicular distance from the line of an applied force to the pivot point.

- Lines of force that pass through the pivot point cause no torques.

- The center of gravity (CG) of an object is the point from which all the weight of an object is considered to act.

KINEMATICS

- Displacement is the straight-line distance between two points.

- Velocity is the time-rate change in displacement.

- Acceleration is the time-rate change in velocity.

- Free fall is the condition where the only force acting on an object is the earth's gravitational attraction.

- All objects in free fall near the earth are accelerated toward the earth at a constant acceleration of 9.8 m/s^2.

MOTION IN TWO DIMENSIONS

- Objects in free fall that are moving in a curved path can be viewed as having linear motion on both the x and y axis simultaneously.

- The horizontal motion (x axis) and the vertical motion (y axis) of a projectile are independent of one another.

- The time during which an object is in free fall is the length of time an object can be moving along the x axis when the object exhibits curvilinear motion.

NEWTON'S LAWS OF MOTION

- Newton's First Law of Motion is called the Law of Inertia

- Newton's Third Law of Motion is called the Action-Reaction Law

- Newton's Second Law of Motion stated in equation form is $F = ma$.

- Frictional forces oppose the movement of objects

- The coefficient of friction is defined as the ratio of the frictional force to the normal force of an object $U = \dfrac{F_f}{N}$.

- The normal force (F_N) always acts perpendicular to the surface from which it emanates.

- Force is a vector quantity.

WORK AND ENERGY

- Energy cannot be created nor can it be destroyed.

- Work is the product of a force and a displacement.

- Kinetic Energy is the energy of a moving object.

- Potential Energy is the energy of position or condition.

- Work, potential energy, and kinetic energy are the same quantities.

- The rate at which work is done is called power

MOMENTUM

- The symbol P is used to represent momentum.

- mv also represents momentum.

- Ft is an impulse. It produces a change in momentum $m\Delta v$.

- The law of conservation of momentum is stated: The momentum of an isolated system remains constant.

CIRCULAR AND ROTARY MOTION

- The force that produces uniform circular motion is called centripetal force.

- Newton's Law of gravitational force describes the mutual force of attraction between any two bodies in the universe.

- Kepler's laws describe the motion of the planets and satellites (third law) in the solar system.

- The actual weight of an object depends on its position in a gravitational field.

- Weightlessness is caused by the constant free fall of a body in orbit.

- Angular quantities all have linear equivalents (analogs), so the angular equations are identical to the linear equations except that θ, ω, and α must be substituted for s, v, and a.

- A rolling or spinning wheel exhibits both linear motion and angular motion, which are related by the tangential quantities.

Chapter 3

WAVES

CHAPTER 3

WAVES

WAVE PROPERTIES

Waves are energy carriers. We are familiar with water waves, light waves, and waves in a string, but there are other types of waves as well. The different types of waves have many similarities and behave alike in many respects. We will begin our discussion of waves by looking at their common characteristics.

If we were to stand on an ocean pier under which water waves were continuously passing, we would notice several things. The waves pass under the pier at a constant rate (frequency) while moving toward the beach (velocity), and the distance between the high points of the waves (wave length) is constant.

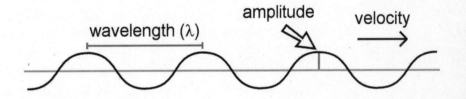

The drawing above shows a set of water waves moving past a fixed point. The wavelength (λ), or distance between waves, is defined as the distance from any point on one wave to the same point on a following or a preceding wave. The rate at which the waves move past the point is their velocity (v), and the number of waves occurring during a given time (number per sec) is the frequency (f).

Amplitude is a measure of the distance above or below the equilibrium position of the wave.

wavelength (λ) has the units $\dfrac{\text{meters}}{\text{wave}}$

frequency (f) has the units $\dfrac{\text{waves}}{\text{meters}}$

velocity (v) has the units $\dfrac{\text{meters}}{\text{sec}}$

The velocity of a wave can be calculated when the frequency and the wavelength are known.

$$v = \lambda f$$

$$v = \left(\frac{\text{meters}}{\text{wave}}\right)\left(\frac{\text{waves}}{\text{sec}}\right)$$

$$v = \frac{\text{meters}}{\text{sec}}$$

The time required for one wave to pass a given point is called the *period* of the wave (*T*). The period is the inverse of the frequency.

$$f = \frac{1}{T} \quad T = \frac{1}{f}$$

Suppose a stone were dropped into the middle of a pond from a height. The event would cause a set of waves to radiate out away from the place where the stone entered the water.

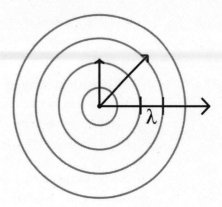

As we look at the event from above, the curvature of each wave front changes with distance. As the wave front moves further from the center it becomes less and less curved. The arrows are called *rays* and represent the straight line direction in which a single point on the wave front is moving. Rays are always perpendicular to the wave front.

Two or more waves can pass through the same point (super-position) at the same time, causing a situation called *interference*. Interference is constructive when waves reinforce one another's amplitudes, and it is destructive when waves cancel one another's amplitudes.

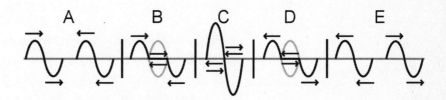

Diagrams A through E show two identical waves, x and y, traveling in opposite directions on a string.

- Diagram A shows the waves approaching one another.

- Diagram B shows that a very short time later the first part of wave x reaches the same place as the first part of wave y (superposition). The negative amplitude of wave x has destructively interfered with the positive amplitude of wave y.

- Diagram C shows both waves at the same place in time where constructive interference occurs.

- Diagram D is the same as Diagram B except that the trailing parts of the two waves are superimposed on one another.

- Diagram E shows the two waves completely separated and moving in opposite directions away from one another.

Mechanical Waves

Waves that require a physical medium in which to travel are mechanical waves. Examples are sound waves, water waves, and the vibrating waves in string instruments.

Electromagnetic Waves

Waves not needing a physical medium are called electromagnetic waves. Light, X-rays, radio waves, and cosmic waves are examples of electromagnetic waves.

Waves are sometimes classified by their method of generation. There are longitudinal (compressional) waves and transverse waves. The longitudinal wave (such as sound) is generated parallel to the direction of movement (propagation) of the wave.

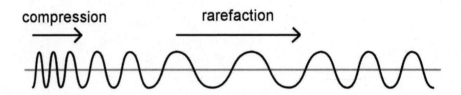

A Slinky held at both ends can be used to illustrate longitudinal mechanical waves. Compressing the spring (*c*) and then releasing it allows the compression to travel down the spring. Stretching the spring and releasing it would cause a stretched area or rarefaction (*R*) to travel through the spring in a similar way.

A transverse wave (light) is generated in a manner perpendicular to the direction of movement (propagation) of the wave.

The transverse wave shown above is produced by the oscillating (vibrating) system. The amplitude of the oscillations becomes the amplitude of the waves, and the rate at which oscillation occurs is the frequency.

The *Doppler Effect* explains the change in pitch of a siren or whistle as it approaches or recedes from the listener. It also explains the color shifts of stars and galaxies that are moving in the cosmos.

The frequency at which waves are generated from a siren, for example, (stars, too) is constant. Should either the source of the waves or the listener move, or both, the sound of the waves undergoes an apparent change. If the source and the listener are moving closer to one another, the waves are encountered at a higher rate, causing the pitch to increase (increasing frequency). If the source and listener are receding from one another, the waves are encountered at a lower rate, causing the pitch to decrease (decreasing frequency). When stars are involved, the frequency shift exhibits a color change. Stars approaching us shift the light waves toward higher frequencies, the blue shift. Stars receding from us shift the light rays toward lower frequencies, the red shift. The Doppler Effect is the method astronomers use to determine the relative motion of stars and galaxies in space.

REFLECTION

Waves that travel to and are incident upon (collide with) a barrier are bounced back (reflected) and inverted.

The surface most often associated with the reflection light rays is a mirror. Mirrors can be flat (a plane mirror) or curved (most common). A mirror can be on the inside of the curve (concave) or on the outside of the curve (convex). Light rays that strike the surface of a mirror, or anything for that matter, are incident rays. The rays that bounce off the surface are reflected rays. A perpendicular line drawn to the surface of a mirror is called the normal.

The law of reflection can be stated as follows: The angle of incidence equals the angle of reflection.

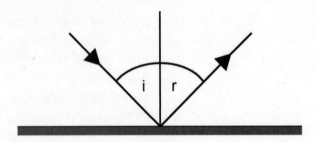

A spherical concave mirror reflects light toward a point on the central radius called the focal point. The radius of curvature is the distance from the mirror to its center if the mirror were a full sphere. This is called the principal axis.

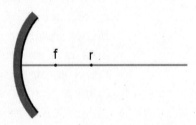

Concave spherical mirrors are important tools in science because of their ability to focus incident light. The point where incident rays are focused is called the focal point and is one half the radius of curvature.

$$f = \frac{r}{2}$$

Two rules worth remembering about light rays that strike a concave mirror are:

1. Any light ray that is moving parallel to the principal axis and is incident to the mirror will be reflected though the focal point.
2. Any light ray that passes through the focal point and is incident to the mirror will be reflected parallel to the principal axis.

Light rays from objects (*O*) placed in front of a concave mirror produce images (*I*).

The images produced may be real (projectable onto a screen) or virtual (appearing to be located on the other side of the mirror); they may be enlarged (magnified) or shrunk (reduced); or they may be right side up (erect) or upside down (inverted).

The following diagrams illustrate the position of the image when the object is placed in various locations in front of the mirror.

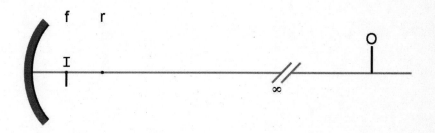

Object distance is considered infinite.
Light rays are parallel as they approach and strike the mirror.
Image is located at *f*. It is reduced, inverted, and real.

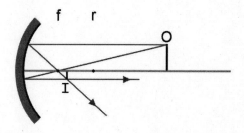

Object is located outside *r*, but not at infinity.
Image is located between *f* and *r*. It is reduced, inverted, and real.

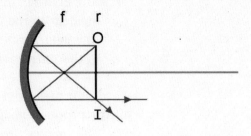

Object is located at *r*.
Image is located at *r*. It is the same size as the object, inverted, and real.

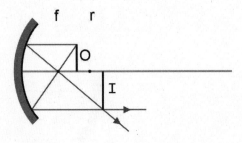

Object is located between *r* and *f*.
Image is located beyond *r*. It is magnified, inverted, and real.

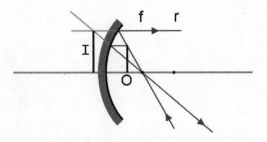

Object is located inside *f*.
Image is located behind the mirror. It is reduced, erect, and virtual.

The letters I and O are used to represent the height of the image (I) and the height of the object (O). The distance from the mirror to the image is labeled q and the distance from the mirror to the object is labeled p.

Mirrors are used in a variety of ways throughout the world. Shopkeepers use convex mirrors to keep an eye on the aisles of their stores, and sharp corners on roadways have mirrors set out so drivers can see the road ahead. The magnifying capability of mirrors allows astronomers and laboratory researchers to perform their work.

This capability of a mirror is based upon the set of ratios (of the object and image heights) compared to the distance of the object and the image from the mirror.

$$\frac{h_i}{h_0} = \frac{q}{p}$$

Convex spherical mirrors produce images that are always virtual. The focal length for convex mirrors is always negative.

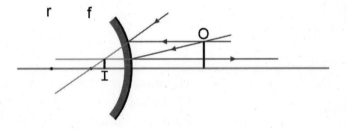

Object is located in front of the mirror.
Image is located behind the mirror and appears to be inside it. It is reduced, erect, and virtual.

The equation that describes the location of an image in a mirror is called the mirror equation.

$$\frac{1}{f} = \frac{1}{p} + \frac{1}{q}$$

The focal length (f) is positive for concave mirrors and negative for convex mirrors. If the image (q) or the object (p) are located in front of the mirror, they are positive. If the image (q) and/or the object is/are located behind the mirror, it is negative.

Example

Let's do a typical reflection problem.

Find the location of the image for an object that is placed 37 cm in front of a mirror having a focal length of 3.6 cm. Describe the image.

Solution

$$\frac{1}{f} = \frac{1}{p} + \frac{1}{q}$$

rearranges to

$$\frac{1}{f} - \frac{1}{p} = \frac{1}{q}$$

$$\frac{1}{3.6\text{cm}} - \frac{1}{37\text{cm}} = \frac{1}{q}$$

$$.277\text{cm} - .027\text{cm} = \frac{1}{q}$$

$$\frac{1}{q} = .025 \text{ cm} = 4\text{cm}$$

The image is located 4 cm from the mirror. The object is outside the radius of curvature ($2f = 7.2$ cm), and the image is located between r and f. It is reduced, inverted, and real.

Now we'll use the original information from the problem above, but we'll replace the concave mirror with a convex mirror.

$$\frac{1}{-f} = \frac{1}{p} + \frac{1}{q}$$

rearranges to

$$\frac{1}{-f} - \frac{1}{p} = \frac{1}{q}$$

$$\frac{1}{-3.6\text{cm}} - \frac{1}{37\text{cm}} = \frac{1}{q}$$

$$-.277\text{cm} - .027\text{cm} = \frac{1}{q}$$

$$\frac{1}{q} = -.304 \text{ cm} = -3.29\text{cm}$$

The image is located 3.29 cm behind the mirror (the negative sign for q). It is reduced, erect, and virtual.

REFRACTION

Waves that move into a new medium bend as they enter the medium. All waves can be refracted, but our discussion here will be limited to light. The light beam shown below passes from air into a cube of plastic.

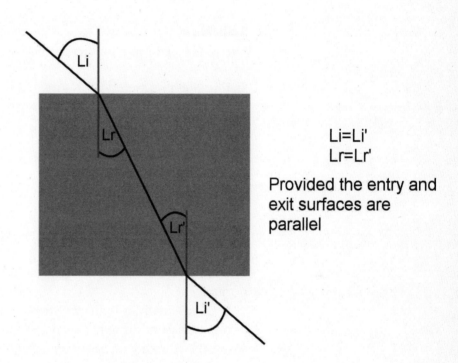

Li=Li'
Lr=Lr'

Provided the entry and exit surfaces are parallel

At the air/plastic boundary, the light ray bends (refracts) toward the normal when the light ray passes into the plastic. The ray moves in a straight line while in the plastic until it reenters the air. At the plastic/air boundary the light ray bends (refracts) away from the normal.

When light enters an optically more dense material, it refracts toward the normal. When it enters an optically less dense material, it refracts away from the normal.

The mathematical relationship between the velocity of light in one material (usually air) compared to another material was determined to be

$$n_1 \sin\theta_1 = n_2 \sin\theta_2 \text{ (Snell's Law)},$$

where n is the index of refraction of the material through which light is passing.

Example

A typical Snell's Law problem is one where a scuba diver shines a light upward into the air from under the water. The light beam makes an angle of 30° from the vertical. What is the angle of the light beam as it enters the air?

Solution

The index of refraction (n) for water is 1.33 and for air is 1.

Stating Snell's Law

$$n_1 \sin\theta_1 = n_2 \sin\theta_2$$

$$\sin\theta_2 = \frac{n_1 \sin\theta_1}{n_2}$$

$$\sin\theta_2 = \frac{(1.33)(.5)}{1} = .655$$

$$\sin\theta_2 = 40.5°$$

The light beam will enter the air at an angle of 40.5° from the normal.

Occasionally, a light ray strikes the surface boundary between two materials at an angle (called critical angle) that is too large (from the normal) to pass through the interface between the materials. The light ray is reflected from the surface where it becomes "trapped" inside the material, a condition called total internal reflection. The sparkle of a diamond and optic fiber lights and cables are examples of total internal reflection.

Lenses are important because they can focus light. Convex lenses converge light rays passing through them toward the focal point f. This kind of lens is called convergent. Concave lenses separate light rays passing through them as if the separated light rays had originated at the focal point. This kind of lens is called divergent. The two light rays of which to take note are:

• A light ray that is parallel to the principal axis and is incident upon the lens will be refracted through the focal point (on the other side of the lens).

- A light ray that passes through the focal point and is incident upon the lens will be refracted parallel to the principal axis (on the other side).

   Light rays from object (*O*) placed in front of a curved lens produce images (*I*). The diagrams below illustrate the position of the image when the object is placed in various positions.

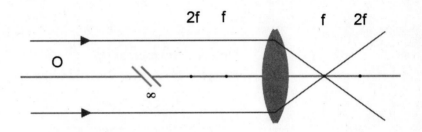

Object distance is considered infinite.
Light rays are parallel.
Image is located at *f*. It is reduced, inverted, and real.

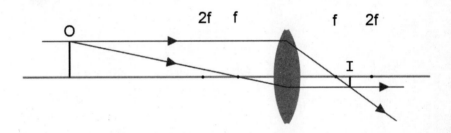

Object distance is outside *2f* but not infinite.
Image is located between *2f* and *f*. It is reduced, inverted, and real.

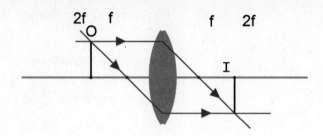

Object is located at 2*f.*
Image is located at 2*f.* It is same size as object, inverted, and real.

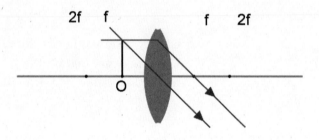

Object is at *f.*
Image is at infinity.

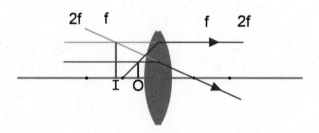

Object inside *f.*
Image same side and outside object; magnified, erect, and virtual.

The lens equation $\dfrac{1}{f} = \dfrac{1}{p} + \dfrac{1}{q}$ is the same as the equation used for

mirrors. Remember though, the image distance (*q*) is positive when on the opposite side of the lens.

Concave lenses produce virtual images.

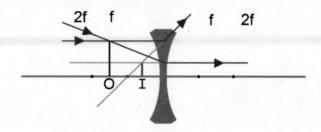

As with the mirror equation, the lens equations can be used to locate an image.

Example
An object is placed 20 cm from a convex lens of 8 cm focal length. Locate and describe the image.

Solution

$$\frac{1}{f} = \frac{1}{p} + \frac{1}{q}$$

Rearrange and substitute:

$$\frac{1}{f} - \frac{1}{p} = \frac{1}{q}$$

$$\frac{1}{8cm} - \frac{1}{20cm} = \frac{1}{q}$$

$$.125cm - .05cm = \frac{1}{q}$$

$$\frac{1}{q} = .075cm = 13.25cm$$

The image is located 13.25 cm from the lens on the side opposite from the object. It is reduced, inverted, and real.

POLARIZATION

Polarization is a phenomenon that applies only to transverse waves. Light is a transverse wave and is commonly the object of polarization. Let's examine polarization by considering a rope tied to a fixed end. Vibrating the rope up and down produces waves that travel down the rope.

Should we stand beside the rope and hold a meter stick vertically beside the rope, there is no problem.

The rope vibrates on the vertical axis, and the meter stick is oriented on the vertical axis. If we change the orientation of the stick to the horizontal axis, the vertical vibrations in the rope strike the horizontal meter stick.

Transverse waves are almost completely stopped when they reach the meter stick.

We can take these results a step further and apply them to light. Light is considered a transverse wave that only differs from our rope example in that light vibrates 360° around the line path of the light ray.

source

ray
direction

The polarized eyeglasses many people wear restrict the intensity of the light that reaches their eyes by using a device (polarizer) that only allows light vibrating on one plane to pass through to the eye.

sun

eye

The result is similar to holding a meter stick over a rope that is vibrating up and down, but with the plane polarizer, every plane but one is polarized at the same time.

DIFFRACTION AND INTERFERENCE

Water waves approaching a fixed object in their path tend to move around the object and continue on their way. The ability of waves to bend around obstacles in their path is called *diffraction*. Likewise, waves that strike a barrier in which there are openings have the ability to pass through the opening. The opening acts as a new source of waves that radiate out from the source.

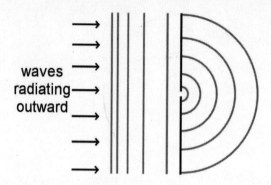

Suppose the barrier has two holes. Then each hole acts as a new source of waves.

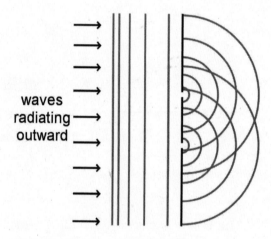

The area of waves beyond the barrier is filled with a confusion of waves crossing one another. A series of peaks and troughs exists as waves both constructively and destructively interfere with one another.

Thomas Young (1801) tested light in this manner using a double slit. Since the confused waves were light waves, Young decided he could project the results onto a screen. Young learned that the light waves would interfere with one another in a way that produced areas of constructive interference (light spots) and destructive interference (dark spots).

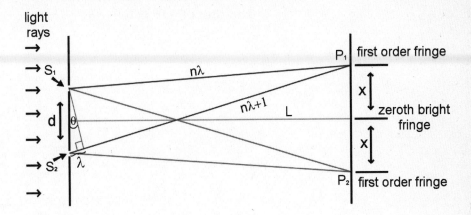

The light traveling from Slit 1 (S_1) travels a number of whole wavelengths ($n\lambda$) to reach the screen at P1. Additionally, the light from Slit 2 (S_2) would travel the same number of whole wavelengths plus one more, $n\lambda + 1$. Typically more than one bright spot on the fringe is visible. The central (zeroth) fringe is the fringe where the light path is exactly equal for both S_1 and S_2. The first fringe on either side of the zeroth fringe is called the first order fringe, the second is the second order fringe, etc. The number of the fringe is the number of extra wavelengths traveled by the light ray on the longest path.

$$n\lambda = d \sin\theta$$

Example

Let's find the wavelength of the green-yellow mercury spectral line. The grating used has a spacing of 1×10^{-6}m, and the angle between the zeroth and first fringe is 33.1°. Write the equation and remember $n = 1$ in this case.

$$n\lambda = d\sin\theta \text{ and } n = 1$$
$$\lambda = d\sin\theta$$
$$\lambda = (1\times 10^{-6}\text{m})(.541)$$
$$\lambda = 5.46\times 10^{-7}\text{m or } 546.1\text{m}$$

If the angle to the fourth order fringe of a blue light is known to be 3.9°, and the distance between slits is .0025 cm, find the wavelength of the light.

Solution

Remember this is the 4th order fringe, thus $n = 4$.
The sine of $3.9°$ is 6.8×10^{-1}.

$$n\lambda = d\sin\theta \text{ and } n = 4$$

$$\therefore 4\lambda = d\sin\theta$$

$$\lambda = \frac{\left(\dfrac{.0025\text{cm}}{100\text{cm/m}}\right)(6.8\times10^{-2})}{4}$$

$$\lambda = 4.25\times10^{-7} \text{ or } 425nm$$

CHAPTER SUMMARY

- Waves are periodic vibrations that carry energy.

- Interference can be constructive or destructive.

- The velocity of a wave is a product of its frequency and wavelength $v = \lambda f$.

- Sound is a longitudinal wave.

- Light is a transverse wave.

- Mirrors reflect light.

- The law of reflection is stated as $\angle i = \angle r$.

- A concave mirror reflects light toward the focal point.

- A convex mirror reflects light as if the rays had passed through a focal point on the other side of the mirror.

- The mirror equation $\dfrac{1}{f} = \dfrac{1}{p} + \dfrac{1}{q}$ is the same for both concave and convex mirrors: f is positive for concave mirrors, and f is negative for convex mirrors.

- Light passing between two transparent materials is refracted at the surface boundary of the materials.

- Snell's Law is $n_1 \sin\theta_1 = n_2 \sin\theta_2$ where n is the index of refraction for the materials, and θ is the angle of refraction.

- A convex lens (converging) refracts light toward a focal point.

- A concave lens (diverging) refracts light as if it had passed through a focal point and the other side of the lens.

- The lens equation $\dfrac{1}{f} = \dfrac{1}{p} + \dfrac{1}{q}$ is identical in form to the mirror equation. However, q is positive when the image is located on the opposite side of the lens from p the object.

- Light that has had all its vibrations eliminated except for those on a single plane is plane polarized.

- Diffraction is the ability of waves to bend around barriers placed in their way.

- Interference is the constructive or the destructive superposition of waves with one another.

Chapter 4

HEAT AND THERMODYNAMICS

CHAPTER 4

HEAT AND THERMODYNAMICS

TEMPERATURE

The atoms and molecules of which matter is made are constantly in motion. The more energy they contain, the faster they move. The kinetic energy the particles have is called internal energy. A hot body has more internal energy than a cold body. The measure of the internal energy of a body is called temperature. The temperature of an object is not dependent on the amount of the substance present and can be measured with a thermometer.

- Temperature scales are the method by which the heat energy of bodies can be compared. They are often based on an arbitrary point.

- The Fahrenheit scale was devised to read 0°F as the coldest temperature reached on earth and 100°F as the hottest material temperature on the earth. The freezing point of water is 32°F and its boiling point is 212°F.

- The Celsius scale was devised to measure between the freezing and boiling points of water. The freezing point of water on the Celsius scale is $0°C$, and the boiling point of water is $100°C$.

- The Kelvin or absolute scale places $0K$ at the point where there is no heat, thus no lower temperature is possible. Zero on the Kelvin scale is absolute, thus absolute zero means no heat energy is present. *Note the degree sign is not used on the Kelvin or absolute scale.*

- There are 180 degrees between the freezing and boiling points of water on the Fahrenheit scale.

- There are 100 degrees between the freezing and boiling points of water on the Celsius scale.

- The Kelvin scale places the freezing point of water at $273K$ and the boiling point of water at $373K$, which is also a 100-unit difference. The Celsius and the Kelvin scales have a 1:1 relationship. Thus to change $°C$ to K, all that's necessary is to add 273 to the Celsius temperature.

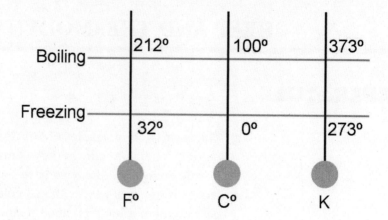

THERMAL PROPERTIES OF MATTER

Thermal energy is the energy substances possess when their temperature is greater than absolute zero. As energy is added, most substances expand. You have probably seen the open joints in concrete or on bridges—they are there to allow room for the expansion of the concrete as the seasons change. Continued addition of heat energy can cause solids to change into liquids or liquids to change to gases. These are called phase changes.

- Solids change to liquids by melting.
- Liquids change to solids by freezing.
- Liquids change to gases by evaporation.
- Gases change to liquids by condensation.

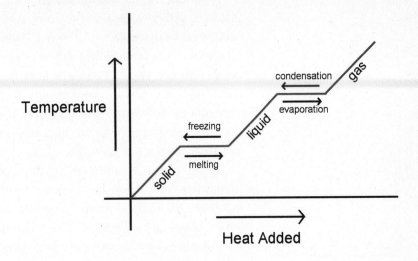

Above is a generalized heat and temperature graph for materials. Note the increase in temperature in the substance until a phase change begins to occur. During a phase change all the heat energy added to the material is converting the substance from one phase to another. The temperature remains constant. The temperature does not begin to rise again until the phase change is complete. Reversing the process means removing heat. Should we apply the graph to water, we can say that during the freezing/melting phase, both liquid water and ice are present. Likewise, during the condensation/evaporation phase, both liquid water and steam are present. The graph is flat during these processes, showing that no temperature change occurs during a phase change.

The heat required to change a substance from a solid to a liquid is called *heat of fusion*. The heat required to change a substance from a liquid to a gas is called *heat of vaporization*. Typically the heat of vaporization is greater than the heat of fusion for a given substance.

Expansion and Contraction
When the temperature of a substance is raised, the atoms and molecules of the substance have more energy. This causes the distance between the atoms and molecules to increase. As a result, the material expands. Lowering the temperature of a substance causes the distance between atoms and molecules to decrease or shrink.

Heat Transfer
Heat can be transferred between substances in several ways. Every case of heat transfer involves the movement of heat from an area of high heat content to an area of low heat content.

Conduction is the transfer of heat through an object such as a fireplace poker. One end of the poker is cool to the touch while the other end of the poker (in the fire) is very hot. Conduction can only take place in a body when different parts of the body are at different temperatures. The direction of heat flow is from the higher temperature end to the lower temperature end. The rate of conduction depends on the material in question, the cross-section area of the object, the difference in the temperatures between two points, and inversely on the length of the object.

Convection is the term applied to heat transfer from one place to another by the actual movement of the atoms and molecules of the material. A radiant heater is a good example of this. When the heater is in operation, air molecules are heated. The heated air expands, becomes less dense, and rises away from the heater. Cooler unheated air "falls" into the place vacated by the previously heated air, where it too is heated and rises. The continuous rise and replacement of heated air circulates warm air throughout an enclosed space.

Radiation is the only heating/cooling process where no physical medium is necessary. The sun's energy heats the atmosphere, the oceans, and the land through the vacuum of space. Radiant energy from the sun also provides the light necessary for photosynthesis in plants.

A wall that was heated by the sun during the day radiates heat at night, thus cooling itself. Radiant energy is emitted by all warm bodies and is a form of electromagnetic energy. Thermos bottles keep liquids hot or cold because they do not absorb heat, but rather reflect it back into the substance within the vacuum bottle, which keeps heat within the substance. Cold substances stay cold inside a Thermos because the bottle is a poor heat emitter and does not allow heat to easily pass into the cold substance within.

KINETIC THEORY

The following three statements compose the basis of the kinetic theory:

1. All matter is made of very small particles called atoms and molecules.
2. The particles of matter are in constant random motion.
3. The particles of matter experience perfectly elastic collisions with one another and with the walls of their containers.

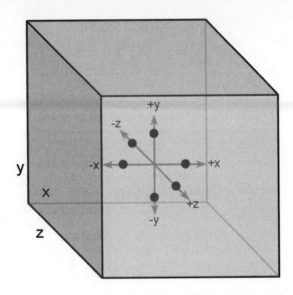

The particles of a gas in a closed container move in a random manner. However, there is a certainty that the enclosed gas molecules are moving toward or away from one of the walls of the container. Eventually, the gas particles strike one of the sides of the container. The impact each particle exerts on the container wall is its *momentum*, which is a product of the particle's mass and its velocity.

The number of times the container wall is struck by the gas particles within depends on the number of gas particles in the container and the velocity at which the particles are moving. The faster the particles move, the faster they travel the distance to the container wall and the more often the particles strike the container wall. The enclosed gas particles have constant mass, which means the momentum of the gas only changes when the velocity of the particle changes. If the particle moves more slowly, then its kinetic energy decreases; if it moves faster, its kinetic energy increases. A higher number of particles within the container will collide with the walls more often than a lower number of particles.

The measure of the rate at which gas particles strike the container walls and their momentum is called *pressure*. Pressure is directly related to the number of particles and their kinetic energy. We can use the temperature of gas as a measure of its kinetic energy.

Generally we can say:

As the temperature increases ↑   Pressure increases ↑

As the number of particles increases ↑   Pressure increases ↑

Example

So far the container in which the gas is held has been constant in its volume. Let's consider a gas in a cylinder with a movable piston.

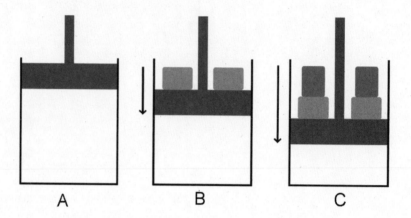

The diagrams show a gas enclosed in a cylinder that has a movable piston. Diagram A shows the gas under normal conditions. If we add weight to the outside of the piston in Diagram B, the pressure exerted on the enclosed gas is increased and its volume is reduced. In Diagram C, we add even more weight to the piston and the pressure on the gas increases again. The pressure and volume of the enclosed gas are indirectly related.

Pressure increases ↑   Volume decreases ↓

Solution

We can sum these relationships with an equation called the Ideal Gas Law.

$$PV = nRt$$

$P = $ pressure, expressed in $\dfrac{N}{m^2}$ or Pa

$V = $ volume, expressed in m^3 (or compatible units)

$N = $ number of moles and/or $n = \dfrac{\text{mass of gas}}{\text{molecular mass}}$

$R = $ gas law constant $\left(8.314 \dfrac{J}{(\text{mole})(K)} \right)$

$T = $ temperature in Kelvins

1 atmosphere of pressure $= 1.01 \times 10^5 \ Pa$ or $101 KPa$

Standard temperature and pressure are defined as 1 atmosphere of pressure and a temperature of 273 K.

Any gas that obeys the Ideal Gas Law is called an ideal gas.

Example

A 500cm^3 ($5 \times 10^{-4} m^3$) container is filled with chlorine gas. How many moles of the gas are in the container at *STP*?

Solution

$PV = nRt$

State and rearrange the equation.

$$\frac{PV}{RT} = n$$

$$n = \frac{(1.01 \times 10^5 \, Pa)(5 \times 10^{-4} m^3)}{(8.314 \dfrac{J}{mole \bullet K})(273K)}$$

$$n = 2.2 \times 10^{-2} \text{ moles} = .022 \text{ moles}$$

Boyle's Law and Charles' Law

The relationship between pressure and volume was studied by Robert Boyle (1627–1691), who gave us the statement called *Boyle's Law.*

Boyles' Law states that when the temperature of a gas is kept constant, the pressure will vary inversely with the volume.

A few years later, Jacques Charles (1746–1823) added his statements about the relationships between pressure, temperature, and volume, which are known as *Charles' Law*.

1. If the pressure of a gas is held constant, the volume of a gas is directly proportional to its absolute temperature.
2. At constant volume, the pressure of a gas is proportional to the absolute temperature.

Boyle's Law can be stated as an equation.

$$P_1 V_1 = P_2 V_2$$

Charles' Law can also be stated in equation form.

$$\frac{V_1}{T_1} = \frac{V_2}{T_2} \text{ or the variation } \frac{P_1}{T_1} = \frac{P_2}{T_2}$$

Combining the three equations above gives another useful equation called the *Combined Gas Law*.

$$\frac{(P_1)(V_1)}{T_1} = \frac{(P_2)(V_2)}{T_2}$$

Notice a difference in the *Combined* Gas Law compared to the *Ideal* Gas Law ($PV = nRt$).

Pressure and volume units may be expressed in any units that are compatible to one another. Temperature, though still relative to absolute or Kelvin values, may be left in Celsius values because the Celsius and Kelvin temperatures have a relationship of $1°C$ per $1K$. For this reason, Celsius degrees may be used provided both temperatures are from the Celsius scale. Fahrenheit temperatures must always be converted.

USING THE GAS LAWS

Example

A 40L ($4 \times 10^{-3} m^3$) gas tank is filled with Helium gas at a temperature of $20°C$ (293K) and a pressure of $2.5 \times 10^5 Pa$. Find the mass of Helium gas in the container (the atomic mass of Helium $= 4 \frac{g}{mole}$).

Solution

This is an *Ideal Gas Law* problem.

$$PV = nRT \quad \text{rearrange}$$

$$n = \frac{PV}{RT} \quad \text{remember } n = \text{number of moles of the gas}$$

$$\text{mass} = \frac{(P)(V)(\text{atomic mass})}{(R)(T)}$$

$$\text{number of moles} = \frac{\text{mass}}{\text{atomic mass}}$$

$$\text{mass} = \frac{(2.5 \times 10^5 \, Pa)(4 \times 10^{-3} m^3)\left(4 \frac{g}{mole}\right)}{\left(8.314 \frac{J}{mole}\right)(293K)}$$

$$\text{mass} = 1.642g$$

Example

A gas occupies 4.5L at *STP.* What new volume will the gas occupy if its temperature is raised to 325K and the pressure changes to 1.75 *atm*?

Solution

This problem is a combined gas law problem. Let the original conditions be P_1, V_1, and T_1 and the new conditions be P_2, V_2, and T_2. The missing value in the problem is the volume (V_2).

$$\frac{(P_1)(V_1)}{T_1} = \frac{(P_2)(V_2)}{T_2}$$

Rearranging to find V_2 :

$$V_2 = \frac{(P_1)(V_1)(T_2)}{(P_2)(T_1)}$$

$$V_2 = \frac{(1atm)(4.5L)(325K)}{(1.75atm)(273K)} = 3.06L$$

Notice in this example that the atmosphere (*atm*) for pressure units works, as do the liters for volume.

THERMODYNAMICS

LAWS OF THERMODYNAMICS

We will begin our discussion of thermodynamics with what is called an isolated system, or simply, a system. All the matter and energy in the system is totally separated from everything else. By definition, the internal energy (U) of a system is the sum of all the potential and kinetic energy contained within that system. When heat (Q) is added to a system, (ΔU) is positive, and when heat (Q) is removed from a system, (ΔU) is negative.

The first law of thermodynamics is a restatement of the law of conservation of energy. The special circumstance is that the first law of thermodynamics only addresses *heat* energy. When a quantity of heat (Q) is added to a closed system, the internal energy (U) of the system will increase by the same amount, minus any work (W) done by the system.

$$\Delta Q - \Delta W = \Delta U$$

or

$$\Delta Q = \Delta U + \Delta W$$

Since a thermodynamic system is concerned with the transfer of heat, one of the ways such a system interacts with its surroundings will always be heat transfer. Heat transfer can occur in many ways, but the most common way in a thermodynamic system is through *work*. Work is done by a system when some of the heat that is added to that system is converted to mechanical energy. Work can be positive or negative.

(Remember, Work = $F \cdot s \cdot \cos\theta$). This can be illustrated by investigating a gas enclosed in a cylinder.

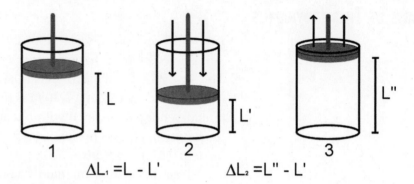

$\Delta L_1 = L - L'$ $\Delta L_2 = L'' - L'$

- Diagram 1 shows an enclosed gas.

- Diagram 2 shows that gas compressed. The gas has been reduced in volume (work done on the gas), so the quantity ΔW from the first law statement is negative. ΔL is the distance the piston moved inward as the gas was compressed.

- Diagram 3 shows the gas after it has expanded. The volume has increased as the gas inside the cylinder has done work on the piston when it expanded, thus the work is positive.

The second law of thermodynamics can be stated two ways:

1. No heat engine can have an efficiency of 100%.
2. Any ordered system will tend to become disordered.

The first of these statements makes it clear that losses due to friction, combustion, and heat transfer prevent any heat engine (such as cars) from being 100% efficient. Most automobiles are around 40% efficient.

    The second statement predicts the movement of heat from hot objects (ordered) to cold objects (disordered). This means that entropy is a measure of disorder.

THERMODYNAMIC PROCESSES INVOLVING GASES

Gases, like all other matter, have a specific heat capacity. This means they can absorb heat energy when they are in contact with a hotter source and can pass heat energy to a colder source. They also undergo several processes unique to gases, which are useful in the operation of devices called heat engines.

These processes are:

Isobaric: A process that occurs at constant pressure.
Isochoric: A process that occurs at constant volume.
Isothermal: A process that occurs at constant temperature.
Adiabatic: A process in which no heat enters or leaves a system.

The work done *by* an enclosed gas is positive work.
Work done *on* an enclosed gas is negative work.

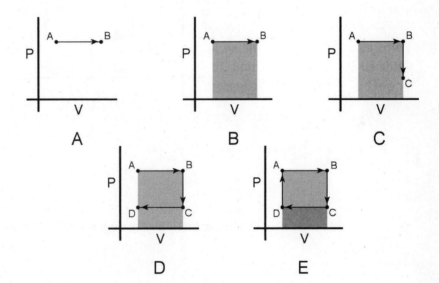

Diagram A shows an enclosed gas expanding at constant pressure. The piston moves outward and the system does positive work. The quantity of work done is equal to the pressure and the change in volume ($P\Delta V$) and is the area under the *P-V* curve. To do additional work, the piston must be able to repeat the process, but if the piston moves back from B to A, all the work already done will be lost. The solution to returning the piston to point A without losing the work already done is to lose just some of the work. The gas is allowed to contract adiabatically to point C. At that point, work is done on the system and the volume is reduced to point D in an isothermal process. The gas undergoes an adiabatic expansion during which the system returns to its starting point at point A, and the cycle can begin again. The positive work done by the system is enclosed under the curve ABCDA. Under the A → B curve, the work done is positive. The gas expands and does work *on* the system. Under the C → D curve, work is done on the gas. Therefore, the result is negative work as the system does work on the gas by reducing its volume.

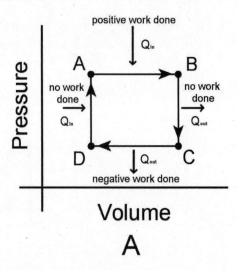

The diagram above represents an idealized thermodynamic cycle.

The diagram below represents a Carnot cycle.

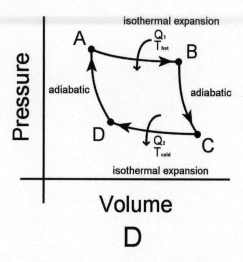

During processes AB and BC, positive work is done, but during processes CD and DA, negative work is done. The net work done by the system is the area enclosed by ABCDA.

The value of the work done can be calculated by subtracting the value of Q_2 from Q_1 ($Q_1 - Q_2$ = Work).

The ratio of the output temperature compared to the input temperature of the gas is used to calculate the efficiency of the heat engine $\left(1 - \dfrac{T_c}{T_h} = \text{Efficiency}\right)$.

Another way to find the efficiency of a heat engine is to compare the output heat (Q_{out}) with the input heat (Q_{in}) of the engine: $1 - \dfrac{Q_c}{Q_h}$.

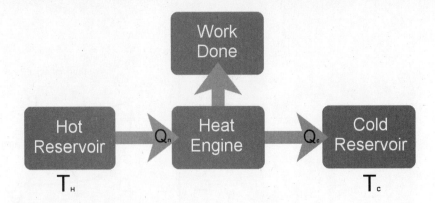

The flow chart above shows a generalized diagram of a heat engine. Heat from the hot reservoir (Q_h) flows from a high temperature area to a low temperature area. Between the two areas some of the heat energy is used to do work. The remaining heat (Q_c) becomes the exhaust.

When a heat engine is run in the opposite direction from the flow chart above, cooling occurs. Many devices, such as refrigerators, air conditioners, and freezers, can perform cooling. Another example is the heat pump. This device cools in the same way as the other cooling devices: the reverse of the normal movement of heat from a heat engine to produce a reversed flow chart.

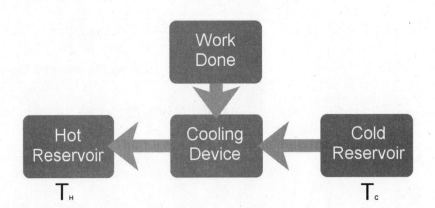

Peterson's SAT II Success: Physics

CALORIMETRY

When a hot object and a cold object are brought into contact with one another, heat flows from the hot object into the cold object until both objects reach the same temperature. This flow, hot→cold, is a characteristic of heat energy. When both objects reach the same temperature by their contact with one another, *thermal equilibrium* has been reached.

The heat that has been transferred from the hot object to the cold object is called heat energy. Heat energy is not the same as thermal energy. Thermal energy is the energy possessed by an object that makes up the energy of the individual atoms and molecules of the substance. The difference between the two is that heat energy flows from one object to another because of a temperature difference between the two objects.

The study of how heat transfers between objects that are in contact with one another is called *calorimetry*.

All heat is a form of energy, and so the unit for measuring thermal energy is the Joule. Several other units are also used to measure heat energy. The BTU, or British Thermal Unit, is used in conjunction with the Fahrenheit temperature scale. Another commonly used heat unit is the calorie (cal).

The heat energy required to change the temperature of a substance by 1 degree is defined as the specific heat capacity (specific heat) of the substance. It is represented by a lower case *c*. In addition, the heat required to raise the temperature of a substance by 1 degree is dependent on the amount of the substance present. If a standard mass of 1 gram of the substance is used as a reference, the relationship between mass, temperature, specific heat, and heat content can be stated as:

$$Q = cm\Delta T$$

When two different substances are in contact with one another and the specific heat of one substance is different from the specific heat of the other substance, the heat that transfers between them (ΔQ) to reach equilibrium will always be the same for both substances.

Take, for example, a closed system with 1 gram of aluminum in contact with 1 gram of lead. The heat that flows from the hot substance, in this case lead, must equal the heat flow into the cold substance, the aluminum.

$$Pb \qquad = \qquad Al$$

$$\Downarrow \qquad\qquad \Downarrow$$

$$Q = cm\Delta T \quad = \quad Q = cm\Delta T$$

The heat flow Q is the same for both, giving the following equation:

$$(cm\Delta T)_{Pb} = (cm\Delta T)_{Al}$$

Notice that the heat flow into the aluminum and out of the lead *is* the same, but the change in the temperature of each substance will *not* be the same.

The specific heat for lead is $.13\dfrac{Joules}{(g)(°C)}$, while the specific heat for aluminum is $.88\dfrac{Joules}{(g)(°C)}$.

Just looking at the difference in the specific heat of the two, we can see that it takes almost seven times as much heat to change the temperature of the aluminum by 1 degree Celsius as it does to change the lead by the same amount.

Not only do substances require a specific amount of heat to be added (or removed) to change their temperature, they require additional heat energy in order to change phase.

The specific heat capacity of ice is $2.1\dfrac{Joules}{(g)(°C)}$. As long as ice is at a temperature below $0°C$, heat must be added to change the temperature of the ice. The temperature of the ice will continue to rise until it reaches $0°C$. Once the ice reaches its melting point, all the heat energy added to the ice is used to change the ice to water (heat of fusion). After all the ice is melted, any heat added to the water raises its temperature until the boiling point of the water is reached. Note that the specific heat of ice is different from that of water, which is $4.184\dfrac{Joules}{(g)(°C)}$.

When the water reaches its boiling point, all the heat added to the system is used to change the boiling water to steam (heat of vaporization). Once again, when all the water has been changed to steam, the temperature of the steam begins to rise. The specific heat of steam $\left(1.92\dfrac{Joules}{(g)(°C)}\right)$ is different from both that of ice and of water.

PROBLEM SOLVING IN CALORIMETRY

Students who are doing calorimetry problems should realize that they are completing an energy ledger, just as in bookkeeping. All the heat lost by an object(s) will *always* be gained by one or more other objects. That's a statement of the first law of thermodynamics.

Example
How much heat is required to change the temperature of 500g of water from 10°C to 50°C? The specific heat for water is:

$$4.184\frac{Joules}{(g)(°C)}$$

Solution

$$\Delta Q = cm\Delta T$$

$$\Delta Q = \left(4.184\frac{Joules}{(g)(°C)}\right)(500g)(50°C-10°C)$$

$$\Delta Q = 83,680 J$$

Example
Now we'll do the same problem using iron. The specific heat of iron is:

$$.46\frac{Joules}{(g)(°C)}$$

Solution

$$\Delta Q = cm\Delta T$$

$$\Delta Q = \left(.46\,\frac{Joules}{(g)(°C)}\right)(500g)(50°C - 10°C)$$

$$\Delta Q = 9200J$$

Notice that it takes more than nine times as much heat energy to heat the water as it does to heat the iron. This is in keeping with what we would expect by looking at the specific heats of the two materials. Water has a specific heat nine times larger than the specific heat of iron.

Example:

Here is another type of Calorimetry problem with which you should be familiar.

The temperature of 300g of water is 20°C. If 12,500J of heat energy is added to the water, what will the temperature of the water change to?

Solution:

Start with the calorimetry equation:

$$\Delta Q = cm\Delta T$$

$$\Delta Q = cm(t_f - t_o)$$

$$12,500J = \left(4.184\,\frac{Joules}{(g)(°C)}(300g)(t_f - 20°C)\right)$$

$$12,500J = \left[\left(1255.2\,\frac{Joules}{(g)(°C)}(t_f)\right)\right] - (25,104J)$$

$$12,500J + 25,104J = \left[\left(1255.2\,\frac{Joules}{(g)(°C)}(t_f)\right)\right]$$

$$\frac{37604J}{1255.2\,Joules} = t_f$$

$$29.96°C = t_f$$

Example:

The last problem to take a look at is similar to one you may have already seen in your high school laboratory.

During a laboratory experiment a student places 50g of copper, which is at a temperature of 100°C, into a Styrofoam cup (the cup effectively can be ignored in this problem) that contains 200g of water at a temperature of 25°C. The copper remains in the water until thermal equilibrium is reached. Predict the final equilibrium temperature of the system. The specific heat of the water is

$$4.182 \frac{Joules}{(g)(°C)}, \text{ and the specific heat of copper is } .39 \frac{Joules}{(g)(°C)}.$$

Solution

Before starting to solve the problem, we need to remember what is happening in the system.

1. Copper loses heat. Heat loss is negative.
2. Water gains heat. Heat gain is positive.

Start by stating the heat change. *Be sure to watch your signs.*

Copper (Cu)		**Water (H$_2$O)**
$-\Delta Q$		$+\Delta Q$
$-(cm\Delta T)$	$=$	$+(cm\Delta T)$
$-\left[cm(t_f - t_o)\right]$	$=$	$+\left[(cm(t_f - t_o)\right]$
$-\left[(.39 \frac{Joules}{(g)(°C)})(50g)(t_f - 100°C)\right]$	$=$	$+\left[(4.184 \frac{Joules}{(g)(°C)}(200g)(t_f - 25°C)\right]$
$-\left[(19.5\frac{J}{°C}t_f) - (1950J)\right]$	$=$	$+\left[(+836.8\frac{J}{°C}t_f) - (26,131.25J)\right]$
$(-19.5\frac{J}{°C}t_f) + (+1950J)$	$=$	$(+836.8\frac{J}{°C}t_f) - (26,131.25J)$
$26,131.25J + 1950J$	$=$	$+836.8\frac{J}{°C}t_f + 19.5\frac{J}{°C}t_f$
$28,081J$	$=$	$856.3\frac{J}{°C}t_f$
$\dfrac{28,081J}{J}$	$=$	t_f
$32.8°C$	$=$	t_f

It is important to keep the correct sign for heat loss and heat gain throughout the entire problem. Do not multiply the sign through the problem until you are ready to remove the brackets and parentheses.

CHAPTER SUMMARY

- There are no temperature changes during a phase change.

- Most substances expand when they are heated and contract when they cool. Water is a notable exception.

- The Kinetic Theory explains the actions of gases.

- The ideal gas law is $PV = nRT$.

- The combined gas law is $\dfrac{(P_1)(V_1)}{T_1} = \dfrac{(P_2)(V_2)}{T_2}$.

- Robert Boyle determined the relationship between the pressure and the volume of an enclosed gas.

- Jacques Charles determined the relationship between the pressure and temperature of a gas at constant volume.

- Jacques Charles determined the relationship between the volume and temperature of a gas kept at constant pressure.

- The first law of thermodynamics is a restatement of the law of conservation of heat energy. $\Delta Q = \Delta U + \Delta W$

- The second law of thermodynamics states that no heat engine can have efficiency equal to 100%.

- An alternate statement of the second law is that an ordered system tends to become disordered.

- The work done by a heat engine is the area under its P–V curve.

- A heat engine operating in reverse produces cooling.

- Calorimetry is the study of heat transfer between objects.

- The specific heat capacity of a substance is the heat energy required to change the mass of one gram of a substance by one degree Celsius.

- A substance that loses heat has a negative change of heat $(-\Delta Q)$.

- A substance that gains heat has a positive change of heat $(+\Delta Q)$.

Peterson's SAT II Success: Physics

Chapter 5

ELECTRICITY AND ELECTROMAGNETISM

CHAPTER 5

ELECTRICITY AND ELECTROMAGNETISM

ELECTROSTATICS

Electrostatics is a study of charges that are not moving. The source of all charge is the atoms from which all things are formed. If an atom loses or gains electrons, the natural charge balance (equal numbers of protons and electrons) is disturbed. This produces an ion, or charged particle. The only part of an atom capable of moving to form an ion is the electron, which carries a charge of $-1.6 \times 10^{-19}C$. The charge carried by a proton is the same value as the charge on the electron, but it is a positive charge. *Hence, all charge is due either to an excess of electrons (negatively charged bodies) or a deficiency of electrons (positively charged bodies).*

- Negatively charged objects are produced by moving electrons onto an object. This happens when an object is touched by another object that contains excess electrons.

- Positively charged objects are produced by allowing electrons to drain *away* from an object being charged *to* an object deficient in electrons.

- The forces between charged bodies are repulsion or attraction. Like charges repel one another. Unlike charges attract one another.

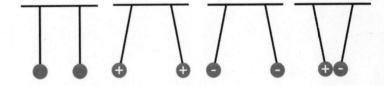

- The first diagram shows a pair of pith balls. The balls are uncharged and hang straight down.

- The second and third diagrams show pith balls charged with like charges; the balls repel one another.

- The last shows unlike charges on the pith balls, which attract one another.

COULOMB'S LAW

The equation describing how charged particles affect one another is called Coulomb's Law.

$$F = K \frac{(q_1)(q_2)}{r^2}$$

$F = $ force

$k = $ a constant whose value is $9 \times 10^9 \, N \frac{m^2}{C^2}$

$q = $ charges on the bodies

$r = $ distance between bodies in m

One coulomb of charge is a very large charge. It takes 6.25×10^{18} excess electrons to produce a charge of $1C$.

If two blocks of iron, each weighing 10 N and with a $1C$ charge, were placed on a surface where the frictional force between the blocks and the surface was 10 N, and the blocks did not move, they would have to be located 30 km apart.

$$F = K \frac{(q_1)(q_2)}{r^2}$$

$$r = \sqrt{K \frac{(q_1)(q_2)}{F}}$$

$$r = \sqrt{\left(9 \times 10^9 \, N \frac{m^2}{C^2}\right)\left(\frac{(1C)(1C)}{10N}\right)}$$

$r = 30,000 \, m \quad$ or $\quad$ 30 km

Example

Here is an example of a commonly seen electrostatics problem. Two electrons are located 10 mm apart. What happens to the force between them if the distance between them is halved (to 5 mm)?

Solution

$$F = K \frac{(q_1)(q_2)}{r^2}$$

$$F = 9 \times 10^9 \, \text{N} \frac{m^2}{C^2} \left[\frac{(1.6 \times 10^{-19} C)(1.6 \times 10^{-19} C)}{(.01m)^2} \right]$$

$$F = \frac{2.304 \times 10^{-28} \, \text{N} \bullet m^2}{1 \times 10^{-4} m^2}$$

$$F = 2.3 \times 10^{-24}$$

That's the force operating on the particles at a distance of 10 mm. Now we'll solve for the force at 5 mm so we can compare them.

We know everything remains exactly the same in the problem except the separation, which halves, so all we do is use the numerators in the first equation with a new distance inserted into the denominator.

$$F = K \frac{(q_1)(q_2)}{r^2}$$

$$F = \frac{2.3 \times 10^{-28} \, \text{N} \bullet m^2}{(2.5 \times 10^{-5} m)^2}$$

$$F = 9.2 \times 10^{-24} \, \text{N}$$

Comparing the two forces:

$$\text{Ratio of forces} = \frac{9.2 \times 10^{-24} \, \text{N}}{2.3 \times 10^{-24} \, \text{N}} = \frac{4}{1}$$

The force on the electrons is four times greater at a distance of 5 mm than it is at 10 mm.

Solution 2

Let's use an intuitive approach to solving the same problem. We apply a little thought to the situation and save some of the calculations we need to perform.

Since everything in the problem remains the same except the separation distance, which is halved, we can say the ratio of the two distances also gives the ratio of the two forces as $\left(\dfrac{1}{2}\right)^2$. Clearly we have a 1:4 ratio, which tells us that the force changes by 4 times as much when the distance between the two electrons is halved.

ELECTRIC FIELDS

The forces that charged bodies exert on one another can be explained with a concept called electric field. The electric field exists about cell-charged bodies. Bodies that are positively charged have electric fields that *exit* from them (positive electric fields). Bodies that are negatively charged have electric fields that are *directed into* them (negative electric fields).

Electric fields are represented by field lines, which always enter or leave a charged body perpendicular to the surface of the body. The field lines are representative of the path that a hypothetical charge (called a test charge) would follow near a charged body.

A test charge is not real, so its characteristics can be defined.

- The test charge can be affected by an electric field, but it does not affect the electric field.

- The value of a test charge is +1C. The test charge is represented by Q.

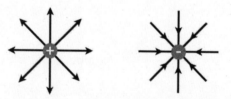

The positive test charge is repelled from the positive charged point, and it is attracted to the negative point (called point charges).

Two things you should remember about point charges are:

1. Field lines originate in and leave positive charges, and they enter and end in negative charges.
2. Field lines are closer together where the electric field is strongest.

The strength of the electric field E is defined as the force exerted on a positive test charge Q placed in the electric field.

$$F = EQ$$

When charged bodies are near one another their electric fields interact with one another.

The field lines of the like charges do *not* cross one another, which produces repulsive forces. The field lines of the unlike charges work concurrently, producing an attractive force.

The electric field can be applied to a pair of charged parallel plates. The electric field between parallel plates operates in the same direction as point charges. The field lines leave the positive plate and enter the negative plate perpendicular to the two surfaces. Between the two plates the electric field lines are parallel to one another.

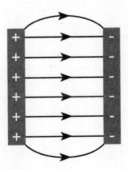

The only place the field lines are *not* parallel is at the edges of the parallel plate.

The parallel plates can be charged by hooking a battery to each side of the plates, producing a potential difference. A positively charged particle can be moved from the negative plate to the positive plate by exerting a force on it. The two plates are separated by a distance d, so the particle has work done on it to move it from the negative plate to the positive plate.

When charge is added to a body, work is required. The potential that can build upon the body is dependent on the magnitude of the charge deposited on the body, as well as the distance between the charges on the body.

The ratio of the charge to the potential is called *capacitance*, which is a constant. A device designed to accept charge while building potential is called a capacitor. Capacitance is measured in *farads*. The farad is defined as a charge of one coulomb per volt.

$$C = \frac{Q}{V}$$

Capacitors are important parts of electrical circuits and will be addressed below when we discuss circuits.

The potential difference between one terminal of a battery and the other terminal of the battery is called the *volt (V)*. The volt is a measure of the work that must be done to move a charged body against an electric field or is the work that can be obtained by letting a charged body move with an electric field.

The *electron volt (eV)* is a term used to describe the energy an electron gains as it is moved through a potential difference of 1 volt. Thus, an electron moved through a potential of 1 volt gains a potential of $1eV$, while the same electron moved through a potential of $50V$ gains a potential of $50eV$.

Electrical potential energy is used to perform mechanical work.

ELECTRIC CIRCUITS

An electric circuit is defined as a pathway for charge to flow from high potential to low potential. When charge flows from high to low potential, it is ordinarily caused to do work, such as running a fan motor or lighting a light bulb.

Charge flow in an electric circuit is called current (I), and its unit is the ampere (A). A flow of 6.25×10^{18} electrons is required for a charge flow of $1\frac{C}{s}$, which is equal to 1 ampere of current.

As charge flows, frictional forces resist the movement of electrons through the conducting wire. The resistance of an object requires charge to do work in order to flow. Useful work is obtained when the resistance is a light bulb, compressor motor, or a computer. The source of charge can be a battery or other device that acts as a source of charge. The higher the potential of the source, the greater the current provided. Batteries and other like devices provide a constant voltage, which is why they are called direct current (DC) sources. The more resistance a DC circuit has in it, the lower the current that can develop.

OHM'S LAW

The German scientist George Ohm (1787-1854) stated the relationships described above and combined them into what is called *Ohm's Law*.

$$V = I R$$

The potential difference is in volts (*V*), the electric current *I* is in amperes (*A*), and the resistance *R* is in ohms (Ω).

Example
Let's try a problem using Ohm's Law.

What current flows in a circuit that has an applied voltage of 6*V* and a total resistance of 12Ω?

Solution

$$V = IR$$

$$I = \frac{V}{R}$$

$$I = \frac{6V}{12\Omega}$$

$$I = .5A$$

In order to increase the current, let's say double it to 1*A*, we would either have to halve the resistance or double the applied voltage, showing the inverse relationship between resistance and current and the direct relationship between voltage and current.

SERIES AND SERIES PARALLEL CIRCUITS

A source of electrical potential sometimes has a single task, such as to operate a flashlight bulb. But just as often the power source is used to perform many tasks through several different pathways. The first example we will discuss is the single task or series circuit; and the second type is called a parallel circuit.

SERIES CIRCUITS

Series circuits have only one pathway in which current can flow. Every unit of charge flowing in a series circuit must pass through every position of the circuit.

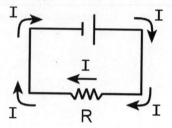

When more than one resistor is in a series circuit, the value of each resistor is added together to give the total resistance.

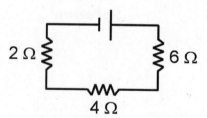

$$R_t = R_1 + R_2 + R_3 + R\ldots$$

The total resistance for the circuit shown is 12Ω.

$$R_t = 2\Omega + 4\Omega + 6\Omega$$

$$R_t = 12\Omega$$

PARALLEL CIRCUITS

Parallel circuits have two or more pathways through which current can flow. The total value of the current depends on the parallel resistance offered against the current flow. Since current and resistance are indirectly related, the highest resistance will allow less current to flow, and the lowest resistance will allow more current to flow.

The total resistance of a set of parallel resistors is found in the following manner:

$$\frac{1}{R_t} = \frac{1}{R_1} + \frac{1}{R_2} + \frac{1}{R_3}$$

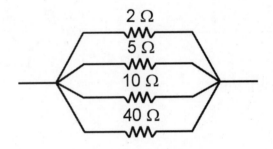

$$\frac{1}{R_t} = \frac{1}{2\Omega} + \frac{1}{5\Omega} + \frac{1}{10\Omega} + \frac{1}{40\Omega}$$

$$\frac{1}{R_t} = .5\Omega + .2\Omega + .1\Omega + .025\Omega$$

$$\frac{1}{R_t} = .825$$

$$R_t = 1.21\Omega$$

The value of the final resistance shows another characteristic of parallel resistances. *The total resistance of a set of parallel resistors is always equal to or less than the value of the smallest resistor in the parallel set.* When an extremely large resistor (500 meg-ohms) is in parallel with an extremely small resistor, the total resistance is equal to the smallest resistor. When a set of parallel resistors are all of equal resistance, we can divide the resistance value of one of them by the total number of resistors in parallel to find the resistance of the parallel system.

Example

Let's do a problem where elements of both the series circuit and the parallel circuit are combined.

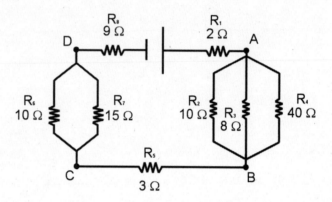

1. Find the total resistance for the circuit.

The first step to solve the problem is to find the equivalent resistance for the R_2 - R_3 - R_4 parallel set of resistors:

$$\frac{1}{R_t} = \frac{1}{R_1} + \frac{1}{R_2} + \frac{1}{R_3}$$

$$\frac{1}{R_t} = \frac{1}{10\Omega} + \frac{1}{8\Omega} + \frac{1}{4\Omega}$$

$$\frac{1}{R_t} = .25\Omega$$

$$R_t = 4\Omega$$

Next we find the equivalent resistance for the R_6 - R_7 pair.

$$\frac{1}{R_t} = \frac{1}{R_6} + \frac{1}{R_7}$$

$$\frac{1}{R_t} = \frac{1}{10\Omega} + \frac{1}{15\Omega}$$

$$\frac{1}{R_t} = .1667$$

$$R_t = 6\Omega$$

Finally, we add the two parallel equivalent values to the values of R_1, R_5, and R_8, yielding:

$$R_t = 2\Omega + 4\Omega + 3\Omega + 6\Omega + 9\Omega$$
$$R_t = 24\Omega$$

2. Use Ohm's Law to find the total current in the circuit.

$$V = IR$$

$$I = \frac{V}{R}$$

$$I = \frac{24V}{24\Omega}$$

$$I = 1A$$

3. Find the voltage change between points B and C.

This may seem difficult at first, but remember Ohm's Law. The current passing through R_5 is 1A, and the resistance is 3Ω.

$$V = IR$$
$$V = (1A)(3\Omega)$$
$$V = 3V$$

4. Find the voltage change between points A and B.

Again, the problem seems more difficult than it really is—it's another Ohm's Law problem. The total current passing through the parallel resistors is 1A, and the equivalent resistance is 4Ω.

$$V = IR$$

$$V = (1A)(4\Omega)$$

$$V = 4V$$

POWER

Power in circuits is the rate at which electric energy is used. The power capability of the circuit elements is the product of the voltage and the current.

$$P = VI$$

Through substitution from Ohm's Law, we see two other ways to calculate power:

$$P = (I^2)(R) \text{ and } P = \frac{V^2}{R}.$$

Power is an important quantity in circuits. The voltage source must have enough power to operate the devices in the circuit. Furthermore, the devices in the circuitry will burn out and open if their power capacity is not large enough to perform work at the required rate. Remember, power is the rate at which work is done. The power requirement for a circuit or a circuit element can be calculated if any two of the Ohm's Law quantities are known.

Example
A typical power calculation could require you to find the power requirement for a resistor in a circuit.

Find the power dissipated by a 4Ω resistor that has a .05A current passing through it.

.05 A

4 Ω

Solution

$$P = I^2 R$$

$$P = (.05A)(4\Omega)$$

$$P = .01 \text{ Watt}$$

Another type of power question you could be asked would require you to find the total resistance in a circuit, then solve to find either the total power requirement of the circuit or the power requirement for a single element in the circuit.

Example

Find the power requirement for the series-parallel circuit shown below:

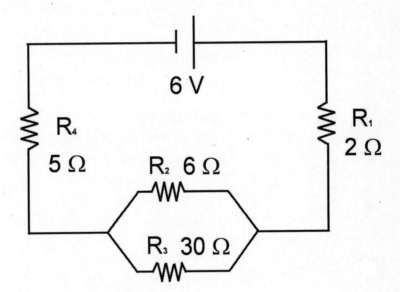

Solution

To find the total power for the circuit you first must find the total resistance. We find that the total resistance for the circuit is 9Ω. With this information we can now solve for the power required to run the circuit with $P = \dfrac{V^2}{R}$.

$$P = \frac{V^2}{R}$$

$$P = \frac{(6V)^2}{9\Omega}$$

$$P = 4 \text{ Watts}$$

Another question might involve one of the parallel resistors in the diagram above. The current in the circuit would be required to solve the problem.

Example

Find the power capacity for R_3 in the circuit above.

Solution

First we find the total current with Ohm's law.

$$I = \frac{V}{R}$$

$$I = \frac{6V}{9\Omega}$$

$$I = .66A$$

The next step is to calculate the voltage change across the two parallel resistors (R_2 and R_3).

$$V = (I)(R)$$
$$V = (.66A)(5\Omega)$$
$$V = 3.3V$$

With this information the actual current in R_3 can be found by using Ohm's Law.

$$I = \frac{V}{R}$$

$$I = \frac{3.3V}{30\Omega}$$

$$I = .11A$$

Next we calculate the power.

$$P = (V)(I)$$
$$P = (2.5V)(.11A)$$
$$P = .275 \text{ Watts}$$

Note: $\dfrac{V^2}{R}$ across the parallel resistors does not work because each resistor has a different current through it.

CAPACITORS

Capacitors (previously mentioned) are parallel plate devices that are capable of storing electric charge and releasing (discharging) it as needed. Their effectiveness is enhanced by placing a non-conductive material, called a *dielectric*, between the two plates. The energy (in the form of the charge) stored by a capacitor is $E = \frac{1}{2}CV^2$.

Capacitors placed in an electric circuit do not allow a steady current to flow. Instead, they build charge between their two plates over a period of time until the potential of the capacitor is almost equal to the applied voltage. When a capacitor is fully charged in a DC circuit, current cannot flow until the capacitor is discharged, because the capacitor acts like an open circuit element.

Capacitors used in an electric circuit can be in series or in parallel. The total capacitance (C_t) for capacitors in a parallel circuit is found by adding the values of the capacitors in parallel with one another. You should note that this technique is the opposite of the technique we used to find the value of the resistance of parallel resistors.

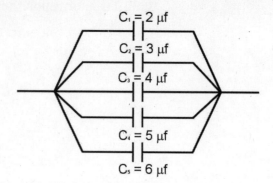

The six capacitors in the diagram have values of 2, 3, 4, 5, and 6 micro farads, respectively. The total capacitance is found by adding them together.

$$C_t = C_1 + C_2 + C_3 + C_4 + C_5$$

$$C_t = 2\mu f + 3\mu f + 4\mu f + 5\mu f + 6\mu f$$

$$C_t = 20\mu f$$

The total capacitance for capacitors in series with one another is found by the reciprocal method. (Again this is just the opposite of resistors in series).

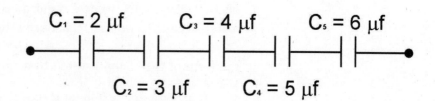

$$\frac{1}{C_t} = \frac{1}{C_1} + \frac{1}{C_2} + \frac{1}{C_3} + \frac{1}{C_4} + \frac{1}{C_5}$$

$$\frac{1}{C_t} = \frac{1}{2\mu f} + \frac{1}{3\mu f} + \frac{1}{4\mu f} + \frac{1}{5\mu f} + \frac{1}{6\mu f}$$

$$\frac{1}{C_t} = .5\mu f + .33\mu f + .25\mu f + .2\mu f + .1667\mu f$$

$$C_t = 1.45\mu f$$

AMMETERS AND VOLTMETERS

Ammeters and voltmeters are used to monitor electric circuits.

Ammeters measure the current flowing in a circuit. They have a low resistance, which keeps them from interfering with the circuit. This is necessary because they are hooked in a series with a circuit being measured, and a large resistance would decrease the current being measured with the meter.

Voltmeters are used to measure voltage changes in a circuit. They have a high resistance and are used in parallel with the circuit being measured. The high resistance in the voltmeter causes all but the tiniest fraction of current to pass through the circuit being measured, which prevents the voltmeter from interfering with the circuit.

MAGNETS AND MAGNETIC FIELDS

The properties of naturally occurring magnetic rocks have been known for several thousand years. The Chinese knew that a piece of iron could be magnetized by putting it near lodestone, and sailors have been navigating with magnetic compasses for nearly a thousand years.

Some characteristics of magnets that you should know and remember are:

1. Magnets have poles. The north-seeking pole is the north pole of the magnet. The south-seeking pole is the south pole of the magnet.
2. Like poles of magnets repel one another and unlike poles of magnets attract one another.
3. Magnets can induce demagnetized ferrous materials to become magnetized.
4. Temporary magnets cease acting like magnets as soon as the permanent magnet is removed.
5. Permanent magnets retain their magnetism for a long time.

A magnet field is said to exist in the region where a compass experiences a force upon it. Magnetic fields form around magnets. The magnetic field exits the north pole of a magnet and enters the south pole of a magnet.

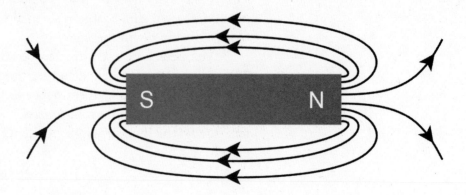

Magnetic field lines act much the same as electric field lines when magnetic poles are brought near one another. That is, *the magnetic lines of force do not cross.* You could say that the repulsive force the north pole of a magnet exerts on another similar magnetic pole is a manifestation of the lines of force not crossing one another.

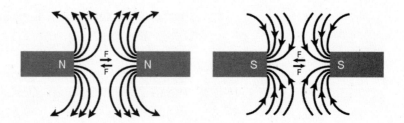

The attraction between unlike poles also can be explained in a manner similar to the electric field.

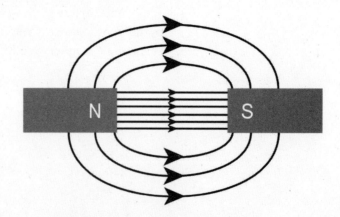

Peterson's SAT II Success: Physics

Some magnets exert large repulsive or attractive forces on other magnets regardless of how physically close the two magnets are to one another. The way these magnets repel or attract is an indication of their magnetic field strength, but this does not give an accurate measure of the actual strength of the magnetic field.

A more accurate method for determining the magnetic field strength is to use a term called *magnetic flux.* The number of magnetic field lines within a given area is called magnetic flux, and it represents the strength of the magnetic field B. Magnetic fields exert a force on current carrying wires. The force the wire experiences is the product of the length of the wire in the field, the magnitude of the current, and the strength of the magnetic field.

$$F = B_\perp IL$$

Note the perpendicular sign behind the B. The maximum force is exerted when a current carrying wire is perpendicular to the magnetic field. The direction of the force exerted on the wire can be found by using the right-hand rule.

Right-hand rule:

1. Point your right thumb in the direction of the current flow in the wire.
2. Point the fingers of your right hand in the same direction as the field lines (toward the south pole).
3. The force exerted on the wire by the magnetic field will be in the same direction as your palm points.

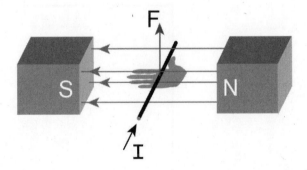

The diagram above shows a current carrying a magnetic field. According to the right-hand rule, the wire will experience a force in the upward direction. When the force exerted on a wire in a magnetic field is known, the magnetic field (B) can be determined.

Example

A .5m length of wire carries a 6A current within a magnetic field. The wire is at right angles to the field and experiences a force of .45N. What is the strength of the magnetic field?

Solution

$$F = B_\perp IL$$

$$B_\perp = \frac{F}{(I)(L)}$$

$$B_\perp = \frac{.45N}{(6A)(.5m)}$$

$$B_\perp = .15\frac{N}{A \bullet M} = .15 \; tesla \; (T)$$

A current-carrying wire is a source of a magnetic field too. This is the reason the wire has a force exerted on it when it is in a magnetic field.

Let's place a compass beside a wire hooked to a battery with an open switch.

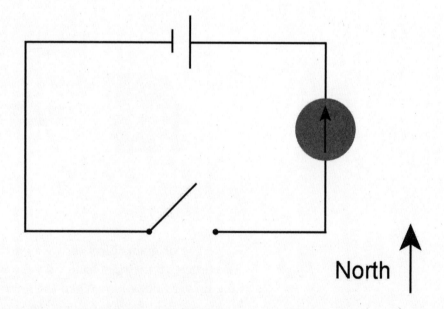

North

Notice that with the switch open the compass points correctly to the north. When the switch is closed the compass points in a different direction.

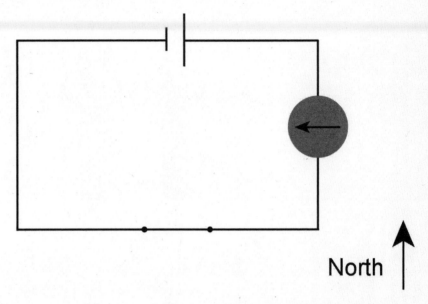

A force must affect the compass to cause it to point in a different direction. The current in the wire is the source of this force. The direction of the magnetic field around the current-carrying wire can be found by using a variation of the right-hand rule.

1. Point the thumb of your right hand in the direction of the current.
2. Grasp the wire and wrap you fingers around the wire.
3. Your fingers point in the same direction as the orientation of the magnetic field around the wire (see below).

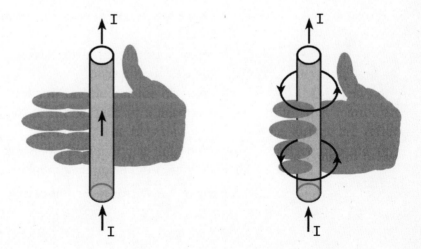

When two current-carrying wires are side by side, their magnetic fields interact, causing the wires to attract one another or to repel one another.

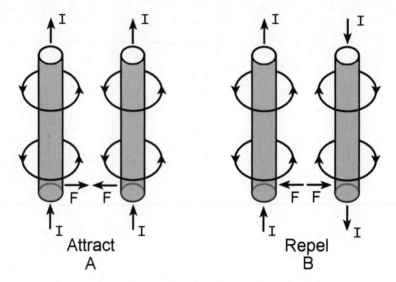

Notice the arrows in diagram A. Think of this situation as opposite magnetic fields, that attract one another. The arrows in diagram B head in the opposite direction. Think of this situation as like magnetic fields that repel one another.

Electric currents consist of moving charges. It is only natural to expect a charged object to experience a force when it is moving within a magnetic field. The right-hand rule can be applied to charged particles within a magnetic field. Unlike the current in a wire that followed its pathway in the wire, a charged particle can have its pathway changed by the force applied to it.

Reviewing the right-hand rule:

1. Point the thumb of your right hand in the direction the particle is moving.
2. Point your fingers in the direction of the field (toward the south pole of the magnet).
3. Your palm faces in the direction the force is applied to the particle. This is the direction the particle will move.

The charged particle has a charge q on it, and its velocity is v. The definition of current is a number of moving charges. Thus, we can say $F = B_\perp IL$ for a current-carrying wire.

The current in a wire is made of a number of individual charges that are moving at a high velocity. For a single charged particle, the charge on the particle and the velocity with which it is moving can be equated to the current and the length of the wire. This leads to the following equation, which describes the force exerted on a moving particle in a magnetic field.

$$F = B_\perp qv$$

Unless the particle leaves the magnetic field, the direction of the force on the particle keeps changing as the path of the particle changes. The particle will move in a circular path as the force on it remains constant in magnitude, and the direction continually changes.

Any time an object moves in a circular path, a centripetal force (F_c) is involved. In fact, the force applied to the charged particle by the magnetic field is a centripetal force.

$$F = Bqv \text{ and } F_c = \frac{mv^2}{r}$$

Clearly the (F) from the magnetic field is the same as the (F_c) from the centripetal force, leading to the following equation:

$$Bqv = \frac{mv^2}{r}$$

As you can see, the radius of the circular pathway taken by the particle can be determined. Likewise, it is apparent that the strength of the magnetic field can be changed, thus affecting the radius of the circle. This is the principle which operates our television sets and computer monitors.

MAGNETIC INDUCTION

More than 99% of the electrical power used in the United States is generated by converting mechanical energy into electrical energy for heating, lighting, cooking, etc. This process is called *electromagnetic induction* and was discovered in 1831 by Michael Faraday and John Henry.

A current can be induced in a wire in several ways. One is to place a closed loop of wire in a magnetic field and move the wire. Remember our discussion of the force applied to a current-carrying wire? The movement of the wire within the magnetic field causes a force to be generated in the wire, which in turn forces free electrons in the wire to move, thus generating a current in the wire.

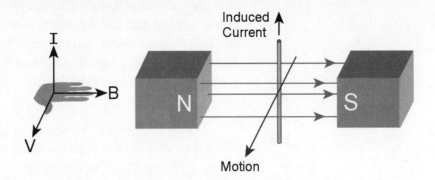

The direction of an electric current induced into a wire can be predicted by using the right-hand rule.

1. Point the thumb of the right hand in the direction of motion of the wire.
2. Point the fingers of the right hand in the direction of the magnetic field.
3. Your palm will point in the direction of the force and the induced current.

The magnitude of the induced current is dependent on several different things.

1. **The strength of the magnetic field.** A stronger magnetic field has more flux density, meaning more field lines to cross. The induced current will be larger when the magnetic field is stronger.
2. **The rate at which the wire is moved in the magnetic field.** The faster the wire is moved through the magnetic field, the more magnetic field lines will be cut, generating a larger current.
3. **The length of the wire in the magnetic field.** Again, the longer the wire, the more magnetic field lines it will cut through, generating more current flow.

The movement of a wire in a magnetic field causes the free electrons to move because their electrical potential is raised. We already know that current flows from high potential to lower potential. This difference in potential is called the induced *EMF*, which is in volts. We also know that the length of the wire (*L*), the strength of the magnetic field (*B*), and the rate at which the wire is moved in the magnetic field (*V*) affect the induced current as well.

The following represents the relationship between the induced voltage and the moving magnetic field in which a wire is placed. (The wire may be moved in a stationary magnetic field too.)

$$EMF = BLV$$

Power-generating plants induce current into lengths of wire on a large scale. Electrical power is generated by using long loops of wire that are wrapped in such a manner that they are in continuous contact with magnetic field lines. The loops of wire are rotated within the magnetic field at a constant rate to produce the type of electricity called alternating current or AC.

A simplified drawing of an AC generator is shown below.

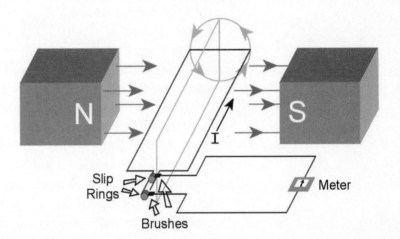

The current and voltage produced in the AC generators is not steady as in DC systems. Both current and voltage increase and decrease each time the loop of wire in the magnetic field turns a full 360°. The diagram below shows a comparison between AC and DC voltages.

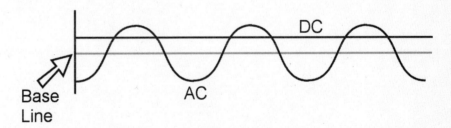

The AC peaks rise above the DC voltage because the effective voltage is equal to .707 the value of the maximum voltage. This is called the *RMS value.*

The process of moving the generated electricity from the power-generating stations to the houses and businesses that use it is called *power transmission*. This is accomplished by the use of wires that lead from the power plants to the location where the power is used. Sometimes the power plant is located hundreds of miles from the user. It is easy to see that the total resistance of the wires increases with the distance that the electricity is transmitted, and according to Ohm's Law, the increased resistance would cause the current to be reduced. Just the act of overcoming the resistance from the wires would cost the power companies a great deal of money, and, in fact, the current would melt the wires because it would have to be extremely large. Power companies therefore transform the electricity they generate into high voltage, which reduces the current in the wire to a mere fraction of what it would be at a low voltage (perhaps 240*V*). The transmission voltage is instead very high, approaching 18,000*V* or more.

The device used to increase or decrease voltage is called a *transformer.* Transformers are made of two separate coils of wire that are wound close to and around one another but that are electrically insulated from one another. The side of the transformer where the voltage is applied is called the *input,* or primary side. The side of the transformer where the new voltage is removed is called the *output,* or secondary side. When a current is passed through the primary transformer wire, a magnetic field emanates from the wire. The magnetic field from the primary side coils cuts through the coils of the secondary side, inducing a current into the secondary side of the transformer (see below).

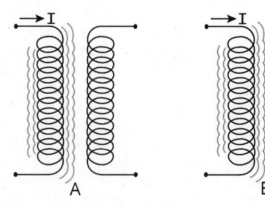

Transformers that reduce the applied voltage are called step-down transformers. Those that increase the applied voltage are called step-up transformers. The ratio of the input voltage and the output voltage is determined by the ratio of the number of turns of wire in the primary and the secondary sides of the transformer.

$$\frac{\text{Secondary Voltage}}{\text{Primary Voltage}} = \frac{\text{Number of Secondary Coils}}{\text{Number of Primary Coils}}$$

$$\frac{V_s}{V_p} = \frac{N_s}{N_p}$$

Here is a pair of transformer problems for you to try.

Example

Suppose you have a calculator that can use two $1.5V$ batteries in series ($3V$) or can use a transformer attachment to save battery power. We know the secondary side of the transformer has 30 turns. How many turns of wire does the primary side of the transformer have? The transformer uses household voltage when it is plugged into the electrical outlet, so we know the input voltage is $120V$.

Solution

$$\frac{V_s}{V_p} = \frac{N_s}{N_p}$$

$$\frac{(V_p)(N_s)}{V_s} = N_p$$

$$\frac{(120V)(30\text{turns})}{3V} = N_p$$

$$1200 \text{ turns} = N_p$$

Example

Another problem might require you to calculate the voltage produced in a transformer.

A step-down transformer contains 900 turns of wire in its secondary side. There are 30,000 turns of wire in the primary side, which has an input voltage of 8000 volts. What is the output voltage of the secondary side of the transformer?

Solution

$$\frac{V_s}{V_p} = \frac{N_s}{N_p}$$

$$V_s = \frac{(V_p)(N_s)}{N_p}$$

$$V_s = \frac{(8000V)(900\text{turns})}{30,000\text{turns}}$$

$$V_s = 240V$$

CHAPTER SUMMARY

- Charged particles are called ions.

- Electrostatic charge is caused by the transfer of electrons from one object to another object.

- Objects with a positive charge have a deficiency of electrons.

- Objects with a negative charge have an excess of electrons.

- Like charges repel, and unlike charges attract.

- The unit of charge is the coulomb.

- Electric fields exist around all charged objects.

- Electric field lines leave a positively charged object.

- Electric field lines enter a negatively charged object.

- Electric field lines are parallel between charged parallel plates.

- The electric field between a pair of parallel plates is uniform.

- Capacitors store electric charge or energy.

- Batteries supply energy to electric circuits. The energy is measured in volts (V).

- Current is the flow of charged particles and is measured in amperes (A).

- Resistance is opposition to current flow, and it is measured in ohms (Ω).

- The resistance of a series circuit is the sum of resistors in the circuit.

- The resistance of a parallel branch of a circuit is equal to the reciprocal of the sum of the reciprocals of the resistors in parallel.

- Like magnetic poles repel, and unlike magnetic poles attract.

- Magnetic field lines leave north poles and enter south poles to form closed loops.

- The intensity of a magnetic field called magnetic flux is measured in $\frac{N}{(A)(m)}$, or tesla.

- A current carrying wire within a magnetic field experiences a force equal **to** $F = B_\perp L$.

- The direction of the force on a current-carrying wire within a magnetic field can be determined by using the right-hand rule.

- A charged particle moving through a magnetic field experiences a force equal to $F = B\,q\,v$.

- The direction of the force on a charged particle in a magnetic field can be determined by using the right-hand rule.

- The right-hand rule states the following:
  1. Point the thumb of the right hand in the direction of the current or the motion of the particle.
  2. Point the fingers of the right hand in the direction of the magnetic field (toward the south pole).
  3. The palm of the right hand points in the direction of the applied force.

- The force applied to a moving particle in a magnetic field provides the centripetal force to move the particle in its circular path.

- Faraday and Henry simultaneously discovered magnetic induction.

- The right-hand rule can be used to determine the direction of a magnetically induced force and current.

- A generator converts mechanical energy into electrical energy.

- Alternating currents and voltages are generated by revolving a wire coil in a magnetic field.

- Transformers change high voltage to low voltage by stepping down the voltage.

- Transformers change low voltage to high voltage by stepping up the voltage.

Chapter 6

MODERN PHYSICS

CHAPTER 6

MODERN PHYSICS

PARTICULATE THEORY OF LIGHT

Sir Isaac Newton studied the continuous spectrum early in the seventeenth century. He passed a beam of sunlight through narrow openings into a darkened room. A white spot from the light beam appeared on the wall, and when Newton placed a prism into the path of the light beam, the white light disappeared and was replaced by what is called a *continuous spectrum*. Newton noticed that the spectrum was displaced slightly to the side of the light path. He also observed that the colors of the spectrum always appeared in a continuous band in the same order. The red light always appeared closest to the original path of the light path, followed by orange, yellow, green, blue, and violet, which was always deflected most from the original path of the white light. Newton recognized the bending of light (refraction) as the same process that occurred with water waves. Since the light exhibited the same characteristics as water waves, the wave nature of light was easy to visualize.

Max Planck spent the years from about 1890 to 1905 reviewing the results of Heinrich Hertz's experiments regarding the radiation of hot objects. Planck noticed that the results of Hertz's experiments could not be explained in terms of wave theory, but could be explained if the energy in radiation was carried in bundles or packets of light, which he called *quanta*. Planck theorized that the energy of the light was proportionally related to the frequency, which meant that the higher the frequency of the light, the higher the energy of the light. Planck related his idea to the equation:

$$E = hf$$

where E is the energy, f is the frequency, and h is Planck's constant. It's value is $6.6 \times 10^{-4} \, J \cdot S$.

Planck's theory is useful because it relates the frequency of light to the energy carried by the light. The light quanta suggested by Planck also shows that the line spectra emitted by energized atoms are a unique set of frequencies that can best be explained by the particle theory (quanta) of light.

Albert Einstein used the quantum theory expressed by Planck to explain the photoelectric effect. Through the photoelectric effect, electrons are energized by light that is shined onto the surface of a photosensitive metal. Einstein concluded that when an electron is struck by a quanta of light (he called them photons) the electron gains enough energy to be ejected from the surface of the metal.

Einstein reached this conclusion through an experiment where a negatively charged zinc plate emitted photoelectrons when struck by an ultraviolet light, but not when visible light was used. Further, when the plate was given a positive charge neither ultraviolet light nor visible light produced electron emission.

Only light of the correct frequency could energize electrons from the surface of the metal. Einstein stated that the electron absorbs or releases energy one photon at a time. He concluded that the higher the frequency of the light, the greater its energy. Thus, yellow light carries less energy than green or blue light. In fact, the continuous spectrum is arranged in order by the energy of the frequency of the light. Einstein also showed that light possessing the largest amount of energy (the highest frequencies) is refracted the most by a prism. Thus, the more a beam of light is refracted by a prism, the more energy it possesses.

We can compare the energy content of different photons by using Planck's equation to calculate the energy of photons of the different colors. The relationship between different light colors and their wavelengths is given in the chart below. We'll use it to help us perform the energy calculations for the different light colors.

Example

Light Color	Wavelength	Frequency
Red	$7.7nm(7.7 \times 10^{-7} m)$	$3.9 \times 10^{14} Hz$
Orange	$6.3nm$	$4.8 \times 10^{14} Hz$
Yellow	$5.8nm$	$5.2 \times 10^{14} Hz$
Green	$5.3nm$	$5.7 \times 10^{14} Hz$
Blue	$5.6nm$	$6.5 \times 10^{14} Hz$
Violet	$3.8nm$	$7.9 \times 10^{14} Hz$

Solution

Now let's calculate the energy of a photon of yellow light.

$$E = hf$$

$$= (6.6 \times 10^{-34} J \bullet s)(5.2 \times 10^{14})$$

$$= 3.14 \times 10^{-19} \frac{Joules}{photon}$$

Notice the units for energy in the answer. The seconds have disappeared. That's because the Hertz units used in the frequency really are either vibrations/sec (wave nature) or photons/sec (particulate nature). The chart below is the same as the previous chart but with a new column added to show the energy of the photon for a particular light color.

Light Color	Wavelength	Frequency	Photon Energy
Red	$7.7nm (7.7 \times 10^{-7} m)$	$3.9 \times 10^{14} Hz$	$2.6 \times 10^{19} J / photon$
Orange	$6.3nm$	$4.8 \times 10^{14} Hz$	$3.2 \times 10^{-19} J / photon$
Yellow	$5.8nm$	$5.2 \times 10^{14} Hz$	$3.4 \times 10^{-19} J / photon$
Green	$5.3nm$	$5.7 \times 10^{14} Hz$	$3.8 \times 10^{-19} J / photon$
Blue	$5.6nm$	$6.5 \times 10^{14} Hz$	$4.3 \times 10^{-19} J / photon$
Violet	$3.8nm$	$7.9 \times 10^{14} Hz$	$5.2 \times 10^{-19} J / photon$

Look at the chart. The relationship between the wavelength, the frequency, and energy of the photon of light is clear. The higher the frequency of the light, the more energy the photon carries. The longer the wavelength of the light, the lower the energy content of the photon.

PHOTOELECTRIC EFFECT

When we apply the quantum theory to the photoelectric effect, we must realize that the KE of the ejected electron is directly related to the energy it receives from the incident photon, minus the energy (W) required to remove the electron from the surface of the metal (work function).

$$KE = hf - W$$
$$1/2 \ mv^2 = hf - W$$

We see from the equation above that no electrons can be emitted from the surface of the metal unless the product of the frequency and Planck's constant is greater than the work function (W). In addition, the kinetic energy of the ejected electron depends upon the frequency of the photon and the work function of the metal. As we have seen from the chart of the color, frequency, and photon energy, the energy of the emitted photon is very small. A more convenient method to measure the energy of the electron (whether it absorbs or emits the photon) is to use an energy scale that is of the same magnitude as the electron: the electron volt (eV). The electron volt is defined as the quantity of work required to move an electron through a potential difference of 1 volt. (Remember, 1 volt is equal to 1 Joule per coulomb of charge.)

$$Work = QV$$

$$1ev = (1.6 \times 10^{-19} C)(1V)$$

$$1eV = 1.6 \times 10^{-19} J = 6.25 \times 10^{18} \frac{eV}{J}$$

Using this relationship, we will go back and recalculate the energy of a photon of yellow light in eV.

$$E = hf$$

$$= (6.6 \times 10^{-34} J \bullet s)(5.2 \times 10^{14} Hz)\left(6.25 \times 10^{25} \frac{eV}{J} \right)$$

The following problem illustrates the usefulness of the electron volt when working with photo-voltaic materials.

Example

The work function of a metal is given as $2.46eV$. What is the kinetic energy of the photons ejected from the surface of the metal when a light with a frequency of $8.2 \times 10^{14}\ Hz$ shines on the metal?

Solution

The work function is the minimum energy required to dislodge an electron from the surface of the metal, and it must be subtracted from the energy of the incident photons.

$$\text{KE} = hf\left(\frac{1eV}{1.6\times10^{-19}\ \dfrac{J}{eV}}\right) - W$$

$$\text{KE} = (6.6\times10^{-34}\ J \bullet s)(8.2\times10^{14}\ Hz)\left(6.25\times10^{18}\ \frac{eV}{J}\right) - 2.46eV$$

$$\text{KE} = 3.38eV - 2.46eV$$

$$\text{KE} = .92eV$$

When the wavelength of the light is known, we can restate the equation in the following manner:

$$\text{E} = h\frac{c}{\lambda}\left(6.25\times10^{18}\ \frac{eV}{J}\right) - W$$

The threshold energy for any photovoltaic metal is simply the work function of the metal. The work function is represented by the symbol (Φ), pronounced "phi."

The work function of a metal is equal to the energy of the photon that energizes the electron.

$$\text{E} = hf$$

The threshold frequency of the light can be calculated if the work function is known.

Example

Find the threshold frequency for a metal that has a work function of 5.10 eV.

Solution

$$\Phi = hf$$

$$f = \frac{\Phi}{h}$$

$$f = \frac{5.1eV}{6.6 \times 10^{-34} J \bullet s}$$

$$f = 7.73 \times 10^{33} Hz$$

The frequency obtained is very high, in the ultraviolet range.

Example

What is the threshold wavelength for a metal that has a work function of 4.28 eV?

Solution

For this problem we use the equation:

$$\Phi = h\frac{c}{\lambda}$$

$$\lambda = \frac{hc}{\Phi}$$

$$\lambda = \frac{(6.6 \times 10^{-34} J \bullet s)(3 \times 10^{8} m/s)}{4.28eV}$$

$$\lambda = 4.63 \times 10^{-26} m/wave$$

Again we obtain a value that places the light into the ultraviolet range.

Peterson's SAT II Success: Physics

We'll do one more problem. This time, try to find the work function of a light that approaches the infrared range. The limit of visible light in the red range is 3.9×10^{14} *Hz*. Calculate the work function:

$$\Phi = hf\left(\frac{1eV}{1.6\times10^{-19}J}\right)$$

$$= (6.6\times10^{-34}J \bullet s)(3.9\times10^{14}Hz)\left(6.25\times10^{18}\frac{eV}{J}\right)$$

$$= 1.61eV$$

Shortly after Einstein's work with the photoelectric effect, Niels Bohr made the suggestion that the normal laws of physics did not apply to the micro-world of the atom and its parts. Bohr maintained that electrons existed in an orbit about the nucleus where they would stay indefinitely. Indefinitely, that is, unless the electron received energy to cause it to move away from the nucleus. Bohr's concept was that the electron only left its usual position near the nucleus (ground state) by absorbing quanta of light, which it gave up to return to its ground state. Bohr used Planck's energy equation to support his theory about the electrons around the atomic nucleus.

$$E = hf$$

Bohr thought the electrons in their orbits would emit energy based upon their distance from the nucleus. He stated the relationship as:

$$\Delta E = E_2 - E_1$$

RELATIVITY

When Einstein predicted that photons should have the characteristics of a particle, he included momentum. He stated that the momentum of the photon should be $P = \frac{hf}{c}$, which led to $P = \frac{h}{\lambda}$.

Proof for Einstein's theory about the momentum of a proton was accidentally found by the American scientist Arthur Compton. Compton was studying the scattering of X-rays by passing them through an easily penetrable solid. During his experiments using a block of carbon, Compton noticed that he kept obtaining a small change in wavelength, which he decided to investigate. He considered the wavelength to be approximately the size of a single atom, and since the X-ray energy is so large, the energy needed to knock a single atom of the carbon is negligible compared to the total energy of the X-ray. The X-ray photon was deflected in the collision with the carbon electron, while the electron had a velocity impressed on it. Applying the laws of conservation of momentum and energy to the collisions produced the conclusion that the X-ray photon does have momentum.

Louis de Broglie investigated one of Bohr's theories while contemplating the dual nature of the electron. He found that by assuming the electron to be capable of having wave properties, he could explain one of Bohr's assumptions about electrons. de Broglie postulated that moving particles could have wave properties, leading to the following:

$$\text{deBroglie wavelength} = \lambda = \frac{h}{mv}$$

where mv = momentum of a photon

Should we attempt to calculate the wavelength of a large object (not on atomic scale), we find the wavelength of the object to be very small, which makes the waves undetectable.

Example

A 900 kg automobile is being driven down the road with a velocity of 30 m/s. What de Broglie wavelength would the car emit?

Solution

$$\lambda = \frac{h}{mv}$$

$$\lambda = \frac{6.6 \times 10^{-34} J \bullet s}{(900 Kg)(30 \text{m/s})}$$

$$\lambda = 2.4 \times 10^{-38} \text{m/wave}$$

That is an incredibly small wavelength. A diffraction grating would be unable to separate on it enough for an angle to be produced for measurement.

REFERENCE FRAMES

One of the most difficult concepts to accept is that the length of a meter stick, or the mass of an apple, or even the ticking of a clock can change without any of the items being broken, damaged, or in disrepair. The relative length, mass, or rate of movement of these items is expected to remain the same relative to other like items. The key word is *relative*. You see, the comparison only remains the same for the objects when they are in the same reference frame.

What is a reference frame? Just think of driving down the road at a velocity of 70 km/hr. When you pass a telephone pole, the telephone pole flashes by in an instant. Your reference frame is the inside of the car. The windows, the dash, the seats, and yourself are not moving in reference to one another. Outside, the rest of the world flies by at 70 km/hr.

Now let's suppose you are seated in the backseat of the moving vehicle with all the windows closed. You toss a wad of paper from your side of the car to the passenger on the other side of the car. That person catches the paper wad and throws it right back to you. As far as you're concerned, the paper wad flew straight across the back of the car in both instances.

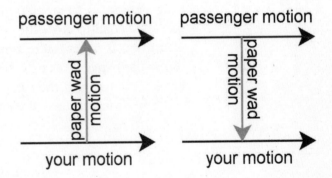

Let's suppose the top of your car is transparent, and an observer in a tall tower is looking down on the events as they take place in the car. To that person, your game of catch looks like this:

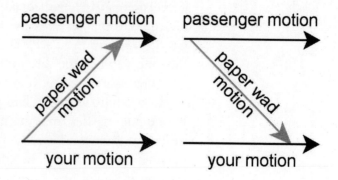

You and the person in the tower see the events in the back of the car in a very different way. For purposes of clarity, the numbers we use in the following discussion will be exaggerated a little, but the idea will still be relevant and may be easier to grasp. Your speed in the car (70 km/hr) is about 20 m/s. Let's say you and your friend both toss the paper wads with a speed of 10 m/s. The car (remember the exaggeration) is 10 m wide. From your perspective, the paper wad takes 1 second to cross the width of the car. Everything inside the car is just fine as far as you're concerned. The car is 10 m wide, you threw the paper at 10 m/s, and it takes 1 second for the paper to cross the interior of the car.

The observer outside the car sees things differently.

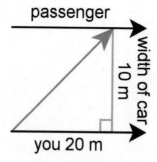

During the 1 second time span, the paper wad flew from one side of the car to the other, while the car itself moved a distance of

(20m)(1 sec) = 20m. The width of the car is 10m, so the path of the paper wad as seen by the outside observer is the hypotenuse of the triangle shown. To the outside observer it is 22.4 m long, and the velocity with which you throw the paper wad is considerably faster than 1 m/s. In fact, the observer measures the velocity of the paper wad to be 22.4 m/s.

When discussing relativity, you must always be aware that the reference frame is the key. One of the conclusions we can draw about reference frames is that the laws of mechanics are the same in all reference frames moving at constant velocity with respect to one another. In addition, all motion is relative to some reference frame.

Now that we have discussed reference frames, let's proceed to Einstein's theory. Einstein postulated that

1. all the laws of physics are the same for all observers moving at constant velocity with respect to one another.
2. the speed of light in a vacuum is the same for all observers regardless of the motion of the source of light or the motion of the observer.

SIMULTANEITY

Let's first look at the second postulate of Einstein's theory. We will return to the car, but instead of a wad of paper, we will use a beam of light, and instead of a second passenger we will use a mirror to reflect the light. In addition, the velocity of the car will be increased to .75 the speed of light. Inside the car, however, nothing changes as far as you are concerned. Things are just as they were when you traveled at 70 km/hr.

Example
The light beam you send from your side of the car crosses the car, strikes the mirror, and returns to your side of the car. The light travels the ten meters to the mirror and the 10 meters from the mirror in 6.67×10^{-8} s at a velocity of 3×10^8 m/s.

Solution
The question is, what does the outside observer see? The answer? The outside observer sees the light beam complete the trip in the same amount of time as you do. This means that the light traveled either a longer distance in the same period of time, thereby breaking one of the postulates of the theory of relativity, or, unlikely as it may seem, the outside observer was in a frame of reference where time passed more quickly.

The reason for the conclusion is that the person in the car sees the light travel from the origin, strike the mirror, and return to him, which is expressed as:

$$\Delta t = \frac{\text{distance}}{\text{speed}}$$

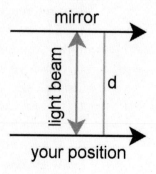

The distance d is the separation of the two sides of the car, yielding $\Delta t = \dfrac{2d}{c}$ for the round trip.

The outside observer sees things differently.

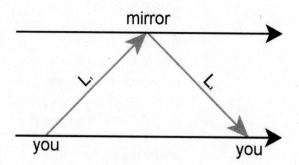

The path length the outside observer sees is considerably longer than the one seen by the person in the car. This means:

$$\Delta t_0 = \frac{L_1 + L_2}{c}$$

$$L_1 = L_2$$

yielding

$$\Delta t_0 = \frac{2L}{c}$$

Since c must be the same for both parties, Δt and Δt_0 cannot be the same.

Einstein related the difference in time for the two observers with the relativistic equation:

$$\Delta t_0 = \frac{\Delta t}{\sqrt{1 - \left(\frac{v}{c}\right)^2}}$$

Δt is the time on the moving clock.

Δt_0 is the time on the stationary clock.

Let's take a look at what this means in terms of the two people. Suppose the person in the car is moving at .75 the speed of light. What time will pass on the rider's clock if the observer in the tower measures a 30-minute time span?

$$\Delta t_0 = \frac{\Delta t}{\sqrt{1 - \left(\frac{v}{c}\right)^2}}$$

$$\Delta t = (\Delta t_0)\left(\sqrt{1 - \left(\frac{v}{c}\right)^2}\right)$$

$$\Delta t = (\Delta t_0)\left(\sqrt{1 - (.75c)^2}\right)$$

$$\Delta t = 19.8 \text{ minutes}$$

The rider in the car moving at .75 c only measures a time of 19.8 minutes on a clock, while the outside observer measures a time of 30 minutes.

The relativistic equation shows that the clock in the moving car moves more slowly. This fact leads to the following statement about time dilation.

Clocks in a moving reference frame run more slowly.

$$\sqrt{1-\left(\frac{v}{c}\right)^2}$$

The equation is called the relativistic factor.

Now that we have seen the time dilation part of Einstein's theory of relativity, the question arises about mass and other quantities. According to Einstein's relativistic equation, an object that has a length of 1 meter will be shorter to an outside observer. Let's take a look at length.

LENGTH CONTRACTION

Example

A hypothetical traveler going to Alpha Centauri will be in a spaceship that can travel at .85 the speed of light. How will the traveler experience the trip compared to an observer on earth?

Solution

We already know the clocks on the spaceship will move more slowly. That means the time on the earth ticks away faster. Substituting the distances into the relativistic factor instead of time yields the answer.

$$d_t = (d_0)\left(\sqrt{1-\left(\frac{v}{c}\right)^2}\right)$$

d_t = distance according to the spaceship traveler
d_0 = distance traveled to and from the star according to the known measurement

The distance to Alpha Centauri is approximately 4.5 light years, so we multiply by 2 to find the round trip distance.

Substituting and solving, we have:

$$d_t = 9 \text{ light years} \left(\sqrt{1-\left(\frac{v}{c}\right)^2}\right)$$

$$d_t = 4.74 \text{ light years}$$

The traveler finds the distance to the star and back again to be 4.74 light years instead of the 9 light years measured by earthbound observers.

RELATIVISTIC MASS—ENERGY RELATION

As stated earlier, the postulates of Einstein's theory of relativity tell us that no object can be accelerated beyond the speed of light. According to Newton's laws of motion, any object *could* be accelerated to the speed of light if given enough time. To be consistent with the laws of momentum, Einstein determined that the mass of an object must increase when its velocity increases. This led him to conclude:

$$m = \frac{m_0}{\sqrt{1 - \left(\dfrac{v}{c}\right)^2}}$$

This means an electron moving at nearly the speed of light gains mass. Let's use .98c, for example,

$$m_e = \frac{9.11 \times 10^{-31}\,\text{kg}}{\sqrt{1 - (.98)^2}}$$

$$m_e = 4.57 \times 10^{-30}\,\text{kg}$$

This shows us that the mass of an electron moving at .98 the speed of light has a mass 5 times larger than its rest mass. Should we use .999C, the mass of the electron increases to 2×10^{-29} kg. This is a mass 22 times larger than the rest mass of the electron.

The closer an object approaches to the speed of light, the larger its mass becomes, meaning an increasingly large quantity of energy must be input to accelerate the object as it nears the speed of light. The kinetic energy equation becomes:

$$KE = (m - m_0)(c^2)$$

Notice the change in mass requires more and more energy to increase the speed of the object. This finally leads to the equation:

$$E = mc^2$$

This is perhaps Einstein's most famous equation, and it is the equation that eventually lead to the development of nuclear weapons and nuclear power.

The equation showing the relationship between mass and energy predicts that if any mass can be accelerated to the velocity of light squared, an immense amount of energy will result.

What energy is required to accelerate a 10g mass of matter to the speed of light?

$$E = mc^2$$

$$E = \left(\frac{10g}{\frac{1000g}{kg}} \right) (3 \times 10^8 \, m/s)^2$$

$$E = 9 \times 10^{14} \, J$$

That is enough energy to heat 2151 m³ of water from 0°C to boiling. That is a cube of water approximately 13m × 13m × 13m. That's quite a lot of energy, and from just 10g of matter!

CHAPTER SUMMARY

- Max Planck theorized the particulate nature of light.

- Planck's constant is $6.6 \times 10^{-34} J \bullet s$.

- Albert Einstein used Planck's particulate nature of light theory to explore the photoelectric effect.

- Planck called light particles quanta.

- Einstein called light particles photons.

- The higher the frequency of the light, the more energy it carries.

- Photons of light have the ability to energize electrons from some metals.

- The ability of photons of light to knock electrons from the surface of some metals is called the photoelectric effect.

- The work function of a metal is equal to $\Phi = hf$.

- Louis de Broglie theorized the existence of matter waves.

- The two postulates of Einstein's theory of relativity are:
  1. The speed of light in a vacuum is the same for all observers.
  2. The laws of physics are the same for all observers moving at a constant speed.

- Moving clocks tick out time more slowly than still clocks.

- The relativistic equation is $\sqrt{1 - \left(\dfrac{v}{c} \right)^2}$.

- The relativistic mass of an object is much greater than its rest mass, leading to the equation $E = mc^2$.

Chapter 7

THE ATOM

CHAPTER 7

THE ATOM

THE ATOM

The outer part of the atom is the realm of the electron. Similar to a lead sinker on a string that is being swung around the fist that holds it, the electron is a tiny particle that is usually found at the outer edge of an atom's radius, but always outside the nucleus. Another similarity is the difference in mass of the sinker compared to the hand. The electron has a mass $\frac{1}{1836}$ that of the proton in the nucleus. Adding to the mysterious nature of the electron is its ability to be located at various distances from, but not in, the nucleus.

Electrons were first noted by Jean Perrin (1870–1942) as a greenish beam in a cathode ray tube (so named because the beam came from the cathode). A little later (1897) J.J. Thompson determined the charge to mass ratio for an electron. Twelve years later (1909) Robert Millikan found the charge on an electron in his famous "Oil Drop Experiment." Another calculation by Millikan gave him the mass of the electron.

Charge per electron = $1.6 \times 10^{19}C$
Mass per electron = 9.1×10^{-31}kg

As we discussed in Chapter 6, Sir Isaac Newton studied the continuous spectrum that was visible when sunlight was passed through a glass prism. His observations led to another interesting discovery. Scientists noticed that the spectrum caused by energized gases in discharged tubes produced lines of color that were the same color as portions of the continuous spectrum.

Each different gas produces a different set of lines (called line spectrum) that can be matched into the continuous spectrum. As we saw in Chapter 3, $V_{wave} = \lambda f$. We can show the velocity of light to be the product of the wavelength and the frequency with this calculation.

The known frequency of blue light is 6.5×10^{-14} (Hz), and its wavelength is 4.6×10^{-5}cm. Multiplying the two yields:

$$V = (4.6 \times 10^{-5} \text{cm/wave})(6.5 \times 10^{14}\, Hz)$$
$$V = (2.99 \times 10^{-10}\ \text{cm/s})$$
$$V = 3 \times 10^{8}\ \text{m/s}$$

Clearly the velocity of light.

BOHR'S ATOM

The Danish physicist Niels Bohr suggested that electrons absorbed energy when they were struck by photons of light, and when they returned to their non-energized state, they emitted the absorbed energy in the form of light. Thus, an electron either absorbs or releases energy to change its state. Bohr stated his theory in the following equation:

$$\Delta E = E_2 - E_1$$

Bohr next used Max Planck's equation, which converts the energy of a light wave into the energy of a photon.

$$\Delta E = \hbar f$$

E = energy

f = frequency

$\hbar$ = Planck's constant = $6.6 \times 10^{-34}\, Joule \bullet \sec$

Since only line spectra occurred when an elemental gas tube was energized, Bohr concluded that the line spectra showed that the electrons occupied specific orbits around the nucleus of the atom. He called the permitted orbits *energy states*. The orbit closest to the nucleus was called the ground state of the electron. It represented the orbit with the least amount of energy content for the electron. When an electron absorbed energy it jumped to a new "higher" energy state and was considered energized. An energized electron could only occupy specific quantified orbitals, and each new orbital required a different amount of energy for an "excited" electron to be able to occupy the orbital. When an excited electron returned to a lower energy state, it gave up the energy it had absorbed in the form of light. Bohr's equation predicted the result as:

$$f = \frac{E_2 - E_1}{\hbar}$$

From the equation we see that if we are given the frequency of the light we can calculate the wavelength. The reverse is also true for calculating the frequency from the wavelength. Given the frequency of the light, we can also calculate the energy of the emission.

Example
A blue-colored light from the line spectrum of hydrogen is found to have a frequency of $6.17 \times 10^{14} Hz$. How much energy is emitted by the electron as it falls to a new orbital?

Solution

$$\Delta E = \hbar f$$

$$(6.6 \times 10^{-34} J \bullet s)(6.17 \times 10^{17} photons/s)$$

That is a tiny amount of energy, but if a mole of electrons is considered, the energy is substantial.

$$E_{mole} = (6.022 \times 10^{23} photons/mole)(4.07 \times 10^{-19} Joules/photon)$$

$$E = 2.45 \times 10^5 Joules/mole$$

_____ $n = 7$

_____ $n = 6$

_____ $n = 5$

_____ $n = 4$

_____ $n = 3$

_____ $n = 2$

_____ $n = 1$

Bohr visualized the orbital energies around the nucleus as similar to the steps of a ladder. Much as you gain potential energy as you climb up the rungs of a ladder, electrons were required to absorb energy in order to jump from a lower energy orbital to a higher energy orbital. A "jump" by an electron meant the electron moved from a low "n" number to a higher "n" number. A fall meant the electron gave up energy (emitted energy) in order to fall from a high "n" number to a lower "n" number.

The absorption of energy is considered a negative quantity, and the emission of energy is considered a positive quantity. Unfortunately the Bohr model could not account for the spectrum of atoms with more than one electron and consequently was replaced with a new one. The new atomic spectra model was derived from the field of quantum mechanics. Quantum mechanics explains not just the spectral lines for the hydrogen, but also the spectral lines of the heavier elements too, because it approaches the location of an electron as probable states, rather than a definite place, a concept that in effect releases the electron from a rigid set of positions and allows it to vary its location according to the conditions affecting it. *Quantum mechanics predicts where an electron is most likely to be at a given time based on the energy of that electron.* By using probability instead of restricting the orbital placement, the energy changes electrons exhibit when they are excited can be accurately predicted.

Left alone, electrons fall to their lowest energy state, which in the case of the hydrogen electron is $-13.6eV$, and is called the ground state or $n = 1$ level. Note the negative sign. The negative sign represents the energy required to raise the electron to an excitation level high enough to remove it from the atom. That is the potential where the electron has absorbed enough energy to escape from its atom and is called $E = 0$. The values for the first five excitation states are shown on the energy-level diagram below:

$-.54eV$	_____	$n = 5$
$-.85eV$	_____	$n = 4$
$-1.51eV$	_____	$n = 3$
$-3.4eV$	_____	$n = 2$
$-13.6eV$	_____	$n = 1$

It should be noted that each change in level, whether as absorption or emission, is a discrete quantity of energy. Every electron rising from $n = 2$ to $n = 3$ must absorb $1.89eV$ of energy. Anything less and the electron cannot change its excitation state to the next highest level. Energy in excess of the amount required to move the electron from $n = 2$ to $n = 3$ has no effect unless the additional energy is exactly enough to raise the electron to the next highest (or more) excitation level. When the electron emits energy, the energy is again quantized in discrete values that are the exact energy differential between the higher and the lower energy levels. The electron may fall two or more energy levels, but in that case the energies given off are again quantized. Thus, the energy difference between $n = 4$ and $n = 3$ would be emitted as one color of light, and $n = 3$ and $n = 2$ energy would be emitted as another color of light.

Example

Let's do a problem where an electron absorbs energy.

A hydrogen atom is at $n = 2$ energy level when it absorbs energy and jumps to the $n = 4$ level. How much energy did the electron absorb?

$-.54eV$ _____	$n = 5$
$-.85eV$ _____	$n = 4$
$-1.51eV$ _____	$n = 3$
$-3.4eV$ _____	$n = 2$
$-13.6eV$ _____	$n = 1$

Solution

Determining the energy required to raise the electron from $n = 2$, where its energy is $-3.4\ eV$, to $n = 4$, where its energy is $-.85eV$, is a matter of finding the difference between the two energy levels.

$$\Delta E = E_3 - E_1$$
$$\Delta E = (-3.4eV) - (-.85eV)$$
$$\Delta E = (-3.4eV) + (.85eV)$$
$$\Delta E = -2.55eV$$

Note the negative sign. The electron must absorb 2.55eV to rise from the $n = 2$ potential to the $n = 4$ potential.

Example

The next problem is one where the electron emits energy and falls from a higher potential to a lower potential (toward the ground state).

An electron at $n = 3$ emits energy as it falls from $n = 3$ to $n = 1$. How much energy did the electron lose?

$-.54eV$	_____	$n = 5$
$-.85eV$	_____	$n = 4$
$-1.51eV$	_____	$n = 3$
$-3.4eV$	_____	$n = 2$
$-13.6eV$	_____	$n = 1$

Solution

The energy emitted by the electron as it changes from $n = 3$ to $n = 1$ is:

$$\Delta E = E_3 - E_1$$

$$\Delta E = (-1.51eV) - (-13.6eV)$$

$$\Delta E = (-1.51eV) + (13.6eV)$$

$$\Delta E = +12.09eV$$

Note the positive sign. When the electron falls to its ground state, it emits all the energy it had absorbed to reach the excited state.

THE NUCLEUS

All matter is made of atoms. Except for hydrogen, atoms consist of protons and neutrons in the nucleus and the electrons that are always found outside the nucleus. (Hydrogen is made of electrons and protons only.) Atoms are electrically neutral; when an atom has gained or lost electrons, the result is an ion. The number of protons in the nucleus of an atom is the *atomic number*, called the (Z) number. Because all atoms are electrically neutral, this is the number of electrons, too. All atoms of a particular element contain the same number of protons; however, they may have different numbers of neutrons.

Peterson's SAT II Success: Physics

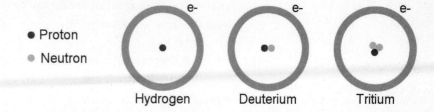

Notice that the hydrogen, deuterium, and tritium (above) each have one proton and one electron. The difference between them is the number of neutrons in the nucleus. The sum of the protons in a nucleus plus the number of neutrons is called the mass number, or (A) number. Elements with the same atomic number but a different mass number are called isotopes.

The number of neutrons in the nucleus can be found by subtracting the Z number from the A number (A-Z). Atoms and their isotopes are expressed by writing the A number over the Z number, followed by the symbol of the element.

$$_8^{15}O \text{ is oxygen 15, and } _8^{16}O \text{ is oxygen 16.}$$

You may notice on the periodic table of the elements that for the most part, the mass number of the elements is a decimal. That's because the number on the periodic table represents the atomic mass number of all the isotopes of the element of the type in discussion averaged together in their natural abundance. *The isotope number or mass number of an element has absolutely nothing to do with the atomic number of the element.* Isotopes of any given element with the same mass number are the same element because they all have the same number of protons in the nucleus. The mass of the atom listed on the periodic table is actually the relative mass of each of the elements compared to one another.

The actual mass of an atom should be the sum of the masses of its individual parts. An atom of $_6^{12}C$ *should* have the mass of 6 protons plus 6 neutrons plus 6 electrons. We are about to see that this is not necessarily the case.

Before proceeding with the calculation of the mass of the $_6^{12}C$ atom, let's take a look at relative mass. Since atoms are so tiny, their mass is an extremely small number. A convenient way to consider the small masses involved with atoms is the *atomic mass unit* or *amu*.

One *amu* (*u*) is equivalent to 1.6606×10^{-27} kg. The calculation of the mass of a carbon atom is shown below by using both the actual mass, and the amu simultaneously.

Mass of the proton (m_{p+}) $= 1.6726 \times 10^{-27}$ kg or $1.007276u$
Mass of the neutron (m_n) $= 1.6749 \times 10^{-27}$ kg or $1.008665u$
Mass of the electron (m_e) $= 9.1094 \times 10^{-31}$ kg or $5.86 \times 10^{-4}u$

The mass of the proton is approximately 1836 times as great as the electron mass. The mass of the electron is so tiny in comparison to the mass of the nucleus that it is not even considered in most applications.

Continuing to find the mass of the carbon atom we have:

$$(6_{p+})(1.6726 \times 10^{-27} \, kg) = 1.0036 \times 10^{-26} \, kg$$

$$\text{or } (6_{p+})(1.007276u) = 6.043656u$$

$$(6_n)(1.6749 \times 10^{-27} \, kg) = 1.0049 \times 10^{-26} \, kg$$

$$\text{or } (6_n)(1.008665u) = 6.05199u$$

$$(6_{e-})(9.1094 \times 10^{-31} \, kg) = 5.4656 \times 10^{-10} \, kg$$

$$\text{or } (6_{e-})(5.486 \times 10^{-4}u) = 3.2916 \times 10^{-3}u$$

The total mass of the carbon 12 atom is:

$$2.009 \times 10^{-26} \, kg \qquad \text{or} \qquad 12.098932 \, u$$

The mass of the carbon nucleus is found by subtracting the mass of the electrons from the mass of the nucleus:

2.009×10^{-26} kg	mass of atom	$12.098932u$
$(-)5.4656 \times 10^{-30}$ kg	mass of electrons	$(-) \; 3.2916 \times 10^{-3}u$
2.0085×10^{-26} kg	mass of nucleus	$12.095642u$

All the parts of the nucleus, whether they are protons or neutrons, are called *nucleons.*

Two noteworthy facts emerge from the calculations above. The first is the ease with which we can use *amu* values, and the second is the extremely small fraction of the mass of the carbon atom that is electron mass.

$$\frac{3.2916\times10^{-3}u}{12.095642u}=.0002721 \text{ or } 2.7\times10^{-6}\%.$$

As the atoms become larger, the electron mass percentage of the atom decreases to a smaller and smaller percent.

The calculations show that the mass of the carbon–12 nucleus should be 12.095642 u. The actual mass of the carbon nucleus has been found to be 12.01115 u. What happened to the rest of the mass? Remember, the protons carry a positive charge that produces a force of repulsion on other protons. There are 6 protons in the carbon nucleus, and energy is required to hold the protons together against the forces they exert on one another. Einstein's equation ($E = mc^2$) relates the changes in the mass of the nucleus with energy. The missing mass (mass defect) converts into the energy required to hold the positively charged protons together in the nucleus.

Mass defect is the difference between the calculated mass of all the protons and neutrons in a given nucleus compared to the actual mass of the nucleus.

The energy that holds protons together in the nucleus is called *binding energy*. Binding energy results from converting the mass resulting from the mass defect into energy. This energy is necessary to overcome the force of repulsion the protons exert on one another.

When the binding energy is calculated using kilograms as the mass units, the energy is given in joules. More often, the binding energy is measured in units called the *electron volt*. The electron volt is defined as the energy required to move one electron through a potential of one volt.

Using Einstein's equation $E = mc^2$, we find:

$$1u = 931.5 \ MeV$$

This means 1*amu* of mass produces 931.5 *MeV* of energy. Going back to the original oxygen atom, we will find the binding energy for carbon-12.

12.095642u (calculated mass of the carbon nucleus)

(−) 12.011150u (known mass of the carbon nucleus)

.084492u (mass defect of the carbon nucleus)

The binding energy is calculated to be:

(931.5 *MeV/amu*)(.084492 u) = 78.7 *MeV*

Sometimes there is a need to know how much binding energy applies to each nucleon. Calculating the binding energy per nucleon, we have:

$$\frac{78.7MeV}{12 \text{ nucleons}}=\frac{6.56MeV}{\text{nucleon}}$$

Binding energy usually holds the particles in the nucleus strongly together. Elements that fit into this category are the "stable" elements. Some elements that are not held together strongly enough by the binding energy are called "unstable." That is because the unstable element occasionally emits parts or particles called radiation. *The emission of radiation by a nucleus always changes the nucleus in a way that tends to make the nucleus more stable.*

RADIOACTIVITY

Henri Becquerel was studying fluorescence and phosphorescence when he accidentally discovered that photographic plates stored near uranium compounds became fogged. Becquerel reasoned that the photographic plates must have been exposed by something from the uranium. Over the next decade several dozen new radioactive substances were found by scientists, most notably by Pierre and Marie Curie.

Even though the newly discovered radioactive substances were different, all were found to emit just three kinds of radiation: alpha (α), beta (β), and gamma (γ). An experiment in which a sample of radioactive uranium was placed in a lead container with a very small opening showed that each type of radiation has different characteristics.

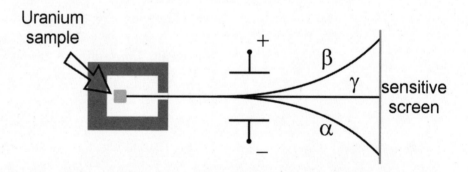

The radiation from the sample could only escape from the lead box by passing through a pinhole opening. As the radioactive particles passed out of the lead box, they were subjected to an electric field. Some of the particles were repelled by the positive and attracted toward the negative plate. These were called alpha (α) rays. Alpha rays were assigned a positive charge because they were deflected away from the positively charged plate when they passed through an electric field. Alpha radiation was found to be less penetrating than the other radiations. Alpha particles are easily stopped by a sheet of paper. The alpha particle is a helium nucleus $_2^4\text{He}$.

The second of the three radiations was repelled by the negative plate and attracted toward the positive plate; these are beta (β) rays. Beta radiation is somewhat more penetrating than alpha particles.

Beta particles are high-speed electrons $\left(_{-1}^{\ 0}e\right)$ capable of penetrating thin metal sheets, but they are stopped by a few millimeters of lead.

The third ray was found to be completely unaffected by the electric field. These high-energy photons, called gamma (γ) rays, were found to be a highly penetrating type of radiation, with the ability to penetrate several centimeters (or more) of lead.

Gamma radiation occurs when a nucleus emits energy. No other changes occur in the nucleus. Beta radiation occurs when a neutron decays into a proton and an electron (combining a proton and an electron yields a neutron.) When alpha particles are emitted, the nucleus changes by the value of a helium nucleus.

Alpha Emission	$_{92}^{238}U \rightarrow {}_{90}^{234}Th + {}_2^4He$
Beta Emission	$_{90}^{234}Th \rightarrow {}_{91}^{234}Pa + {}_{-1}^{\ 0}e$
Gamma Emission	$_{92}^{238}U \rightarrow {}_{92}^{234}U + \gamma$

Notice the examples above are not only radiations, but examples of nuclear equations.

When doing nuclear equations, you should always check the following:

1. The sum of the atomic numbers on both sides of the equation must be equal.
2. The sum of the mass numbers on both sides of the equation must be equal.

NEUTRON ADDITION

$$^{235}_{92}U + ^{1}_{0}n \rightarrow ^{144}_{56}Ba + ?$$

The missing substance on the right side of the equation must contain enough protons and neutrons to balance the number of protons and neutrons on the left side of the equation.

$$\frac{236}{92} - \frac{144}{56} = \frac{92}{36}$$

When the correct number of protons and neutrons have been determined, the appropriate symbol is added to the equation.

$$^{235}_{92}U + ^{1}_{0}n \rightarrow ^{144}_{56}Ba + ^{92}_{32}Kr$$

β emission $\quad ^{92}_{36}Kr \rightarrow ?Zr + 4\,^{0}_{-1}e$

Remember that the electron emission changes a neutron into a proton. There are 4 electrons (B particles) emitted, so 4 neutrons change into protons.

$$^{92}_{36}Kr \rightarrow ^{92}_{40}Zr + 4\,^{0}_{-1}$$

FISSION

The process by which an atomic nucleus splits into two or more parts is called nuclear fission. Nuclear fission occurs when a neutron collides with a nucleus, producing two new "daughter" nuclei that usually have a ratio of (60:40) of the mass of the parent nucleus.

Nuclear power plants generate electricity through the fission of $^{235}_{92}U$.

$$^{235}_{92}U + ^{1}_{0}n \rightarrow ^{140}_{56}Ba + ^{92}_{36}Kr + 4\,^{1}_{0}n + \text{energy}$$

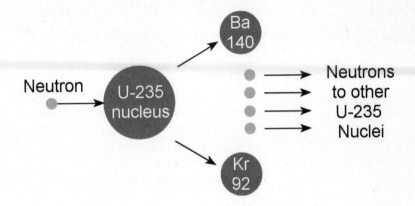

The diagram above illustrates the process through which the uranium nucleus is split to produce the two daughter nuclei and four neutrons. We can calculate the energy released in the reaction by finding the change in mass between the reactant nucleus and neutron and the products.

First we will restate the equation with the known mass of the substances inserted into the equation.

The mass of ^{235}U is $235.0439231u$

The mass of ^{140}Ba is $139.9105995u$

The mass of ^{92}Kr is $91.9261528u$

$$\,_0^1 n + \,_{92}^{235}U \rightarrow \,_{56}^{140}Ba + \,_{36}^{92}Kr + 4\,_0^1 n$$

$$1.008665u + 235.0439231u \rightarrow 139.910599u + 91.9261528u + 4.03466u$$

$$236.05259u \rightarrow 235.8714u$$

The difference in the mass of the reactants on the left is greater than the mass of the products on the right. The laws of conservation of mass and energy require an accounting of the missing mass. That is the mass converted to energy according to $E = mc^2$.

Subtracting we have:

$$236.05259u$$

$$(-)235.87140u$$

$$.18119u$$

The difference between the two is the mass that is converted to energy.

$$E = \left(931.5\frac{MeV}{u}\right)(.18119u)$$

$$E = 168.7785 \; MeV \text{ per } {}^{235}U \text{ atom}$$

We can see that the larger the number of uranium atoms present to fission, the more energy can be obtained from the process. The energy from the reaction is produced when some of the binding energy of the $\,{}^{235}_{92}U\,$ is released. The 4 neutrons represent a net gain of 3 extra neutrons in the reaction. The neutrons continue to strike and fission more uranium nuclei in a reaction called a *chain reaction*. In a nuclear reactor the chain reaction is controlled through the use of non-reactive boron rods.

The two daughter nuclei, $\,{}^{140}_{56}Ba\,$ and $\,{}^{92}_{36}Kr,$ are both radioactive, as are many physical objects that come into contact with reactive materials. One of the major drawbacks in fission reactions is the large amount of radioactive nuclear waste that is produced.

RADIATION

Radioactive waste and other nuclear materials produce radiations that are dangerous to living organisms, causing tissue and genetic damage. The penetrating power of radiation particles depends on the mass of the particle, its energy, and its charge. Alpha radiation damages tissue less than beta radiation because it is less penetrating. Gamma radiation is the most penetrating radiation of all.

The activity of a radioactive sample is the number of radioactive disintegrations a sample undergoes in a unit of time.

$$\text{Activity} = \frac{\Delta N}{\Delta t}$$

The unit for activity is the Bequerel (Bq). The activity of any substance depends upon the number of radioactive nuclei that were originally present (N_0) and the decay constant (λ) of the substance. The decay constant is equal to the ratio between the N_0 and the activity of the substance.

$$\frac{\Delta N}{\Delta t} = \lambda N_0$$

To find out how long it takes for one half of a radioactive substance to decay away ($T_{1/2}$), we use the following equation.

$$T_{\frac{1}{2}} = \frac{.693}{\lambda}$$

The decay curve for a radioactive substance is an exponential curve:

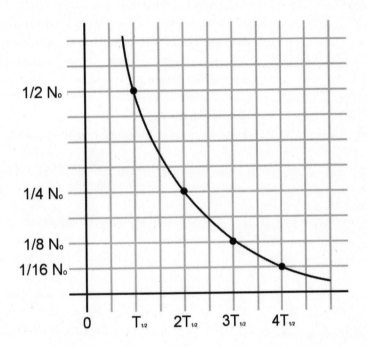

The graph above tells us that one half of a radioactive element has decayed away after one half-life. After two half-lives, 25% of the substance remains, after three it is 12.5%, and so on. After six half-lives, the radioactive material decays to negligible amounts. The remaining percentage of a radioactive substance after six half lives is calculated as follows:

$$\left(\frac{1}{2}\right)\left(\frac{1}{2}\right)\left(\frac{1}{2}\right)\left(\frac{1}{2}\right)\left(\frac{1}{2}\right)\left(\frac{1}{2}\right) \text{ or } \left(\frac{1}{2}\right)^6$$

Yielding .015625 or 1.5625%

The percentage of any radioactive substance is calculated in the

same way. Raise $\frac{1}{2}$ to the power of the number of half-lives, and the

result is the amount of substance left $\left(\frac{1}{2}\right)^n$.

Example
Let's try a problem.

A radioactive isotope of iodine used in medical procedures has a half-life of 2.26 hours. How much of the radioactive iodine will be left in a patient's body 24 hours after 10 grams of the radioisotope of iodine is ingested?

Solution
First we find the number of half-lives in the 24 hour period.

$$\frac{24 \text{ hours}}{2.26 \text{ hours}/\text{half-life}} = 10.6 \text{ half-lives}$$

Next we find the decimal amount of the iodine left.

$$(1/2)^{10.6} = .00064 \text{ or } .064\%$$

Since the patient ingested 10g, the amount of the isotope left is:

$$(10g)(.00064) = .0064g$$

There is almost no radioactive iodine left in the patient's body.

FUSION

When the nucleus is split (through the process of fission), energy is derived from the mass defect that was converted into the binding energy to hold the nucleus together. This shows that the mass of a stable nucleus is less than the mass of the individual parts of the nucleus if they were divided and added together in that manner. The missing mass, or mass defect, provides the necessary mass to provide the binding energy to hold the protons within in the nucleus in spite of their repulsion for one another.

The change in the masses of nuclear parts when they are within a nucleus compared to their masses when they are not within a nucleus is a source of energy in another type of nuclear reaction. *The process of combining small nuclei with other small nuclei to build larger nuclei is called fusion.* During the process of fusing nuclei together, the energy of the reaction is obtained.

Fusion continuously occurs in the stars. These stellar "ovens" eventually produce all the elements known to man by the fusion process. The process also produces large amounts of energy. The energy produced in the sun is the energy that heats the earth.

Fusion in the sun begins with the simplest of the elements, hydrogen.

$$ {}_1^1H + {}_1^1H \rightarrow {}_1^2H + {}_{+1}^{0}e + \upsilon $$

Notice the emission of a $\left({}_1^0 e \right)$ particle (called a positron) in the reaction, which means a proton has changed into a neutron. The positron is an emission which converts a proton into a neutron. The formation of deuterium $\left({}_1^2 H \right)$ is just the first of several steps leading to the formation of helium in the sun. Next is:

$$ {}_1^2H + {}_1^1H \rightarrow {}_2^3He $$

followed by

$$ {}_2^3He + {}_2^3He \rightarrow {}_2^4He + 2{}_1^1H $$

Four protons (hydrogen) have combined to form helium. Now we calculate the energy released in the fusion reaction by finding the mass of the reactants and using the known mass of the products.

Reactants: $(4p+)(1.007276\ u) = 4.029104\ u$
Products: Known mass of helium $= 4.001506\ u$

Subtract the known mass of the helium nucleus from the sum of its parts:

$$ 4.029104\ u - 4.001506\ u = .027598\ u $$

This provides an energy yield of:

$$\left(931.5\frac{MeV}{u}\right)(.027598u) = 25.7\,MeV$$

The energy obtained doesn't seem very large, but remember this is the energy yield from the formation of only *one* helium nucleus.

We can gain a better understanding of how much energy is derived from fusion if we consider a larger number of the fused helium atoms, say 1 mole of helium. There are 6.022×10^{23} atoms of helium in one mole. Multiply the energy from the formation of one helium atom by the number of atoms in one mole of helium.

$$(6.022 \times 10^{23})\,(25.7\ MeV) = 1.55 \times 10^{25}\ MeV$$

That is the equivalent of 2.5×10^{11} Joules, enough heat to raise the temperature of $597m^3$ of water by $100°C$.

The fusion reaction produces a large amount of energy. However, a sustainable fusion reaction has been extremely difficult to achieve. Problems exist with sustaining the reaction and with containing the reaction in a vessel capable of withstanding the immense heat energy produced in the reaction.

Despite this, fusion power has its benefits, a major one of which is the relative cleanliness of the reaction. Hydrogen is the simplest and the smallest of all the elements. It is readily available in large quantities on earth. There would be no fuel shortages for reactors using hydrogen as their fuel. With the exception of some incidental radiations, there is very little radiation produced in the reaction, either as a by-product or a waste product.

PARTICLES

The search for new particles has been aided by the advent of newer and bigger particle accelerators. Early particle accelerators used small particles, protons and neutrons, as projectiles to smash into target particles, or nuclei. As larger accelerators were constructed, larger particles could be accelerated and more energetic collisions could be designed. The most commonly used accelerators used today are *cyclotrons*, *synchrotrons*, and *linear accelerators*. The cyclotron uses magnetic fields to accelerate a particle (usually a proton) in a circular pathway. The synchrotron also uses a circular pathway, but its size is much larger than the cyclotron. The particles in the synchrotron are subject to a constantly changing magnetic field to accelerate the particles. The particle of choice for linear acceleration

is the β particle $\begin{pmatrix} 0 \\ -1 \end{pmatrix} e$. It is accelerated through a straight line to

nearly the speed of light. The advent of the new, more powerful accelerators made possible the formation and discovery of new particles (and antiparticles).

Experiments in high energy-physics have left researchers with a classification problem. The particles that result from high energy collisions do not always lend themselves to the normal mass and charge classification, so scientists devised a way to classify particles according to their interactions.

The interactions are based upon the strength of a particle's interaction with other particles. These interactions, arranged from strongest to weakest, are

- Strong interactions

- Electromagnetic interactions

- Weak interactions

- Gravitational interactions

Particles exhibiting strong interactions are responsible for nuclear force. There are several types of particles that fit into this category, and they are collectively called *hadrons*. Protons and neutrons are in this category.

Electrons have no strong interactions and are categorized as *leptons*. Particles that exhibit electromagnetic interactions have electric charge. Electromagnetic interactions between charged bodies are not as strong as nuclear interactions at short distances (nuclear radius), but they operate over longer distances. Neutral particles have no magnetic interactions.

Radioactive decay and β-emission are examples of *weak interaction*, which is the force involved in the decay of unstable particles into more stable products.

The last of the interactions is the *gravitational interaction*. It does not seem to have any significant effect upon the particle physics world; its importance is in the macro-environment of large bodies.

CHAPTER SUMMARY

- The three basic parts of an atom are the electron, the proton, and the neutron.

- Electrons are the negative part of the atom. They are found outside the nucleus and they are only 1/1836 the mass of a proton.

- Protons are the positive part of the atom. They are found in the nucleus and their mass is 1836 times greater than that of the electron.

- Neutrons are neutral. They have no charge, are found inside the nucleus, and have a mass approximately equal to a proton.

- Electrons occupy discrete levels near their nucleus called orbitals.

- The lowest energy orbital is called the ground state.

- Unexcited electrons normally occupy the ground state $n = 1$.

- Electrons absorb energy to change to a higher energy level.

- Electrons emit energy as they drop to a lower energy level.

- Except for hydrogen, all atoms have neutrons and protons in the nucleus.

- An isotope is a form of an element that has the same atomic number as the element but has a different atomic mass.

- The Z number of an atom is the number of protons in the nucleus.

- The A number of an atom is the number of the protons plus the neutrons in the nucleus.

- Atomic nuclei are held together by energy called *binding energy*.

- The source of the binding energy is the *mass defect*.

- Balanced nuclear equations require that:
  1. the sum of the atomic numbers on both sides of the equation must be equal.
  2. the sum of the mass numbers on both sides of the equation must be equal.

- Nuclear fission is a process by which large atomic nuclei are split to obtain energy.

- Nuclear fusion is a process by which small atomic nuclei are joined to obtain energy.

- Unstable atomic nuclei become more stable by emission of energy or particles in a process called radiation.

- The three types of natural radiation are:
  1. Alpha particles   α
  2. Beta particles   β
  3. Gamma rays   γ

- The length of time required for one half of a radioactive substance to decay away is called its half-life, $T_{1/2}$.

- The activity of a radioactive substance is defined as the number of radioactive disintegration per unit of time.

$$\text{Activity} = \frac{\Delta N}{\Delta t}$$

- A variety of machines called particle accelerators are used in the search for new particles.

- Many newly found particles are particle/anti-particle pairs.

- The four interactive forces are:
  1. Strong interactions
  2. Electromagnetic interactions
  3. Weak interactions
  4. Gravitational interactions

Practice Test 1

PHYSICS TEST

PRACTICE TEST 1

PHYSICS TEST

While you have taken many standardized tests and know to blacken completely the ovals on the answer sheets and to erase completely any errors, the instructions for the SAT II Physics Test differ in an important way from the directions for other standardized tests. You need to indicate on the answer key which test you are taking. The instructions on the answer sheet will tell you to fill out the top portion of the answer sheet exactly as shown.

1. Print PHYSICS on the line under the words *Subject Test (print)*.
2. In the shaded box labeled *Test Code* fill in four ovals:

      —Fill in oval 1 in the row labeled V.
      —Fill in oval 6 in the row labeled W.
      —Fill in oval 3 in the row labeled X.
      —Fill in oval C in the row labeled Y.
      —Leave the ovals in row Q blank.

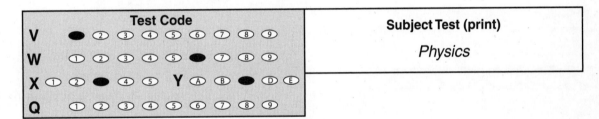

There are two additional questions that you will be asked to answer. One is "How many semesters of physics have you taken in high school?" The other question lists courses and asks you to mark those that you have taken. You will be told which ovals to fill in for each question. The College Board is collecting statistical information. If you choose to answer, you will use the key that is provided and blacken the appropriate ovals in row Q. You may also choose not to answer, and that will not affect your grade.

When everyone has completed filling in this portion of the answer sheet, the supervisor will tell you to turn the page and begin. The answer sheet has 100 numbered ovals, but there are only approximately 75 multiple-choice questions on the test, so be sure to use only ovals 1 to 75 (or however many questions there are) to record your answers.

PHYSICS TEST

Part A

<u>Questions 1–2</u> relate to the diagram below, which shows a set of open-ended pipes with waves vibrating inside them.

<u>Questions 3–5</u> relate to the diagram below, which shows atomic particles moving through a magnetic field.

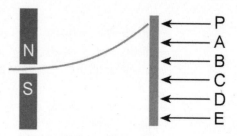

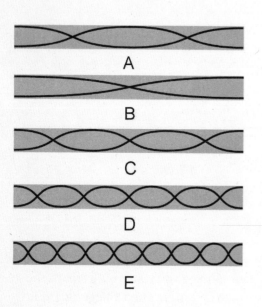

A beam of electrons is deflected in the magnetic field shown. The electrons that have passed through the field strike the screen at point *P.*

3. At which letter would a stream of neutrons strike the screen?

4. At which letter would a stream of protons strike the screen?

5. At which letter would a stream of electrons strike the screen if the poles of the magnet were reversed?

1. Which of the diagrams shows the pipe containing waves with the longest wavelength?

2. Which of the diagrams shows the pipe containing the waves with the highest frequency?

PHYSICS TEST—*Continued*

<u>Questions 6-7</u> relate to the graph below, which shows an object that is thrown almost straight up from the top of a ten-story building.

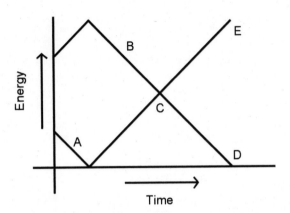

6. At what point on the graph does the potential energy of the object equal the kinetic energy of the object?

7. At what point on the graph does the kinetic energy of the object decrease while the potential energy increases?

<u>Questions 8-10</u> relate to the symbols used in writing nuclear equations. Atomic nuclei are typically written in the form $_{Z}^{A}X$.

Select the choice that provides the best match to each of the questions below.

(A) The number of protons is Z.

(B) The number of neutrons is X.

(C) The symbol of the element is X.

(D) The number of electrons is A.

(E) The mass number is A.

8. Which letter represents the atomic number?

9. Which letter represents the protons plus neutrons in the nucleus?

10. Which letter represents the name of the nuclide?

GO ON TO THE NEXT PAGE

PHYSICS TEST—*Continued*

<u>Questions 11–13</u> relate to the following situation.

A train engine that weighs 5000N stops at the exact center of a bridge. The bridge weighs 75,000N and has two equally spaced pillars that completely support the bridge.

    (A) 75,000N

    (B) 40,000N

    (C) 37,500N

    (D) 2500N

    (E) 0N

Select the choice that provides the best match to each of the statements below.

11. The sum of the torques

12. The force exerted on the ground by a single pillar

13. The upward force exerted by each pillar

PHYSICS TEST—*Continued*

Part B

Directions: Each question or statement below is followed by five possible answers. In each case, select the best possible answer and fill in the corresponding oval on the answer sheet.

14. A carbon atom decays into a nitrogen atom in the equation below. Which of the quantities correctly finishes the equation?

$$^{14}_{6}C \rightarrow {}^{14}_{7}N + ?$$

   (A) Alpha
   (B) Beta
   (C) Gamma
   (D) Neutron
   (E) Neutrino

15. A rocket is launched into the air during a fireworks show. Which of the following statements about the parts of the rocket is appropriate immediately after the explosion?
   (A) They have less mass than they had before the explosion.
   (B) They have more momentum than they had before the explosion.
   (C) They have less momentum than they had before the explosion.
   (D) They have the same momentum as they had before the explosion.
   (E) They have less kinetic energy than they had before the explosion.

16. Two 1 liter containers contain 1 mole each of the same gas at the same temperature. Container A is allowed to expand until the temperature of gas A is reduced by half. Container B is compressed until the temperature of gas B doubles. Both gases are then mixed together in a 2 liter container. Which of the following statements about the gases is correct?
   (A) Both gases gain heat.
   (B) Both gases lose heat.
   (C) Gas A loses heat to gas B.
   (D) Gas B loses heat to gas A.
   (E) The equilibrium temperature of the gases is exactly one half the original starting temperature of the gases.

17. The energy obtained in a nuclear reaction is derived from
   (A) mass defect.
   (B) binding energy.
   (C) fission.
   (D) fusion.
   (E) all of these.

18. Constructive interference between two light beams results in
   (A) a loss of kinetic energy.
   (B) the destruction of the waves.
   (C) the reversal of the direction of the waves.
   (D) a larger wave.
   (E) the refraction of the waves.

GO ON TO THE NEXT PAGE

PHYSICS TEST—*Continued*

19. Two batteries are hooked together in an electric circuit. Which of the following statements is/are true?

    I. Maximum voltage is obtained when the batteries are wired in parallel.
    II. Maximum voltage is obtained when the batteries are wired in series.
    III. Maximum current capacity is obtained when the batteries are wired in parallel.

    (A) I only
    (B) II only
    (C) I and III only
    (D) II and III only
    (E) I, II, and III

20. A goldfish swims through an aquarium by moving its fins and tail. What causes the fish to move forward?

    I. The force the water exerts on the goldfish
    II. The force the tail of the goldfish exerts on the water
    III. The force the fins of the goldfish exert on the water

    (A) I only
    (B) II only
    (C) I and III only
    (D) II and III only
    (E) I, II, and III

21. A hydrogen electron gains enough energy to rise from the $n=1$ to the $n=5$ energy level. How much energy does it gain?

$-.38eV$	_____	$n=7$
$-.54eV$	_____	$n=6$
$-.85eV$	_____	$n=5$
$-1.52eV$	_____	$n=4$
$-3.39eV$	_____	$n=3$
$-13.6eV$	_____	$n=1$

    (A) $+.88\ eV$
    (B) $+2.54\ eV$
    (C) $+10.21\ eV$
    (D) $+12.09\ eV$
    (E) $+12.75\ eV$

22. A 50 g cube of ice is added to 500 g of boiling water. Which of the following is most likely to occur?

    (A) The ice cube vaporizes before it strikes the bottom of the container.
    (B) The water boils more vigorously because the hot water draws cold from the ice cube.
    (C) The water in the container stops boiling during the phase change of the ice to water.
    (D) The more dense ice cube sinks in the less dense hot water.
    (E) Steam bubbles form on the ice cube.

PHYSICS TEST—*Continued*

23. An unmanned exploratory space vehicle is accelerated to .85*c* as it leaves the solar system. Years later a stationary extra-terrestrial watches the vehicle pass and measures the length of the vehicle to be 12.64 m. What was the length of the vehicle on earth before it began its trip?
    (A) 8.44 m
    (B) 12.64 m
    (C) 18.23 m
    (D) 24.0 m
    (E) 29.77 m

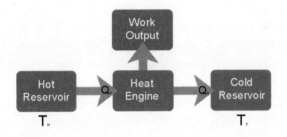

24. The diagrammatic representation of a heat engine above shows which of the following?
    (A) Positive work
    (B) An adiabatic process
    (C) An isobaric process
    (D) An isochoric process
    (E) An isothermal process

25. A force is applied to an object that is free to move. Which of the following statements is correct?
    (A) The frictional force is larger than the applied force.
    (B) The frictional force is smaller than the applied force.
    (C) The weight of the object is larger than the applied force
    (D) The weight of the object is smaller than the applied force
    (E) All of these statements could be correct.

26. Two charged spheres are separated by 2 mm. Which of the following would yield the greatest attractive force?
    (A) +1*q* and +4*q*
    (B) −1*q* and −4*q*
    (C) +2*q* and +2*q*
    (D) −2*q* and −2*q*
    (E) +2*q* and −2*q*

27. An astronaut is standing on an asteroid when he accidentally drops a wrench. He observes that the gravitational acceleration on the asteroid is 2.4 m/s². If he had thrown the wrench at an upward angle instead, he would have found the gravitational acceleration on the asteroid to be
    (A) less than 2.4 m/s².
    (B) toward him at 2.4 m/s².
    (C) downward at 2.4 m/s².
    (D) greater than 2.4 m/s².
    (E) none of these.

GO ON TO THE NEXT PAGE

PHYSICS TEST—*Continued*

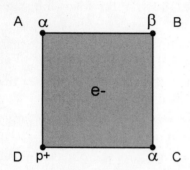

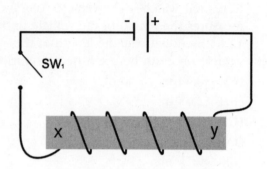

28. The two-dimensional cube in the diagram above has charged objects placed at the corners as shown. An electron that is free to move is placed at the exact center of the cube. In which direction will the electron move?

    (A) It will move toward A.
    (B) It will move toward B.
    (C) It will move toward C.
    (D) It will move toward D.
    (E) It will remain stationary.

29. A white disk and a black disk are placed on top of a snow bank on a sunny day. The black disk sinks deeper into the snow because

    (A) the black disk reflects light better.
    (B) the white disk reflects light better.
    (C) the black disk radiates heat better.
    (D) the white disk radiates heat better.
    (E) both of the disks reflect light and radiate heat at the same rate.

30. Based on the diagram above, which of the following statements describes the quantities induced into the iron core when SW_1 is closed?

    (A) Lines of force emanate from side y.
    (B) Lines of force emanate from side x.
    (C) Side y becomes a south magnetic pole.
    (D) Side x becomes a north magnetic pole.
    (E) The electric field cancels the magnetic field.

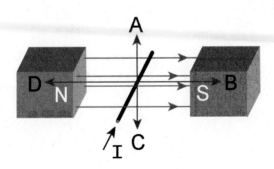

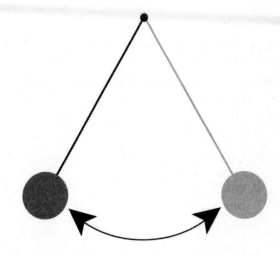

31. A wire within a magnetic field has a current flowing in it as shown. Any force exerted on the wire is in the direction of
    (A) point A.
    (B) point B.
    (C) point C.
    (D) point D.
    (E) No forces are exerted on the wire.

32. A 24 *V* battery is connected to a 4 ohm resistor, causing a current of 5 amperes. What is the internal resistance of the battery?
    (A)   0 W
    (B)   .8 W
    (C)   .4 W
    (D)   1.6 W
    (E)   1.2 W

33. A pendulum is used on Earth and then transported to the moon where it is released and allowed to swing freely. Which of the following statements about the pendulum is correct?
    (A) The period of the pendulum on the moon is greater than it was on Earth.
    (B) The frequency of the pendulum on the moon is greater than it was on Earth.
    (C) The potential energy of the pendulum on the moon is greater than it was on Earth.
    (D) The kinetic energy of the pendulum on the moon is greater than it was on Earth.
    (E) The period, the frequency, the kinetic energy, and the potential energy of the pendulum on the moon are the same as they were on Earth.

GO ON TO THE NEXT PAGE

PHYSICS TEST—*Continued*

34. A girl standing on a high bridge over a creek throws a rock straight down at leaves floating in the creek. Just as she throws the rock she accidentally drops another rock. Neglecting air resistance, which statement best describes the situation just as the rocks reach the water?

    (A) The acceleration of the thrown rock is greater.

    (B) The acceleration of the dropped rock is greater.

    (C) The acceleration of both rocks is the same.

    (D) The average velocity of both rocks is the same.

    (E) The final velocity of both rocks is the same.

35. When does an artificial earth satellite that is in an elliptical orbit experience its greatest centripetal acceleration?

    (A) When it first enters orbit

    (B) When it is nearest the earth

    (C) When it is farthest from the earth

    (D) When it leaves orbit

    (E) Its centripetal acceleration is always the same

36. A sample of a radioactive substance has a half-life of 20 minutes. If the sample's activity is 200 counts/second, what is the number of counts/second after one hour passes?

    (A)   6.25 counts/sec

    (B)   12.5 counts/sec

    (C)   25 counts/sec

    (D)   50 counts/sec

    (E)   100 counts/sec

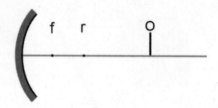

37. An object (*O*) is placed in front of a concave mirror as shown in the diagram above. Which of the following choices best describes the image formed?

    (A) Virtual and magnified

    (B) Real and erect

    (C) Inverted and magnified

    (D) Virtual and reduced

    (E) Real and inverted

38. A very rich boy has an ice hockey practice floor that is essentially frictionless installed in a long refrigerated boxcar. As the train is moving, the boy practices shooting at the goal at the other end of the car. Just as he releases his shot, the train goes around a sharp curve to the left (looking forward in the direction the boy is shooting). Which statement most accurately describes the boy's shot?

    (A) It curves to the right and misses to the right side of the net.

    (B) It curves to the left and misses to the left side of the net.

    (C) It travels straight and misses to the right side of the net.

    (D) It travels straight and misses to the left side of the net.

    (E) It travels straight into the goal.

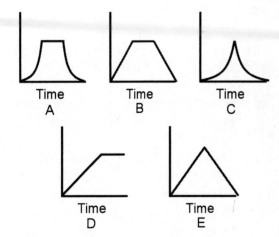

39. The three blocks in the diagram above are identical and are pulled at a constant rate across a surface that has a frictional coefficient of .22. Which of the following statements about the tensions in the connecting strings is correct?

    (A) T_1 is equal to $(T_3 - T_2)$.
    (B) T_1 is equal to $(T_2 - T_3)$.
    (C) T_2 is equal to $(T_3 - T_1)$.
    (D) T_3 is equal to $(T_1 - T_2)$.
    (E) T_3 is equal to $(T_2 - T_1)$.

40. A boxcar rolls down an incline and strikes a stationary boxcar at the bottom of the incline. The two boxcars stick together and roll a short distance before they come to a stop.

    Which of the graphs above shows the total momentum of both boxcars throughout the time they are moving?

    (A) Time A
    (B) Time B
    (C) Time C
    (D) Time D
    (E) Time E

GO ON TO THE NEXT PAGE

PHYSICS TEST—*Continued*

41. At the third maxima on both sides of the zeroth fringe in a Young's double slit experiment, the light
    (A) travels the same distance.
    (B) from the lower opening travels three times farther than light from the upper opening.
    (C) from the upper opening travels three times farther than light from the lower opening.
    (D) from either opening travels 2 wavelengths farther than light from the other opening.
    (E) from either opening travels 3 wavelengths farther than light from the other opening.

42. A professional golfer strikes a golf ball with his driver, imparting a momentum of 8 kg· m/s on the ball. The golf ball strikes a wall and maintains contact for .0025 seconds before it bounces straight backward at the same velocity with which it struck the wall. The momentum of the golf ball is
    (A) 6400 kg·m/s
    (B) 3200 kg ·m/s
    (C) 8 kg·m/s
    (D) .02 kg·m/s
    (E) .01 kg·m/s

43. Two disks of equal mass but different diameter are connected with an axle system that allows them to roll down an incline together. Both disks start and finish at the same time. Which of the following statements best describes the disks?
    (A) Their tangential velocity is the same.
    (B) Their tangential acceleration is the same.
    (C) Their angular velocity is the same.
    (D) Their angular displacement is the same.
    (E) Their angular acceleration is the same.

44. A motorcycle racer starts from rest and accelerates on a straight track at 5 m/s^2. How far does the racer travel in 8 seconds?
    (A) 40 m
    (B) 60 m
    (C) 80 m
    (D) 120 m
    (E) 160 m

45. A photon can eject an electron from the surface of a photovoltaic metal if and only if
    (A) the frequency of the photon is above the activation minimum.
    (B) the wavelength of the photon is above the activation minimum.
    (C) the speed of the photon is above an activation minimum.
    (D) the momentum of the photon is below the activation minimum.
    (E) the momentum of the impacted electron is above the activation minimum.

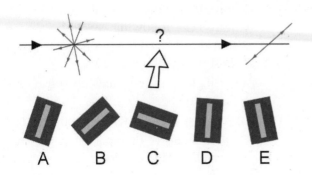

46. Which of the Polaroids in the diagram above will produce the polarized light shown?
    (A) Polaroid A
    (B) Polaroid B
    (C) Polaroid C
    (D) Polaroid D
    (E) Polaroid E

47. Which of the following best describes the condition of an enclosed gas during an isothermal expansion?
    (A) The gas remains at constant pressure.
    (B) The gas remains at constant volume.
    (C) The gas remains at constant temperature.
    (D) The gas remains at constant density.
    (E) The gas remains at constant molarity.

48. The velocity of a moving object is doubled. Which of the following statements about the object is correct?
    (A) The kinetic energy of the object increases by four.
    (B) The displacement of the object increases by four.
    (C) The momentum of the object increases by four.
    (D) The frictional force increases by four.
    (E) None of these quantities increase by four.

49. Two concurrent forces act at right angles to one another. The resultant force is 65N and one of the component forces is 35N. What is the force of the other component?
    (A) 40N
    (B) 45N
    (C) 50N
    (D) 55N
    (E) 60N

50. Which of the following statements is/are correct about an object that has no unbalanced forces applied to it?
    I.   The object has no velocity.
    II. The object has no acceleration.
    III. The object does not move.

    (A) I only
    (B) II only
    (C) I and III only
    (D) II and III only
    (E) I, II, and III

51. When a gas undergoes an adiabatic expansion, its
    (A) energy increases.
    (B) pressure increases.
    (C) volume decreases.
    (D) temperature increases.
    (E) temperature decreases.

GO ON TO THE NEXT PAGE

PHYSICS TEST—*Continued*

52. Two moving electrons enter a strong magnetic field at right angles to the field. The velocity of one of the electrons is four times greater then the velocity of the other electron. Which of the following best describes the ration of the circular radii the two electrons follow?

    (A) The faster electron has a radius two times larger than the slower electron.

    (B) The faster electron has a radius four times larger than the slower electron.

    (C) The faster electron has a radius eight times larger than the slower electron.

    (D) The faster electron has a radius sixteen times larger than the slower electron.

    (E) The faster electron has a radius sixty-four times larger than the slower electron.

53. A pair of a particles (helium nuclei) approach one another head on. Compared to the force they exert on one another at a distance of .066 m, by how much will the force the two particles exert on one another at .033 mm increase?

    (A) 2
    (B) 3
    (C) 4
    (D) 6
    (E) 8

54. According to Einstein's theory of relativity, which of the following would be a correct assumption to make for a traveler in a spaceship traveling at .95c?

    (A) Clocks on the spaceship run more slowly.

    (B) The spaceship will appear shortened.

    (C) The mass of the spaceship increases while it is in motion.

    (D) Light travels at the same velocity for the traveler whether he is moving or not moving.

    (E) All of these assumptions would be correct.

55. The engineer of a train blows the train whistle as he approaches a crossing. A few moments later he hears an echo from the whistle. The engineer hears the echo of the whistle because of

    (A) reflection.
    (B) refraction.
    (C) constructive interference.
    (D) destructive interference.
    (E) Doppler effect.

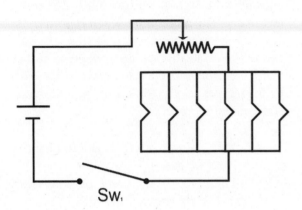

56. The diagram above shows a battery and a variable resistor set at its midpoint resistance in series with a parallel light circuit. Switch l (*SW*1) is closed and the light bulbs illuminate. When the variable resistor is moved slightly to the left (*L*) the bulbs dim a little. When the variable resistor is moved slightly to the right (*R*) the bulbs brighten slightly.

What happens in the circuit when the variable resistor is set all the way to the right?
(A) The lights brighten considerably.
(B) The total circuit resistance increases.
(C) The total circuit current decreases.
(D) The total applied voltage increases.
(E) The total power used in the circuit increases.

57. The density of any substance from the most dense phase to the least dense phase is
(A) gas, liquid, solid
(B) liquid, solid, gas
(C) liquid, gas, solid
(D) solid, gas, liquid
(E) solid, liquid, gas

58. An object that is placed on the edge of a constant speed turntable has
(A) constant linear velocity.
(B) tangential acceleration.
(C) centripetal acceleration.
(D) centrifugal acceleration.
(E) no acceleration.

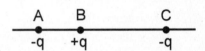

59. The diagram above shows a proton at point B between two electrons at points A and C. The distance from point B to point C is twice the distance from point B to point A. The force the proton experiences at point B is
(A) two times stronger from the electron at A.
(B) three times stronger from the electron at A.
(C) four times stronger from the electron at A.
(D) the same from both electrons.
(E) It is not possible to determine the force the proton experiences from the information provided.

60. A laser beam passes from the air into a piece of plexiglass. All of the following are false EXCEPT
(A) the velocity decreases.
(B) the wavelength increases.
(C) the frequency decreases.
(D) the period decreases.
(E) None of the above is true.

GO ON TO THE NEXT PAGE

PHYSICS TEST—*Continued*

61. A 30 kg child is standing in the back of a stationary 10 kg wagon that is free to move. The child jumps from the wagon into his mother's arms. Which of the following statements is correct at the moment he jumps from the wagon?
    (A) The child's velocity is greater than the wagon's velocity.
    (B) The wagon's velocity is greater than the child's velocity
    (C) The impulse exerted by the child on the wagon is the same as the momentum gained by the wagon.
    (D) The impulse exerted by the wagon on the child is larger than the momentum gained by the child.
    (E) None of these statements is correct.

62. Ice, which has a temperature of $0°C$, is added to 500 g of water that has a temperature of $100°C$. Ice is continually added to the system until it has all melted and no more ice will melt. What is the temperature of the water in the system?
    (A) $50°C$
    (B) $25°C$
    (C) $4.184°C$
    (D) $1°C$
    (E) $0°C$

63. Two similar pith balls are very near to one another, and each is charged with 2 excess electrons. The angle q between q_1 and q_2 is $5.5°$. One electron is removed from q_1 and placed on q_2 so that q_1 has 1 electron and q_2 has 3 electrons. The angle between the pith balls changes to $4°$. Which of the following statements is correct?

    I. The amount of electrostatic charge has decreased.
    II. The electrostatic force between the pith balls has decreased.
    III. Both the electrostatic charge and force have decreased.

    (A) I only
    (B) II only
    (C) I and III only
    (D) II and III only
    (E) I, II, and III

64. Complete the nuclear reaction below by selecting the answer choice that correctly completes the reaction.

$$_1^1H + _3^7Li \rightarrow _4^7Be + ?$$

    (A) $_1^1H$

    (B) $_0^1n$

    (C) $_{-1}^0e$

    (D) α

    (E) Y

Peterson's SAT II Success: Physics

65. A stuntman drives a brand new 800kg sports car off a high cliff at 200 km/hour. At the exact moment that the car is driven off the cliff, an 800kg rock is dislodged and falls straight down toward the ground. Which of the following is a correct statement about the event?

    (A) The car hits the ground first.
    (B) The rock hits the ground first.
    (C) The car and the rock hit the ground at the same time.
    (D) The x velocities of the car and the rock equalize over a period of time.
    (E) The x accelerations of the car and the rock are different

66. A person standing 1.5 m in front of a plane flat mirror would see their image at a distance of

    (A) .75 m
    (B) 1.5 m
    (C) 2.25 m
    (D) 3 m
    (E) 6 m

67. A paperboy rides his bicycle down the street and throws the papers to houses as he rides by them. When a thrown paper leaves his hand, which of the following statements is NOT true about the paper?

    (A) Its velocity changes.
    (B) Its acceleration changes.
    (C) Its displacement changes.
    (D) Its position relative to the earth changes.
    (E) Its position relative to the paperboy changes.

68. A tugboat pulls on an 84,000N barge with a cable having a breaking strength of 15,000N. The maximum acceleration the tugboat can apply to the barge without the cable breaking is

    (A) .75 m/s^2
    (B) 1.0 m/s^2
    (C) 1.25 m/s^2
    (D) 1.5 m/s^2
    (E) 1.75 m/s^2

69. Two equal vectors V and V' are added together. All of the following are possible values for the magnitude of the resultant vector EXCEPT

    (A) 0
    (B) 1/4 V
    (C) 1/2 V
    (D) 2 V
    (E) 4 V

70. A 30N child can push open a 1000N door because

    (A) the torque the child exerts on the door is greater than the torque the door exerts on the child.
    (B) the lever arm through which the child's force is exerted is less than the lever arm through which the door's weight is exerted.
    (C) the door's center of gravity is located at the bottom hinge.
    (D) the door's center of gravity is located at the top hinge.
    (E) the door's center of gravity is located at the doorknob.

GO ON TO THE NEXT PAGE

PHYSICS TEST—*Continued*

71. The kinetic energy a pendulum contains when it passes through its zero displacement may be decreased by
    (A) increasing the mass of the bob.
    (B) increasing the thickness of the string.
    (C) decreasing the length of the string.
    (D) increasing the length of the string.
    (E) decreasing the displacement of the bob.

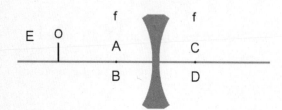

72. An object (O) is placed in front of a convex lens as shown. Which of the positions best describes the location of the image?
    (A) Position A
    (B) Position B
    (C) Position C
    (D) Position D
    (E) Position E

73. During a lacrosse game, an attacking player shoots a low hard shot into the goal. The ball leaves the lacrosse stick and travels into the net very quickly. What happens as the ball flies toward the goal?
    (A) The horizontal acceleration of the ball increases.
    (B) The vertical acceleration of the ball increases.
    (C) The horizontal velocity of the ball is constant.
    (D) The vertical velocity of the ball is constant.
    (E) All the listed quantities are constant.

74. Einstein's theory of relativity is based on which of the following statements?
    (A) Mass and energy are equivalent.
    (B) The velocity of light is a constant.
    (C) Space and time are anomalies.
    (D) All particles have antiparticles.
    (E) Energy is infinite.

75. While a child flies a kite on a breezy day, a burst of wind causes the kite to fly in 1.6 m diameter circles in the sky every second. If the circular motion were converted to a straight down speed, how fast would the kite dive toward the ground?
    (A) 3.14 m/s
    (B) 5 m/s
    (C) 6.28 m/s
    (D) 9.8 m/s
    (E) 15.7 m/s

STOP

IF YOU FINISH BEFORE THE TEST SESSION ENDS, YOU MAY REVIEW YOUR WORK ON THIS TEST ONLY. YOU MAY NOT TURN TO ANY OTHER TEST IN THIS BOOK.

ANSWER SHEET

Leave any unused answer spaces blank.

Test Code										
V	①	②	③	④	⑤	⑥	⑦	⑧	⑨	
W	①	②	③	④	⑤	⑥	⑦	⑧	⑨	
X	①	②	③	④	⑤	Y	Ⓐ	Ⓑ	Ⓒ	Ⓓ Ⓔ
Q		①	②	③	④	⑤	⑥	⑦	⑧	⑨

Subject Test (print)

FOR ETS USE ONLY	R/C	W/S1	FS/S2	CS/S3	WS

1 Ⓐ Ⓑ Ⓒ Ⓓ Ⓔ	21 Ⓐ Ⓑ Ⓒ Ⓓ Ⓔ	41 Ⓐ Ⓑ Ⓒ Ⓓ Ⓔ	61 Ⓐ Ⓑ Ⓒ Ⓓ Ⓔ	81 Ⓐ Ⓑ Ⓒ Ⓓ Ⓔ
2 Ⓐ Ⓑ Ⓒ Ⓓ Ⓔ	22 Ⓐ Ⓑ Ⓒ Ⓓ Ⓔ	42 Ⓐ Ⓑ Ⓒ Ⓓ Ⓔ	62 Ⓐ Ⓑ Ⓒ Ⓓ Ⓔ	82 Ⓐ Ⓑ Ⓒ Ⓓ Ⓔ
3 Ⓐ Ⓑ Ⓒ Ⓓ Ⓔ	23 Ⓐ Ⓑ Ⓒ Ⓓ Ⓔ	43 Ⓐ Ⓑ Ⓒ Ⓓ Ⓔ	63 Ⓐ Ⓑ Ⓒ Ⓓ Ⓔ	83 Ⓐ Ⓑ Ⓒ Ⓓ Ⓔ
4 Ⓐ Ⓑ Ⓒ Ⓓ Ⓔ	24 Ⓐ Ⓑ Ⓒ Ⓓ Ⓔ	44 Ⓐ Ⓑ Ⓒ Ⓓ Ⓔ	64 Ⓐ Ⓑ Ⓒ Ⓓ Ⓔ	84 Ⓐ Ⓑ Ⓒ Ⓓ Ⓔ
5 Ⓐ Ⓑ Ⓒ Ⓓ Ⓔ	25 Ⓐ Ⓑ Ⓒ Ⓓ Ⓔ	45 Ⓐ Ⓑ Ⓒ Ⓓ Ⓔ	65 Ⓐ Ⓑ Ⓒ Ⓓ Ⓔ	85 Ⓐ Ⓑ Ⓒ Ⓓ Ⓔ
6 Ⓐ Ⓑ Ⓒ Ⓓ Ⓔ	26 Ⓐ Ⓑ Ⓒ Ⓓ Ⓔ	46 Ⓐ Ⓑ Ⓒ Ⓓ Ⓔ	66 Ⓐ Ⓑ Ⓒ Ⓓ Ⓔ	86 Ⓐ Ⓑ Ⓒ Ⓓ Ⓔ
7 Ⓐ Ⓑ Ⓒ Ⓓ Ⓔ	27 Ⓐ Ⓑ Ⓒ Ⓓ Ⓔ	47 Ⓐ Ⓑ Ⓒ Ⓓ Ⓔ	67 Ⓐ Ⓑ Ⓒ Ⓓ Ⓔ	87 Ⓐ Ⓑ Ⓒ Ⓓ Ⓔ
8 Ⓐ Ⓑ Ⓒ Ⓓ Ⓔ	28 Ⓐ Ⓑ Ⓒ Ⓓ Ⓔ	48 Ⓐ Ⓑ Ⓒ Ⓓ Ⓔ	68 Ⓐ Ⓑ Ⓒ Ⓓ Ⓔ	88 Ⓐ Ⓑ Ⓒ Ⓓ Ⓔ
9 Ⓐ Ⓑ Ⓒ Ⓓ Ⓔ	29 Ⓐ Ⓑ Ⓒ Ⓓ Ⓔ	49 Ⓐ Ⓑ Ⓒ Ⓓ Ⓔ	69 Ⓐ Ⓑ Ⓒ Ⓓ Ⓔ	89 Ⓐ Ⓑ Ⓒ Ⓓ Ⓔ
10 Ⓐ Ⓑ Ⓒ Ⓓ Ⓔ	30 Ⓐ Ⓑ Ⓒ Ⓓ Ⓔ	50 Ⓐ Ⓑ Ⓒ Ⓓ Ⓔ	70 Ⓐ Ⓑ Ⓒ Ⓓ Ⓔ	90 Ⓐ Ⓑ Ⓒ Ⓓ Ⓔ
11 Ⓐ Ⓑ Ⓒ Ⓓ Ⓔ	31 Ⓐ Ⓑ Ⓒ Ⓓ Ⓔ	51 Ⓐ Ⓑ Ⓒ Ⓓ Ⓔ	71 Ⓐ Ⓑ Ⓒ Ⓓ Ⓔ	91 Ⓐ Ⓑ Ⓒ Ⓓ Ⓔ
12 Ⓐ Ⓑ Ⓒ Ⓓ Ⓔ	32 Ⓐ Ⓑ Ⓒ Ⓓ Ⓔ	52 Ⓐ Ⓑ Ⓒ Ⓓ Ⓔ	72 Ⓐ Ⓑ Ⓒ Ⓓ Ⓔ	92 Ⓐ Ⓑ Ⓒ Ⓓ Ⓔ
13 Ⓐ Ⓑ Ⓒ Ⓓ Ⓔ	33 Ⓐ Ⓑ Ⓒ Ⓓ Ⓔ	53 Ⓐ Ⓑ Ⓒ Ⓓ Ⓔ	73 Ⓐ Ⓑ Ⓒ Ⓓ Ⓔ	93 Ⓐ Ⓑ Ⓒ Ⓓ Ⓔ
14 Ⓐ Ⓑ Ⓒ Ⓓ Ⓔ	34 Ⓐ Ⓑ Ⓒ Ⓓ Ⓔ	54 Ⓐ Ⓑ Ⓒ Ⓓ Ⓔ	74 Ⓐ Ⓑ Ⓒ Ⓓ Ⓔ	94 Ⓐ Ⓑ Ⓒ Ⓓ Ⓔ
15 Ⓐ Ⓑ Ⓒ Ⓓ Ⓔ	35 Ⓐ Ⓑ Ⓒ Ⓓ Ⓔ	55 Ⓐ Ⓑ Ⓒ Ⓓ Ⓔ	75 Ⓐ Ⓑ Ⓒ Ⓓ Ⓔ	95 Ⓐ Ⓑ Ⓒ Ⓓ Ⓔ
16 Ⓐ Ⓑ Ⓒ Ⓓ Ⓔ	36 Ⓐ Ⓑ Ⓒ Ⓓ Ⓔ	56 Ⓐ Ⓑ Ⓒ Ⓓ Ⓔ	76 Ⓐ Ⓑ Ⓒ Ⓓ Ⓔ	96 Ⓐ Ⓑ Ⓒ Ⓓ Ⓔ
17 Ⓐ Ⓑ Ⓒ Ⓓ Ⓔ	37 Ⓐ Ⓑ Ⓒ Ⓓ Ⓔ	57 Ⓐ Ⓑ Ⓒ Ⓓ Ⓔ	77 Ⓐ Ⓑ Ⓒ Ⓓ Ⓔ	97 Ⓐ Ⓑ Ⓒ Ⓓ Ⓔ
18 Ⓐ Ⓑ Ⓒ Ⓓ Ⓔ	38 Ⓐ Ⓑ Ⓒ Ⓓ Ⓔ	58 Ⓐ Ⓑ Ⓒ Ⓓ Ⓔ	78 Ⓐ Ⓑ Ⓒ Ⓓ Ⓔ	98 Ⓐ Ⓑ Ⓒ Ⓓ Ⓔ
19 Ⓐ Ⓑ Ⓒ Ⓓ Ⓔ	39 Ⓐ Ⓑ Ⓒ Ⓓ Ⓔ	59 Ⓐ Ⓑ Ⓒ Ⓓ Ⓔ	79 Ⓐ Ⓑ Ⓒ Ⓓ Ⓔ	99 Ⓐ Ⓑ Ⓒ Ⓓ Ⓔ
20 Ⓐ Ⓑ Ⓒ Ⓓ Ⓔ	40 Ⓐ Ⓑ Ⓒ Ⓓ Ⓔ	60 Ⓐ Ⓑ Ⓒ Ⓓ Ⓔ	80 Ⓐ Ⓑ Ⓒ Ⓓ Ⓔ	100 Ⓐ Ⓑ Ⓒ Ⓓ Ⓔ

PRACTICE TEST 1

ANSWERS AND EXPLANATIONS

QUICK-SCORE ANSWERS

1. B	9. E	17. E	25. E	33. A	41. E	48. A	55. A	62. E	69. E
2. E	10. C	18. D	26. E	34. C	42. C	49. D	56. A	63. B	70. A
3. B	11. E	19. B	27. C	35. B	43. A	50. B	57. E	64. B	71. E
4. D	12. B	20. E	28. D	36. C	44. E	51. E	58. C	65. C	72. D
5. E	13. B	21. E	29. C	37. E	45. A	52. B	59. C	66. D	73. C
6. C	14. B	22. C	30. B	38. C	46. B	53. C	60. C	67. B	74. B
7. A	15. D	23. D	31. C	39. D	47. C	54. E	61. B	68. E	75. B
8. A	16. D	24. A	32. B	40. E					

ANSWERS AND EXPLANATIONS

ANSWERS TO PART A, QUESTIONS 1–13

1. **The correct answer is (B).** There is only 1/2 of a wave shown in the pipe. The wave is 4 times longer than the pipe in which it is vibrating. The equation for finding the length of the pipe is

$$L = n\frac{\lambda}{4}.$$

2. **The correct answer is (E).** There are 4 waves in the pipe, which means the wavelength is much shorter that it is in diagram B. Frequency is the *inverse* of wavelength so as the wavelength decreases the frequency increases.

3. **The correct answer is (B).** The neutrons are uncharged particles and are not affected by the electromagnetic field.

4. **The correct answer is (D).** The protons will deflect in a different direction from the electrons. However, the proton is more massive and therefore will not be deflected as much as the electron is deflected in a field of equal magnitude.

5. **The correct answer is (E).** When the field is reversed, the electron is deflected in the opposite direction with the same magnitude.

6. **The correct answer is (C).** The object has lost exactly half the potential energy it originally had. It has gained the lost potential energy as kinetic energy at the point where the two lines of the graph coincide.

7. **The correct answer is (A).** The object is thrown upwards. The kinetic energy the object possesses when it is first thrown is lost in the conversion to potential energy as the object rises away from the earth while slowing to a stop in the earth's gravitational field.

8. **The correct answer is (A).** The number of protons and the atomic number are the same quantity. The Z number represents the atomic number.

9. **The correct answer is (E).** The number of protons added to the number of neutrons is equal to the mass number of an atom. The mass is represented by the letter A.

10. **The correct answer is (C).** The name of the nuclide is represented by the symbol of the element. The X represents the elemental symbol for any one of the elements.

11. **The correct answer is (E).** The engine stops exactly at the center of the bridge, which means the weight of the train passes through the center of gravity of the bridge. The lever arm is zero, which means there cannot be any torques, because a torque is the product of an applied force and a lever arm.

12. **The correct answer is (B).** The two equally spaced pillars each hold one half of the weight of the bridge. Each also supports one half of the weight of the train engine, which is located at the exact center of the bridge.

$$\frac{75,000\text{N}}{2} + \frac{5,000\text{N}}{2} = 37,500\text{N} + 2,500\text{N} = 40,000\text{N}$$

13. **The correct answer is (B).** Each pillar supports exactly one-half of the weight of the train engine, which is 2,500N and is one-half the weight of the bridge.

ANSWERS TO PART B, QUESTIONS 14–75

14. **The correct answer is (B).** The carbon atom changes into a nitrogen atom. This conversion can only occur if a neutron emits a beta particle as it changes into a proton.

15. **The correct answer is (D).** The momentum before the explosion must equal the momentum after the explosion. Initially, the momentum of the parts was zero; therefore, all the parts moving in all directions could be added together, and they would equal the momentum before the explosion: zero!

16. **The correct answer is (D).** According to the first law of thermodynamics, the internal heat of the system remains the same unless work is done or heat is added to the system. Neither of those two things occurs, so the system of two objects,

one hot and one cold, transfers heat between itself with the hot object losing to the cold object until thermal equilibrium is reached.

17. **The correct answer is (E).** The sum of the individual masses of the parts of a nucleus is less than their mass when they are bound into the nucleus-producing mass defect. The mass from the mass defect is converted into the energy that holds the nucleus together and is released in fission. Fusion also produces energy when individual nuclei are forced to combine (fusion) and form new elements in a process that produces energy.

18. **The correct answer is (D).** Constructive interference is the condition in which two or more waves simultaneously occupy the same point or place (superposition) in a medium. If one wave is negative and the other is positive, the waves cancel. This is destructive interference. If the both waves are positive or negative, then they combine their magnitudes and produce a larger wave at the point of superposition.

19. **The correct answer is (B).** The voltage of the two batteries in series adds together, providing a voltage equivalent to their sum.

20. **The correct answer is (E).** The goldfish is pushed along by the water as a part of the action-reaction force pair as stated in Newton's Third Law.

21. **The correct answer is (E).** The hydrogen must gain $12.75eV$ of energy to be raised to the $n = 5$ level, where its potential is $.85eV$.

22. **The correct answer is (C).** When the ice cube enters the boiling water, the heat in the water immediately begins to change the phase of the ice to water. Consequently, the higher energy phase change (boiling) stops until the lower energy phase change (melting) is complete.

23. **The correct answer is (D).** The relativistic equation is $L_0 = L\sqrt{1-(.85)^2}$. In the eyes of an outside observer, the ship undergoes a contraction.

24. **The correct answer is (A).** The representation of the heat engine shows work being done by the system. The arrow from the heat reservoir points to positive work done by the system. This shows work output, which means the system does work.

25. **The correct answer is (E).** Without more information about the applied force, all of the choices *could* be correct.

26. **The correct answer is (E).** The only pair of charged bodies that would attract one another is the pair of unlike charged spheres. The rest of the pairs are like charges, which repel one another.

27. **The correct answer is (C).** Regardless of the direction of motion for an object in free fall near a large body, the gravitational acceleration exerted by the large body on the smaller body does not change.

28. **The answer is (D).** The electron will be repelled toward point D by the β (beta) particle located at point B. The two alpha particles located at points A and C exert equal attractive forces force on the electron, which keep the electron on a straight line toward the proton at D.

29. **The answer is (C).** The black disk absorbs heat better than the white disk, and it radiates heat away faster.

30. **The correct answer is (B).** To find the correct pole of the electromagnet, use the right-hand rule. Wrap your fingers around the core, pointing them in the direction of the positive flow. Your thumb points to the north pole.

31. **The correct answer is (C).** Use the right-hand rule to find the correct answer. Point your fingers in the direction of the magnetic field lines (toward the south pole), and point your thumb along the wave in the direction of the current flow. Your palm points down toward letter C.

32. **The correct answer is (B).** A voltage of 24 *V* should yield a current of 6*A* when it is hooked to a 4Ω resistor. The internal resistance of the battery is found $I = \dfrac{V}{R_1 + R_B}$. The extra .8Ω of resistance is the internal resistance of the battery.

33. **The correct answer is (A).** Remember, the period of a pendu-

   lum is $T = 2\pi\sqrt{\dfrac{\ell}{g}}$. Notice the g under the square root radical.

   The period of the pendulum is directly related to the gravitational acceleration. The moon's gravity is 1/6 the earth's gravity.
   That means the period of the pendulum on the moon is longer.

34. **The correct answer is (C).** The starting velocity of the two
   rocks is not the same, but once in free fall the acceleration of
   the two rocks is equal.

35. **The correct answer is (B).** The satellite travels at essentially
   the same velocity in its orbit, although its speed does increase at
   its closest approach to the earth. The distance from the satellite
   to the earth also changes while the satellite orbits the earth.
   The closer approach to the earth decreases the radius of the
   orbit, which in turn causes an increase in the centripetal acceleration.

36. **The correct answer is (C).** The sample has three half-lives

   occurring in one hour. $\dfrac{60\,\text{min}}{20\,\text{min}} = 3T_{1/2}$. Next, we have

   $\dfrac{1}{2}^{3} = .0125$. The original counts are multiplied by the amount of

   the sample remaining: $(.0125)(200)\dfrac{\text{counts}}{\text{sec}} = 25\dfrac{\text{counts}}{\text{sec}})$.

37. **The correct answer is (E).** An object placed outside the radius
   of the curvature of a concave mirror produces an image that is
   real, inverted, and reduced.

38. **The correct answer is (C).** The two surfaces (hockey puck and
   ice) are essentially frictionless. The movement of the train
   around a curve has no effect on the puck, which continues to
   move in a straight line. The goal does move around the curve
   with the train. This moves the net to the left, while the puck
   travels in a straight line.

39. **The correct answer is (D).** There are no unbalanced forces because none of the blocks is accelerating. The tension in T_1 is equal to the combined tensions in T_2 and T_3. To find T_3, subtract T_2 from T_1.

40. **The correct answer is (E).** The momentum of the boxcars increases and then decreases as the velocity does the same. The velocity increases and decreases in a linear manner.

41. **The correct answer is (E).** Each bright spot is a point at which waves constructively interfere. The waves combine at whole number wavelength intervals. This means at 1, 2, 3, etc., wavelengths. The third maxima is where a three-wave difference in the path length occurs.

42. **The correct answer is (C).** The collision described in the problem is perfectly elastic because the golf ball had the same velocity when it rebounded from the wall as when it struck the wall. Momentum is conserved perfectly, so the golf ball must have the same momentum after the collision with the wall as it had when it approached the wall before the collision

43. **The correct answer is (A).** Both disks move the same linear distance in the same time period. The smaller disk must make more revolutions to have the same tangential velocity as the large wheel. Since the number of revolutions for the small disk is larger, it also has a large angular acceleration.

44. **The correct answer is (E).** The displacement of the motorcycle rider is found with $s = \dfrac{1}{2}at^2$

$$s = \frac{1}{2}at^2$$
$$= \frac{1}{2}(5 \text{ m/s}^2)(8 \text{ s})^2$$
$$= 160 \text{ m}$$

45. **The correct answer is (A).** Electrons in photovoltaic metals are only energized by the photons that carry enough energy to dislodge the electrons.

46. **The correct answer is (B).** The incoherent light is blocked by Polaroids that are not lined along the same axis as the light vibrations. The only light that can pass Polaroid B is the light shown.

47. **The correct answer is (C).** An isothermal process is a process in which the temperature of the system remains constant.

48. **The correct answer is (A).** The kinetic energy equation is $KE = \frac{1}{2} mv^2$. Every time the velocity of an object doubles, its energy increases by a factor of 4. The momentum is directly related to the velocity, so a doubling of an object's velocity doubles the momentum of the object. The frictional force is a constant force no matter what happens to the velocity.

49. **The correct answer is (D).** The missing vector component is found by using the Pythagorean theorem.

$$y = \sqrt{r^2 - x^2}$$
$$y = \sqrt{(65N)^2 - (35N)^2}$$
$$y = 55N$$

50. **The correct answer is (B).** If there is no unbalanced force applied to an object, the object is not accelerated. An unbalanced force always causes acceleration of the object to which it is applied.

51. **The correct answer is (E).** An adiabatic expansion is a process in which no heat flows into or out of the system. During an adiabatic expansion the gas cools as it expands and does work.

52. **The correct answer is (B).** The radius of the curved path the electron follows in the magnetic field is $r = \dfrac{mv}{Bq}$. Both particles are electrons, which have the same mass, and the force exerted by the magnetic field remains the same, so the only difference is the velocity. The ratio of the velocity of the fast electron compared to the slow electron is 4:1. The fast electron has a radius 4 times larger than the slow electron.

53. **The correct answer is (C).** According to Coulomb's law, the force exerted by two charged bodies on one another is indirectly related to the square of the distance between them. When the distance is halved, they exert four times more force on one another.

54. **The correct answer is (E).** All of the choices are correct. Clocks on the spaceship move more slowly, the length of the spaceship would be contracted, the relativistic mass of the spaceship is greater than the rest mass, and the velocity of light is constant for everyone.

55. **The correct answer is (A).** An echo is the repeat sound heard when the original sound waves strike a fixed object and return toward their origin. This is the process of reflection.

56. **The correct answer is (A).** When the variable resistor is changed to the right, the total resistance in the circuit is decreased. More current flows, and the lights brighten.

57. **The correct answer is (E).** The atoms and molecules of a solid are packed together more tightly than they are in a liquid. Liquid particles are able to slide over one another, but they are still in contact. Gaseous atoms and molecules have gained enough energy to move away from one another.

58. **The correct answer is (C).** An object that is turning undergoes a change in direction. The change in direction is a change in velocity. A change in velocity through a period of time is acceleration. Because the acceleration is directed inward toward the center of rotation, this is a centripetal acceleration.

59. **The correct answer is (C).** The force exerted by a charged particle on another charged particle increases as the inverse of the square of the distance between them. Particle A, which has the same magnitude of charge as particle C, is half the distance from particle B as it is from particle C. Consequently, particle A exerts four times the charge on particle B as particle C does.

60. **The correct answer is (C).** Light slows down in an optically more dense material. Additionally, the wavelength shortens. The frequency remains the same. Since the frequency remains unchanged, the period also remains the same.

61. **The correct answer is (B).** When the child jumps into his mother's arms, he pushes on the wagon as he jumps. The momentum the child gains when he jumps is passed on to the wagon, too. They both have the same momentum, but in opposite directions. The wagon must have a greater velocity since it has less mass.

62. **The correct answer is (E).** The phase change to melt the ice drains all the heat from the water. At $0°C$ ice will no longer melt because all the heat has been removed from the water.

63. **The correct answer is (B).** The same number of charged bodies are still in the system, however, the redistribution of the charge has reduced the force the pith balls exert on one another.

64. **The correct answer is (B).** Add all the atomic numbers (Z numbers) on both sides to balance the proton numbers. Then add all the mass numbers (A numbers) on both sides to balance the mass.

65. **The correct answer is (C).** All objects in free fall near the earth are accelerated toward the earth at the same rate. Even though the car is moving along the x-axis at a high rate of speed, as soon as it clears the edge of the cliff it is in free fall. Both the rock and the car start with a y velocity of zero and reach the ground at the same time.

66. **The correct answer is (D).** The image in a plane mirror appears as far into the mirror as the object is in front of the mirror. The image is 1.5 m into the mirror, and the object is 1.5 m in front of the mirror, which is a total of 3 m from the object.

67. **The correct answer is (B).** Once the paperboy releases the paper from his hand, the paper is in free fall. All objects in free fall near the earth experience the same constant acceleration.

68. **The correct answer is (E).** The maximum tension the cable can withstand is 15,000N. This is the limit to applied force. The barge weighs 84,000N, which is a mass of 8571 kg. Use $F = ma$ to solve the problem.

69. The correct answer is (E). For any value of the vector V and V^1, they are equal in magnitude to one another. Whether they act in the same or opposite directions from one another, all the choices are possible except the value of 4 times V.

70. The correct answer is (A). An unbalanced torque causes motion to occur. The child can push the door open because she applies the unbalanced torque.

71. The correct answer is (E). When the pendulum is displaced, the potential energy the pendulum gains is equal to the height above the zero point to which the pendulum is raised. When the pendulum is released, all the potential energy at its displaced position is converted into kinetic energy. Thus, a smaller displacement gives the pendulum less potential energy, which in turn yields less kinetic energy when the bob moves through the zero point.

72. The correct answer is (D). The image formed by a convex lens when the object is outside the radius of curvature is real, inverted, and near the focal point on the other side of the lens.

73. The correct answer is (C). When the player shoots the ball, there is no force affecting the ball except gravity. Nothing can slow or speed the ball's x velocity, which is the horizontal. It is a constant velocity.

74. The correct answer is (B). One of the basic postulates in Einstein's Theory of Relativity is the speed of light, which is constant for everyone.

75. The correct answer is (B). The kite rotates around a 5 m circumference in 1 second ($C = 2\pi r$). Although the path of the kite is circular, it travels 5 m every second. The velocity is

$$v = \frac{5\text{m}}{1\text{s}} = \frac{5\text{m}}{\text{s}}.$$

Practice Test 2

PHYSICS TEST

PRACTICE TEST 2

PHYSICS TEST

While you have taken many standardized tests and know to blacken completely the ovals on the answer sheets and to erase completely any errors, the instructions for the SAT II Physics Test differ in an important way from the directions for other standardized tests. You need to indicate on the answer key which test you are taking. The instructions on the answer sheet will tell you to fill out the top portion of the answer sheet exactly as shown.

1. Print PHYSICS on the line under the words *Subject Test (print)*.
2. In the shaded box labeled *Test Code* fill in four ovals:

       —Fill in oval 1 in the row labeled V.
       —Fill in oval 6 in the row labeled W.
       —Fill in oval 3 in the row labeled X.
       —Fill in oval C in the row labeled Y.
       —Leave the ovals in row Q blank.

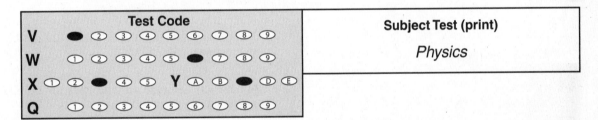

There are two additional questions that you will be asked to answer. One is "How many semesters of physics have you taken in high school?" The other question lists courses and asks you to mark those that you have taken. You will be told which ovals to fill in for each question. The College Board is collecting statistical information. If you choose to answer, you will use the key that is provided and blacken the appropriate ovals in row Q. You may also choose not to answer, and that will not affect your grade.

When everyone has completed filling in this portion of the answer sheet, the supervisor will tell you to turn the page and begin. The answer sheet has 100 numbered ovals, but there are only approximately 75 multiple-choice questions on the test, so be sure to use only ovals 1 to 75 (or however many questions there are) to record your answers.

PHYSICS TEST

Part A

Questions 1–3 relate to the diagram below.

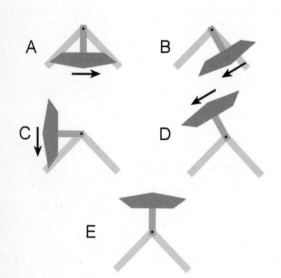

An amusement park ride called DaVinci's cradle swings the riders around a complete circle during the course of the ride.

(A) Point A
(B) Point B
(C) Point C
(D) Point D
(E) Point E

1. Where on the ride is the velocity the largest value?

2. Where on the ride is the potential energy the largest value?

3. Where on the ride are the PE and the KE equal to each other?

Peterson's SAT II Success: Physics

PHYSICS TEST—*Continued*

Questions 4-6 relate to the diagram below.

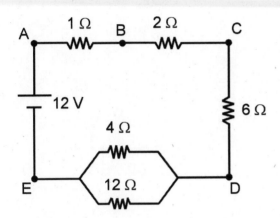

The electrical circuit shown has 1 ampere of current flowing in it. Answer the questions about the parts of the circuit listed between the points below by choosing the letter that correctly represents the quantity in question.

    (A)   Between points A→B
    (B)   Between points B→C
    (C)   Between points C→D
    (D)   Between points D→E
    (E)   Between points E→A

4. Between which two points is the voltage change the largest?

5. Between which two points is the voltage change the smallest?

6. Between which two points is the resistance value the largest?

Questions 7-9

An object is placed in front of an optical device, and an image is obtained. Select the device that would produce the types of images described below.

    (A)   Concave mirror
    (B)   Convex mirror
    (C)   Concave lens
    (D)   Convex lens
    (E)   Flat mirror

7. The image produced is erect, virtual, and reversed from left to right.

8. The image produced is inverted, real, and on the same side of the device.

9. The image produced is inverted, real, and on the opposite side of the device.

GO ON TO THE NEXT PAGE

PHYSICS TEST—*Continued*

Questions 10-12 relate to the electric fields shown in the diagrams below, which represent two charged objects near each other in space.

Questions 13-14 relate to the *P-V* diagram of the heat cycle below. For the gas shown in the diagram, 70*J* of energy is added to the system.

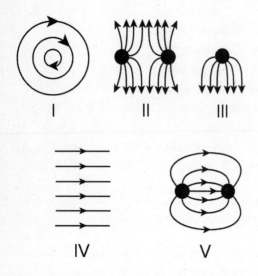

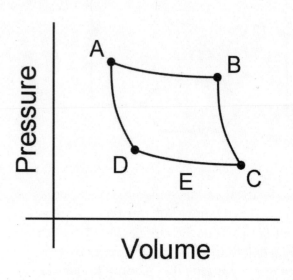

(A)   Drawing I
(B)   Drawing II
(C)   Drawing III
(D)   Drawing IV
(E)   Drawing V

10.   Which drawing represents two like point charges?

11.   Which drawing represents the field from parallel plates?

12.   Which drawing represents two unlike point charges?

(A) A → B
(B) B → C
(C) C → D
(D) D → A
(E) A → B → C → D → A

13.   Where is the heat added to the system?

14.   Where is the exhaust heat released from the system?

> Directions: Each question or statement below is followed by five possible answers. In each case, select the best possible answer and fill in the corresponding oval on the answer sheet.

15. Protons are found in the nucleus of the atom. The nuclear protons with the greatest mass are located
    (A) in the hydrogen atom.
    (B) in the carbon atom.
    (C) in the iron atom.
    (D) in the radon atom.
    (E) in the uranium atom.

16. Four resistors are hooked together in parallel. The resistors have values of 20Ω, 40Ω, 60Ω, and 80Ω respectively. What is the total resistance of the resistors?
    (A) 4.4Ω
    (B) 9.6Ω
    (C) 14.8Ω
    (D) 20Ω
    (E) 25.2Ω

Questions 17-18 refer to the information below.

An Olympic weight lifter lifts a weight bar weighing 2000N straight up to a height of 2.25 m in a time of .65 seconds. The weight lifter stands holding the weight at that height for the next 4 seconds before dropping the weights to the floor.

17. How much work did the weight lifter do while holding the weights overhead?
    (A) 1300 Joules
    (B) 3077 Joules
    (C) 4500 Joules
    (D) 8000 Joules
    (E) No work was done

18. How much power did the weight lifter use to lift the weights overhead?
    (A) 2925 watts
    (B) 3077 watts
    (C) 4500 watts
    (D) 6923 watts
    (E) 9100 watts

GO ON TO THE NEXT PAGE

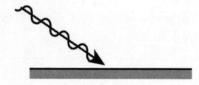

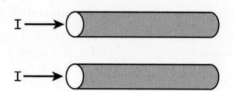

19. A light ray strikes a photovoltaic metal as shown above. Which of the following statements is correct if a voltage is introduced into the metal by the light ray?

    I.   The light ray is a blue light.
    II. The beam is below threshold.
    III. The beam does not contain any photons.

    (A) I only
    (B) II only
    (C) I and III only
    (D) II and III only
    (E) I, II, and III

20. A rescue plane flying at 162 km/hr drops a survival package to a group of stranded skiers from a height of 70 m. After dropping the package the pilot of the plane continues to fly in a straight line. When the package strikes the ground it is
    (A)   85 m behind the plane.
    (B)   170 m behind the plane.
    (C)   255 m behind the plane.
    (D)   462 m behind the plane.
    (E)   directly beneath the plane.

21. In the diagram above, two wires are aligned side by side. They are both hooked into different circuits in which the current is switched on to allow current to flow in each circuit. Which of the following statements is correct?
    (A) The two currents destructively interfere with each other.
    (B) The two currents constructively interfere with each other.
    (C) The two wires attract and move closer.
    (D) The two wires repel and move away.
    (E) The two wires remain still.

22. A species of hummingbird beats its wings 3,300 times per minute. What frequency of sound will a nearby person hear when the hummingbird flies by?
    (A) .003 *Hz*
    (B) .018 *Hz*
    (C) 6 *Hz*
    (D) 55 *Hz*
    (E) 3300 *Hz*

PHYSICS TEST—*Continued*

23. A student uses a magnetic compass to perform a laboratory experiment in the Northern Hemisphere. She then carries the same magnetic compass with her to the Southern Hemisphere, taking care not to damage the compass in any way. When she reaches her destination at the equivalent latitude and longitude in the Southern Hemisphere, she prepares to perform the same laboratory experiment. The student looks at the compass before performing the experiment to see if the compass needle has changed. How has the compass changed?

    (A) The compass needle points 90° to the left of the expected direction.
    (B) The compass needle points 90° to the right of the expected direction.
    (C) The compass needle slowly rotates in a counter-clockwise direction.
    (D) The compass needle slowly rotates in a clockwise direction.
    (E) There has been no change in the compass.

24. An ideal gas is placed in a 4*L* container at a temperature of 300*K* and a pressure of 6 atmospheres. The pressure is held constant while the volume of the gas is halved. What is the new temperature of the gas?

    (A) 1200K
    (B) 600K
    (C) 300K
    (D) 150K
    (E) 75K

25. A photovoltaic metal absorbs a photon of yellow light and immediately emits an ultraviolet photon. This is called

    (A) fluorescence.
    (B) influorescence.
    (C) phosphorescence.
    (D) photoluminescence.
    (E) This is not possible.

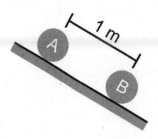

26. Two spheres are at rest on an inclined ramp as shown above. Sphere A has a mass ten times larger than sphere B. Both spheres are released at the same time and roll down the ramp. Which statement best describes the situation by the time sphere B reaches the bottom of the ramp?

    (A) The velocity of sphere A equals the velocity of sphere B.
    (B) The kinetic energy of sphere A equals the kinetic energy of sphere B.
    (C) The potential energy of sphere A equals the potential energy of sphere B.
    (D) Sphere A will catch up to sphere B.
    (E) Sphere B accelerates away from sphere A.

GO ON TO THE NEXT PAGE

PHYSICS TEST—*Continued*

Questions 27-28 relate to the following information.

The frequency of a wave is 4 cycles per second, and its speed is .08 meters per second.

27. What is the period of one of the waves?
    (A) .25 seconds
    (B) .55 seconds
    (C) 3.125 seconds
    (D) .02 seconds
    (E) 12.55 seconds

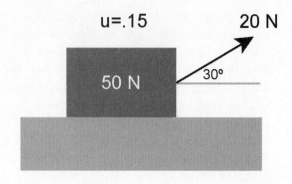

28 What is the wavelength of one of the waves?
    (A) .25 seconds
    (B) .55 seconds
    (C) 3.125 seconds
    (D) .02 seconds
    (E) 12.55 seconds

29. An electric circuit is composed of a pair of parallel 30 ohm resistors in series with a 9 ohm resistor. The current through the 9 ohm resistor is .25 A. What is the voltage applied to the circuit?
    (A) 1.5 V
    (B) 3 V
    (C) 6 V
    (D) 12 V
    (E) 24 V

30. Which of the following best describes the condition of an enclosed gas during an adiabatic compression?
    (A) The internal energy of the gas increases.
    (B) Work is done by the gas.
    (C) Work is done on the gas.
    (D) The gas remains at a constant temperature.
    (E) The temperature of the gas decreases

31. A block resting on the surface shown above has a force of 20N applied. Which statement best describes the force between the block and the surface upon which it rests?
    (A) The normal force is less than 50N.
    (B) The normal force is greater than 50N.
    (C) The normal force is equal to 50N.
    (D) The coefficient of friction increases as the angle increases.
    (E) The coefficient of friction decreases as the angle increases.

$$\underset{88}{226}Ra \rightarrow \underset{86}{222}Rn + ?$$

32. A radium atom decays into a radon atom as shown in the equation above. Which of the quantities below correctly finishes the equation?
    (A) Alpha
    (B) Beta
    (C) Gamma
    (D) Neutron
    (E) Neutrino

35. An object (*O*) is placed in front of a convex lens as shown above. Where is the image located?
    (A) Point A
    (B) Point B
    (C) Point C
    (D) Point D
    (E) Point E

33. A large rimmed hoop with a bowling ball inside it rolls down an incline. Which of the following statements best describes the relationship between the hoop and the bowling ball?
    (A) Their angular accelerations are the same.
    (B) Their angular displacements are the same.
    (C) Their angular velocities are the same.
    (D) Their tangential displacements are the same.
    (E) Their centripetal accelerations are the same.

34. When a net force acts upon an object, the object is
    (A) at rest.
    (B) gaining mass.
    (C) losing mass.
    (D) accelerating.
    (E) moving at constant velocity.

36. In the theory of relativity it is stated that all laws of nature are the same in reference frames that
    (A) accelerate.
    (B) vibrate.
    (C) rotate.
    (D) oscillate.
    (E) move at a constant rate.

37. Which of the following is/are uses for polarized light waves?
    I.   Sunglasses
    II. Remove ultraviolet light
    III. Reveal stress patterns

    (A) I only
    (B) II only
    (C) I and III only
    (D) II and III only
    (E) I, II, and III

38. A .5 kg ball is swinging at the end of a 2 m string that has a tension of 6.25 N in it. Find the speed of the ball as it travels its circular path.
    (A) 3.8N
    (B) 4.4N
    (C) 5N
    (D) 5.6N
    (E) 6.2N

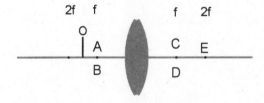

GO ON TO THE NEXT PAGE

39. A solid copper sphere has a charge of .2C placed on it. Which of the following statements best describes the charge distribution for the sphere?
    (A) The charge is equally distributed throughout the entire sphere.
    (B) The charge is concentrated inside the sphere with some charge on the outside.
    (C) The charge is equally distributed on the outside surface of the sphere.
    (D) The charge is equally distributed throughout the inside of the sphere only.
    (E) The charge is concentrated in the center of the sphere.

40. A 30 g icicle that is at a temperature $0°C$ falls 6 meters from the eaves of a house to the ground below. If 5% of the kinetic energy that the icicle possesses when it strikes the ground converts into heat, which of the following is plausible?

    (Note: H_f water $= .335\frac{J}{g}$).

    (A) The ice would become colder during the fall; therefore, no ice would melt.
    (B) This would not happen because it would break the law of conservation of mass.
    (C) Less than .3g of the icicle would melt.
    (D) The frictional work done to stop the icicle's fall would use up all the energy and leave none for anything else.
    (E) The icicle would shatter and the energy would convert into momentum.

41. Any object that is accelerated to near the speed of light experiences which of the following?
    (A) An increase in its length
    (B) An increase in the rate of time passage
    (C) Decrease in energy
    (D) Decrease in momentum
    (E) Increase in mass

42. A bicyclist travels at a constant 25 km/hr for 30 minutes. He coasts for 15 minutes at a constant 20 km/hr and then pedals at a constant 40 km/hr for another 15 minutes. What was the average speed of the cyclist for the past hour?
    (A) 22.5 km/hr
    (B) 25 km/hr
    (C) 27.5 km/hr
    (D) 30 km/hr
    (E) 32.5 km/hr

43. A flat plane is raised until a block resting on its surface just slides down the plane at a constant rate. Which statement(s) is/are true?
    I. The parallel force equals the frictional force.
    II. The weight of the object equals the frictional force.
    III. The perpendicular force equals the normal force.

    (A) I only
    (B) II only
    (C) I and III only
    (D) II and III only
    (E) I, II, and III

44. Two gases are insulated from their surroundings but are in contact with each other so heat can flow between them. One gas is hot at $t = 0$ and the other gas is cold at $t = 0$. After time passes and the gases equilibrate, which of the following will have happened?
    (A) The particles in the cold gas will have slowed in their rate of movement.
    (B) The particles in the hot gas will have increased their rate of movement.
    (C) The temperature of the cold gas will have decreased.
    (D) The temperature of the hot gas will have increased.
    (E) The temperature of the hot gas will have decreased.

45. A driver in an automobile hears a siren behind her and pulls over to let a fire engine pass. The sound of the siren changes as the fire truck approaches, is beside her, and passes her. Which of the following is/are true under these conditions?

    I. The pitch of the sound increases as the fire truck approaches.
    II. The wavelength of the sound increases as the fire truck approaches.
    III. The wavelength of the sound increases after the fire truck passes.

    (A) I only
    (B) II only
    (C) I and III only
    (D) II and III only
    (E) I, II, and III

46 A magician pulls a tablecloth from under a table full of dishes without disturbing the dishes. This act demonstrates that
    (A) gravity holds the dishes still.
    (B) the weight of the dishes is reduced.
    (C) action-reaction forces are in operation.
    (D) the dishes have inertia.
    (E) the dishes have no acceleration.

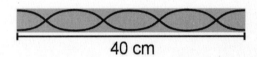

40 cm

47. In the diagram above the open pipe produces a standing wave as shown. What is the frequency of the sound produced in Hertz? (Velocity of sound = 360m/s)

    (A) 900 *Hz*
    (B) 1800 *Hz*
    (C) 720 *Hz*
    (D) 1440 *Hz*
    (E) 2700 *Hz*

GO ON TO THE NEXT PAGE ➤

48. Compare a bucket of boiling water to a cup of boiling water. Which statement(s) can be made about the two containers?

   I.   The heat content of the two is the same.
   II. The temperature of the two is the same.
   III. The bucket of water contains more heat and is therefore hotter

(A) I only
(B) II only
(C) I and III only
(D) II and III only
(E) I, II, and III only

49. Find the total capacitance for three capacitors in parallel with each other. The value of the capacitors is $10\mu f$, $15\mu f$, and $35\mu f$.

(A) $60\mu f$
(B) $50\mu f$
(C) $20\mu f$
(D) $10\mu f$
(E) $5\mu f$

$-.38eV$	_____	$n=6$
$-.54eV$	_____	$n=5$
$-.85eV$	_____	$n=4$
$-1.52eV$	_____	$n=3$
$-3.39eV$	_____	$n=2$
$-13.6eV$	_____	$n=1$

50. A hydrogen electron falls from the $n=3$ to the $n=1$ energy level. Using the chart above, determine how much energy it must release.
(A) $+.97eV$
(B) $+2.85eV$
(C) $+10.09eV$
(D) $+12.21eV$
(E) $+13.06eV$

51. Four 6Ω resistors are available to form a resistor network. Which of the following is NOT a possible value for the total resistance of the resistor combinations?
(A) 24Ω
(B) 12Ω
(C) 8Ω
(D) 6Ω
(E) 1.5Ω

52. A 7.25 kg bowling ball is rolled onto a perfectly level surface at a velocity of 10 m/s. The co-efficient of friction between the surface and the bowling ball is .0025. If the surface is perfectly level and is long enough, how far will the bowling ball roll before it comes to a complete stop?
(A) 20 m
(B) 200 m
(C) 2 km
(D) 20 km
(E) 1/2 km

53. The binding energy of a nucleus is equal to
(A) the average energy of each nucleon.
(B) the energy needed to split the nucleus into its parts.
(C) the mass-energy difference between protons and neutrons.
(D) the energy necessary to overcome the neutron-neutron repulsion.
(E) the energy required to remove a proton from the nucleus.

Peterson's SAT II Success: Physics

Questions 54-55 refer to the graph below, which shows a typical heat and temperature graph for a substance.

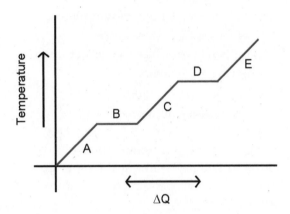

56. When a photon strikes an electron and energizes it, the electron will receive the most energy from the photon if
    (A) the electron does not spin when it is struck.
    (B) the photon has a high velocity.
    (C) the photon has a low velocity.
    (D) the photon has a long wavelength.
    (E) the photon has a high frequency.

54. Which of the levels represents the solid phase of the substance?
    (A) Level A
    (B) Level B
    (C) Level C
    (D) Level D
    (E) Level E

55. During the phase on the graph represented at Level D, the substance is
    (A) evaporating.
    (B) condensing.
    (C) changing phase.
    (D) gaining internal energy.
    (E) All of the above could be correct.

GO ON TO THE NEXT PAGE

PHYSICS TEST—*Continued*

Questions 57-58 refer to the scenario described below.

A light ray passes from a material of low refractive index to one of high refractive index. Which of the pairs of quantities listed below describes the light ray as it strikes and passes through the interface between the two materials? Match the descriptions below with the statement that *best* describes the situation.

57. A part of the light ray remains inside the low refractive index material.
    (A) The angle of refraction is larger than the angle of incidence.
    (B) The angle of refraction is equal to the angle of incidence.
    (C) The angle of reflection is larger than the angle of incidence.
    (D) The angle of reflection is smaller than the angle of incidence.
    (E) The angle of incidence equals the angle of reflection.

58. The light ray inside the material with the higher index of refraction bends toward the normal.
    (A) The frequency of the wave increases.
    (B) The frequency of the wave decreases.
    (C) The velocity of the wave increases.
    (D) The velocity of the wave decreases.
    (E) Interference from reflected waves causes the light ray to refract.

59. A woman dancing in high-heeled shoes accidentally steps on her partner's foot with the heel of her shoe. Even though her partner outweighs her by 400N and can easily lift her off the floor, he feels pain because
    (A) her weight is concentrated into a small area.
    (B) her small foot has a large momentum.
    (C) her foot has a large inertia.
    (D) his foot has no inertia.
    (E) his foot has no momentum.

60. If 50g of water at a temperature of $30°C$ is added to 200g of water at a temperature of $100°C$, what will the new temperature of the water be?
    (A) $68°C$
    (B) $80°C$
    (C) $74°C$
    (D) $86°C$
    (E) $92°C$

61. A radioactive substance is observed to have a count rate of 500 counts/sec. Two hours later the count rate is 62.5 counts/sec. What is the half life of the substance?
    (A) 10 min
    (B) 20 min
    (C) 30 min
    (D) 40 min
    (E) 50 min

PHYSICS TEST—*Continued*

62. A 2.5 kg ball is dropped onto a concrete floor. It strikes the floor with a momentum of 20 kg • m/s and bounces away from the floor with a momentum of 16 kg • m/s. What is the change of momentum of the ball?

    (A) 4 kg • m/s
    (B) 8 kg • m/s
    (C) 32 kg • m/s
    (D) 36 kg • m/s
    (E) 40 kg • m/s

63. Firefighters attempt to squirt water from a hose into a third story window 15 m above the ground. For safety purposes they stand 25 m from the burning building. The water from the hose can only reach the window if

    (A) $t_y > t_x$
    (B) $t_x > t_y$
    (C) $t_y < t_x$
    (D) $t_x < t_y$
    (E) Time has no effect in this case.

64. A 75 g ice cube is added to 450 g of boiling water. The water stops boiling immediately because:
    I.   Heat is melting the ice.
    II. Condensation is occurring.
    III. Phase change occurs.

    (A) I only
    (B) II only
    (C) I and III only
    (D) II and III only
    (E) I, II, and III

65. A spring accelerates a 2 kg cart from rest in a time of .8 seconds, giving it a momentum of 4 kg • m/s. With what force did the spring accelerate the cart?

    (A) .5N
    (B) 1.6N
    (C) 3.2N
    (D) 5N
    (E) 8N

66. New thermos bottles have the ability to keep hot substances hot for several days. The thermos bottles have a highly polished interior made of stainless steel, which makes them almost unbreakable. These thermos bottles keep substances hot by reducing heat loss due to

    (A) absorption
    (B) conduction
    (C) convection
    (D) radiation
    (E) evaporation

GO ON TO THE NEXT PAGE

PHYSICS TEST—*Continued*

Questions 67–68

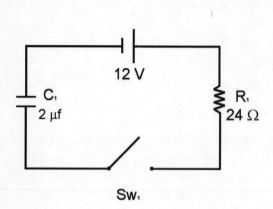

C_1 is an uncharged capacitor (shown in the circuit above). At $t = 0$ the switch *(SW1)* is closed, and C_1 begins to charge.

67. Which of the graphs above best represents the charge on the capacitor as time passes?

(A) Time A

(B) Time B

(C) Time C

(D) Time D

(E) Time E

68. What does graph D show?

(A) The value of the current in the circuit as time passes.

(B) The value of the voltage across the terminals as time passes.

(C) The total value of the resistance as time passes.

(D) The total value of the capacitance as time passes.

(E) None of the above.

PHYSICS TEST—*Continued*

69. An object at rest is placed into free fall at a height of 20 m. What is the velocity of the object when the potential energy equals the kinetic energy?

(A) 8 m/s
(B) 11 m/s
(C) 14 m/s
(D) 17 m/s
(E) There is not enough information to determine the velocity.

70. A rocket sled rides on a frictionless track while a 1000N force from the rockets accelerates the sled. Suddenly the retro-rockets accidentally fire, applying a 1000N force in the opposite direction. The sled will

(A) slow down gradually to a stop.
(B) continue to accelerate.
(C) move at a constant speed.
(D) reverse direction.
(E) not be affected at all.

71. An unknown particle is being studied in a magnetic field of variable intensity and direction. When the magnetic field is turned off, the particle is observed to move toward the earth. When the magnetic field is turned on, the particle is observed to continue to move toward the earth, no matter the strength or the direction of the magnetic field. Which of the particles listed below is most likely the unknown particle?

(A) Beta particle
(B) Alpha particle
(C) Positron
(D) Neutron
(E) Gamma ray

72. Which of the following is an example of a compressional wave?

(A) X-ray
(B) Cosmic ray
(C) Radio wave
(D) Light wave
(E) Sound wave

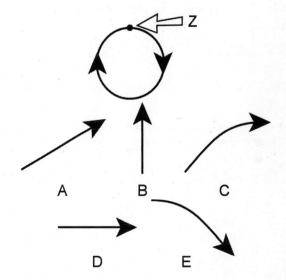

73. An object on a string is traveling in a circular path as shown. If the string breaks when the object is at point *Z*, which pathway will the object follow?

(A) Pathway A
(B) Pathway B
(C) Pathway C
(D) Pathway D
(E) Pathway E

GO ON TO THE NEXT PAGE

PHYSICS TEST—*Continued*

74. Refrigeration is a process through which
    (A) heat is removed from the inside of the refrigerator.
    (B) cold air is produced inside the refrigerator.
    (C) hot air is removed from the inside of the refrigerator.
    (D) hot air is changed to a cold condensate inside the refrigerator.
    (E) hot air inside the refrigerator is expanded to remove its heat.

75. An object is thrown from a moving vehicle. Which of the following statements is not true?
    I.   The velocity of the object changes.
    II. The acceleration of the object changes.
    III. The direction of motion of the object changes.

    (A) I only
    (B) II only
    (C) I and III only
    (D) II and III only
    (E) I, II, and III

STOP
IF YOU FINISH BEFORE THE TEST SESSION ENDS, YOU MAY REVIEW YOUR WORK ON THIS TEST ONLY. YOU MAY NOT TURN TO ANY OTHER TEST IN THIS BOOK

Peterson's SAT II Success: Physics

ANSWER SHEET

Leave any unused answer spaces blank.

	Test Code		Subject Test (print)				
			FOR ETS USE ONLY	R/C	W/S1	FS/S2	CS/S3	WS

Test Code:
- V ① ② ③ ④ ⑤ ⑥ ⑦ ⑧ ⑨
- W ① ② ③ ④ ⑤ ⑥ ⑦ ⑧ ⑨
- X ① ② ③ ④ ⑤ Y Ⓐ Ⓑ Ⓒ Ⓓ Ⓔ
- Q ① ② ③ ④ ⑤ ⑥ ⑦ ⑧ ⑨

1 Ⓐ Ⓑ Ⓒ Ⓓ Ⓔ   21 Ⓐ Ⓑ Ⓒ Ⓓ Ⓔ   41 Ⓐ Ⓑ Ⓒ Ⓓ Ⓔ   61 Ⓐ Ⓑ Ⓒ Ⓓ Ⓔ   81 Ⓐ Ⓑ Ⓒ Ⓓ Ⓔ
2 Ⓐ Ⓑ Ⓒ Ⓓ Ⓔ   22 Ⓐ Ⓑ Ⓒ Ⓓ Ⓔ   42 Ⓐ Ⓑ Ⓒ Ⓓ Ⓔ   62 Ⓐ Ⓑ Ⓒ Ⓓ Ⓔ   82 Ⓐ Ⓑ Ⓒ Ⓓ Ⓔ
3 Ⓐ Ⓑ Ⓒ Ⓓ Ⓔ   23 Ⓐ Ⓑ Ⓒ Ⓓ Ⓔ   43 Ⓐ Ⓑ Ⓒ Ⓓ Ⓔ   63 Ⓐ Ⓑ Ⓒ Ⓓ Ⓔ   83 Ⓐ Ⓑ Ⓒ Ⓓ Ⓔ
4 Ⓐ Ⓑ Ⓒ Ⓓ Ⓔ   24 Ⓐ Ⓑ Ⓒ Ⓓ Ⓔ   44 Ⓐ Ⓑ Ⓒ Ⓓ Ⓔ   64 Ⓐ Ⓑ Ⓒ Ⓓ Ⓔ   84 Ⓐ Ⓑ Ⓒ Ⓓ Ⓔ
5 Ⓐ Ⓑ Ⓒ Ⓓ Ⓔ   25 Ⓐ Ⓑ Ⓒ Ⓓ Ⓔ   45 Ⓐ Ⓑ Ⓒ Ⓓ Ⓔ   65 Ⓐ Ⓑ Ⓒ Ⓓ Ⓔ   85 Ⓐ Ⓑ Ⓒ Ⓓ Ⓔ
6 Ⓐ Ⓑ Ⓒ Ⓓ Ⓔ   26 Ⓐ Ⓑ Ⓒ Ⓓ Ⓔ   46 Ⓐ Ⓑ Ⓒ Ⓓ Ⓔ   66 Ⓐ Ⓑ Ⓒ Ⓓ Ⓔ   86 Ⓐ Ⓑ Ⓒ Ⓓ Ⓔ
7 Ⓐ Ⓑ Ⓒ Ⓓ Ⓔ   27 Ⓐ Ⓑ Ⓒ Ⓓ Ⓔ   47 Ⓐ Ⓑ Ⓒ Ⓓ Ⓔ   67 Ⓐ Ⓑ Ⓒ Ⓓ Ⓔ   87 Ⓐ Ⓑ Ⓒ Ⓓ Ⓔ
8 Ⓐ Ⓑ Ⓒ Ⓓ Ⓔ   28 Ⓐ Ⓑ Ⓒ Ⓓ Ⓔ   48 Ⓐ Ⓑ Ⓒ Ⓓ Ⓔ   68 Ⓐ Ⓑ Ⓒ Ⓓ Ⓔ   88 Ⓐ Ⓑ Ⓒ Ⓓ Ⓔ
9 Ⓐ Ⓑ Ⓒ Ⓓ Ⓔ   29 Ⓐ Ⓑ Ⓒ Ⓓ Ⓔ   49 Ⓐ Ⓑ Ⓒ Ⓓ Ⓔ   69 Ⓐ Ⓑ Ⓒ Ⓓ Ⓔ   89 Ⓐ Ⓑ Ⓒ Ⓓ Ⓔ
10 Ⓐ Ⓑ Ⓒ Ⓓ Ⓔ   30 Ⓐ Ⓑ Ⓒ Ⓓ Ⓔ   50 Ⓐ Ⓑ Ⓒ Ⓓ Ⓔ   70 Ⓐ Ⓑ Ⓒ Ⓓ Ⓔ   90 Ⓐ Ⓑ Ⓒ Ⓓ Ⓔ
11 Ⓐ Ⓑ Ⓒ Ⓓ Ⓔ   31 Ⓐ Ⓑ Ⓒ Ⓓ Ⓔ   51 Ⓐ Ⓑ Ⓒ Ⓓ Ⓔ   71 Ⓐ Ⓑ Ⓒ Ⓓ Ⓔ   91 Ⓐ Ⓑ Ⓒ Ⓓ Ⓔ
12 Ⓐ Ⓑ Ⓒ Ⓓ Ⓔ   32 Ⓐ Ⓑ Ⓒ Ⓓ Ⓔ   52 Ⓐ Ⓑ Ⓒ Ⓓ Ⓔ   72 Ⓐ Ⓑ Ⓒ Ⓓ Ⓔ   92 Ⓐ Ⓑ Ⓒ Ⓓ Ⓔ
13 Ⓐ Ⓑ Ⓒ Ⓓ Ⓔ   33 Ⓐ Ⓑ Ⓒ Ⓓ Ⓔ   53 Ⓐ Ⓑ Ⓒ Ⓓ Ⓔ   73 Ⓐ Ⓑ Ⓒ Ⓓ Ⓔ   93 Ⓐ Ⓑ Ⓒ Ⓓ Ⓔ
14 Ⓐ Ⓑ Ⓒ Ⓓ Ⓔ   34 Ⓐ Ⓑ Ⓒ Ⓓ Ⓔ   54 Ⓐ Ⓑ Ⓒ Ⓓ Ⓔ   74 Ⓐ Ⓑ Ⓒ Ⓓ Ⓔ   94 Ⓐ Ⓑ Ⓒ Ⓓ Ⓔ
15 Ⓐ Ⓑ Ⓒ Ⓓ Ⓔ   35 Ⓐ Ⓑ Ⓒ Ⓓ Ⓔ   55 Ⓐ Ⓑ Ⓒ Ⓓ Ⓔ   75 Ⓐ Ⓑ Ⓒ Ⓓ Ⓔ   95 Ⓐ Ⓑ Ⓒ Ⓓ Ⓔ
16 Ⓐ Ⓑ Ⓒ Ⓓ Ⓔ   36 Ⓐ Ⓑ Ⓒ Ⓓ Ⓔ   56 Ⓐ Ⓑ Ⓒ Ⓓ Ⓔ   76 Ⓐ Ⓑ Ⓒ Ⓓ Ⓔ   96 Ⓐ Ⓑ Ⓒ Ⓓ Ⓔ
17 Ⓐ Ⓑ Ⓒ Ⓓ Ⓔ   37 Ⓐ Ⓑ Ⓒ Ⓓ Ⓔ   57 Ⓐ Ⓑ Ⓒ Ⓓ Ⓔ   77 Ⓐ Ⓑ Ⓒ Ⓓ Ⓔ   97 Ⓐ Ⓑ Ⓒ Ⓓ Ⓔ
18 Ⓐ Ⓑ Ⓒ Ⓓ Ⓔ   38 Ⓐ Ⓑ Ⓒ Ⓓ Ⓔ   58 Ⓐ Ⓑ Ⓒ Ⓓ Ⓔ   78 Ⓐ Ⓑ Ⓒ Ⓓ Ⓔ   98 Ⓐ Ⓑ Ⓒ Ⓓ Ⓔ
19 Ⓐ Ⓑ Ⓒ Ⓓ Ⓔ   39 Ⓐ Ⓑ Ⓒ Ⓓ Ⓔ   59 Ⓐ Ⓑ Ⓒ Ⓓ Ⓔ   79 Ⓐ Ⓑ Ⓒ Ⓓ Ⓔ   99 Ⓐ Ⓑ Ⓒ Ⓓ Ⓔ
20 Ⓐ Ⓑ Ⓒ Ⓓ Ⓔ   40 Ⓐ Ⓑ Ⓒ Ⓓ Ⓔ   60 Ⓐ Ⓑ Ⓒ Ⓓ Ⓔ   80 Ⓐ Ⓑ Ⓒ Ⓓ Ⓔ   100 Ⓐ Ⓑ Ⓒ Ⓓ Ⓔ

PRACTICE TEST 2

ANSWERS AND EXPLANATIONS

QUICK-SCORE ANSWERS

1. A	9. B	17. E	25. E	33. D	41. E	48. B	55. A	62. A	69. C
2. E	10. B	18. D	26. A	34. D	42. C	49. A	56. E	63. C	70. C
3. C	11. D	19. A	27. A	35. D	43. A	50. D	57. E	64. C	71. D
4. E	12. E	20. E	28. D	36. E	44. E	51. B	58. D	65. D	72. E
5. A	13. A	21. C	29. C	37. C	45. C	52. C	59. A	66. D	73. D
6. C	14. C	22. D	30. C	38. C	46. D	53. B	60. D	67. A	74. A
7. E	15. A	23. E	31. A	39. C	47. B	54. A	61. D	68. A	75. B
8. A	16. B	24. D	32. A	40. C					

ANSWERS AND EXPLANATIONS

ANSWERS TO PART A, QUESTIONS 1–14

1. **The correct answer is (A).** The amusement ride is similar to a pendulum. The point at which the potential energy is smallest is the point at which the kinetic energy and the velocity of the pendulum have the largest value.

2. **The correct answer is (E).** The potential energy of the ride is the point at which the cradle is at the greatest height above its resting point.

3. **The correct answer is (C).** The cradle is mid-way between its highest potential energy at E and the lowest potential energy at A. Likewise, the cradle is at the point midway between its largest kinetic energy at point A and its least kinetic energy at point E.

4. **The correct answer is (E).** The largest voltage change occurs between E to A because there is an increase of 12V in the circuit.

5. **The correct answer is (A).** The smallest resistance in the circuit is 1 ohm. The smallest voltage drop in the circuit occurs across the smallest resistance.

6. **The correct answer is (C).** The largest effective resistance in the circuit comes from the 6 ohm resistor even through there is a 12 ohm resistor in the circuit. The 12 ohm resistor is in parallel with a 4 ohm resistor, which gives the parallel network circuit resistance of only 3 ohms.

7. **The correct answer is (E).** A flat mirror reverses an image from left to right while producing a virtual and erect image.

8. **The correct answer is (A).** A concave mirror produces an inverted image that is real and on the same side of the mirror as the object.

9. **The correct answer is (B).** A convex lens produces an inverted, real image that is located on the opposite side of the lens.

10. **The correct answer is (B).** The field shown at A is a magnetic field around a current-carrying device. The field at C is a point charge near a charged plate. The field shown by the letter D is a

Peterson's SAT II Success: Physics

parallel plate field. The field in E is that of attraction between point changes. The field shown at B shows repulsion between the field lines. The repulsive effect is due to a pair of like charged particles.

11. **The correct answer is (D).** The parallel field lines shown in the diagram are from a pair of parallel plates.

12. **The correct answer is (E).** The explanation is the same as the explanation given in question number 10. Left with a choice between B and E, we can see the point charges in diagram E leave one point charge and enter the other point charge. That type of electric field between two point charges is produced when two unlike charges are near each other.

13. **The correct answer is (A).** In the Carnot cycle the heat is added between A→B.

14. **The correct answer is (C).** The release gas or exhaust occurs between C→D in the diagram.

ANSWERS TO PART B, QUESTIONS 15–75

15. **The correct answer is (A).** Due to the mass that is converted in the nucleus (mass defect) to hold the protons together in the nucleus, the proton does not have the same mass when it is inside the nucleus as it has outside the nucleus. The hydrogen proton is the proton that is least affected because it is the only proton in the hydrogen atom.

16. **The correct answer is (B).** The total resistance for a set of resistors in parallel is found by using the sum of the reciprocals. That is to do the following $\frac{1}{R_t} = \frac{1}{R_1} + \frac{1}{R_2} + \frac{1}{R_3} + \frac{1}{R_4}$ yielding the decimal solution $\frac{1}{R_t} = .05 + .025 + .0167 + .0124$. Which is

$$\frac{1}{R_t} = .1042 = 9.6\Omega.$$

17. **The correct answer is (E).** Work is defined as a force applied through a distance. The weight lifter did not move the weights through any distance after he lifted them overhead. He just stood holding the weights overhead, which does not meet the meaning of work in a physics sense.

18. **The correct answer is (D).** Power is the rate at which work is done, $\text{Power} = \dfrac{\text{work}}{\text{time}}$. The weight lifter lifted the weights up from the floor to a distance of 2.25 m above the floor in a time of .65 seconds. The work the weight lifter did to raise the weights can be calculated either by $(F{\cdot}s{\cdot}\cos\theta)$ or by using the potential energy (mgh). Divide the work by the time he took to raise the weights, and the power he develops is 6923 watts.

19. **The correct answer is (A).** We are told in the statement of the situation that a voltage is produced by photons striking the metal. This means the minimum threshold to meet the work function must have been met. This tells us the light is blue light, because the other two statements imply no voltage is produced in the metal.

20. **The correct answer is (E).** This is a curvilinear problem. The package already has the x-axis (horizontal) velocity of the plane. Even though the package accelerates toward the ground, its horizontal velocity remains exactly the same as when it left the plane, and that keeps the package moving along under the airplane until it strikes the ground.

21. **The correct answer is (C).** The two wires have a magnetic field around them caused by the current in the wires. The two fields are in opposition, which weakens them on the sides closest to each other. This allows the un-weakened field on the other (outside) of the wires to push the two wires together

22. **The correct answer is (D).** The frequency at which the humming bird beats its wings is already given in beats per minute. To find the number of wing beats per second (Hz), divide the number of wing beats per minute by 60 seconds.

23. **The correct answer is (E).** The compass is unaffected by the change from the Northern Hemisphere to the Southern Hemisphere. It will work in the same manner all over the world. The magnetic needle points toward the Magnetic North Pole in the Northern Hemisphere.

24. **The correct answer is (D).** The ideal gas law equation $\dfrac{P_1 V_1}{T_1} = \dfrac{P_2 V_2}{T_2}$ converts into $T_2 = \dfrac{V_2 T_1}{V_1}$. $T_2 = \dfrac{(2L)(300K)}{4L} = 150K$.

25. **The correct answer is (E).** The photon of yellow light does not contain enough energy to cause the metal to emit an ultraviolet photon. Remember the energy of a photon is directly related to the frequency of the electromagnetic radiation. The higher the frequency, the higher the energy of the photon of the radiation. Ultraviolet light has a much higher frequency than yellow light, thus its photon is more energetic.

26. **The correct answer is (A).** Both spheres accelerated at the same rate down the same incline for the exact same amount of time. This gives them both the same velocity at the time in question

27. **The correct answer is (A).** The period of a wave is the inverse of the frequency $f = \dfrac{1}{T}$.

28. **The correct answer is (D).** The wavelength is found by dividing the frequency of the waves into the velocity of the waves $\lambda = \dfrac{v}{f}$.

29. **The correct answer is (C).** To solve the problem you must first find the equivalent resistance of the two parallel resistors. The resistors are the same value; so divide 30 ohms by 2, which gives a value of 15 ohms. Add 15 ohms to the 9 ohms in series with the parallel resistors for a total resistance of 24 ohms. The voltage is equal to the current multiplied by the resistance, Ohm's Law. $(24\Omega)(.25) = 6\ V$.

30. **The correct answer is (C).** An adiabatic process is one during which no heat enters or leaves the system. Work is done on the system (the compression of the gas) that keeps the heat content of the system constant.

31. **The correct answer is (A).** Frictional forces always oppose motion, and when the frictional force in the problem is calculated you must remember to add in the downward part of the 20N force to the normal force.

32. **The correct answer is (A).** The mass numbers of the reactants and products must be the same, a mass value of 4 is missing on the product side. Likewise the atomic number on both sides of the equation must be the same. A value of 2 is missing on the

product side, leaving $\begin{smallmatrix}4\\2\end{smallmatrix}$ (a mass number of 4, and an atomic number of 2 as the missing value). This is an alpha particle or $\begin{smallmatrix}4\\2\end{smallmatrix}He$.

33. **The correct answer is (D).** The bowling ball has a smaller radius than the hoop in which it is rolling. All the angular quantities of the bowling ball are larger than those of the hoop. They will both travel the same linear distance, which is the tangential displacement.

34. **The correct answer is (D).** A net force applied to a body causes the body to be accelerated. This is Sir Isaac Newton's second law of motion, *F=ma*.

35. **The correct answer is (D).** The image formed by a convex lens when the object is outside the radius of curvature is real, inverted, and near the focal point on the other side of the lens.

36. **The correct answer is (E).** This is Einstein's statement concerning the relationship between the natural laws of physics and frames of reference. All physical laws are the same for systems that are moving at constant rate.

37. **The correct answer is (C).** Polarizers are used in industry to reveal stress patterns in machinery and tools. Almost everyone has used sunglasses that protect their eyes by polarizing the light to reduce glare.

38. **The correct answer is (C).** The velocity of the ball in its pathway is calculated with the centripetal force equation, $F_c = \dfrac{mv^2}{r}$, which is rearranged to $v = \sqrt{\dfrac{(F_c)(r)}{m}} = \sqrt{\dfrac{(6.25N)(2m)}{.5kg}} = 5N$.

39. **The correct answer is (C).** The charge on a solid conducting body is found on the outside of the object. The charges distribute themselves equally around the outside of the conducting body because of the mutual repulsion the excess charges have for themselves.

40. **The correct answer is (C).** The icicle strikes the ground with a velocity of 10.84 m/s, giving it a kinetic energy $(1/2\ mv^2)$ of 1.76J. Only 5% of the energy is converted to heat, so the energy converted to heat is .088J. It takes .335 J to convert one gram of ice to water, so $\dfrac{.088J}{.335J/g} = .263g$ of ice is converted to water.

41. **The correct answer is (E).** All the answers are stated opposite from their correct relativistic statement except for choice (E).

42. **The correct answer is (C).** During the first 30 minutes (½ hour) the bicyclist travels 12.5 km. The next 15 minutes (¼ hour) the bicyclist travels 5 km, and during the last 15 minutes the bicyclist travels another 10 km. The total distance the bicyclist traveled during one hour is the sum of the three distances, which are 12.5 km + 5 km + 10 km = 27.5 km

43. **The correct answer is (A).** The force down the plane is a component of the weight of the block, which is found by multiplying the weight of the object by the sine θ of the angle to which the plane is raised. This produces a force down the plane, which will accelerate the object when the plane is raised high enough. The frictional force between the block and the plane *always* acts against the motion of the object—in this case, friction operates up the plane. Since there is no acceleration, the frictional force (F_f) opposing the motion of the block exactly equals the downward force (F_{11}).

44. **The correct answer is (E).** The hot gas, which is in contact with the cold gas, will lose heat to the cold gas. The transfer of heat is always from the hot object to the cold object, unless work is done on the system.

45. **The correct answer is (C).** The listener hears the sound waves being bunched together as the siren approaches him, causing the pitch of the sound he hears to increase. When the fire truck passes the listener, the sound waves seem to be spread apart as the pitch of the sound decreases due to the lengthening of the sound waves.

46. **The correct answer is (D).** The inertia of the dishes (Newton's first law) causes them to remain at rest. The fast rate at which the magician pulls the tablecloth from under the dishes keeps the static friction from changing to kinetic friction.

47. **The correct answer is (B).** Look at the pipe carefully and there are two complete waves in the pipe. Since the pipe is 40 cm long, the wavelength of the waves is .2 m. Solve for the frequency of the wave with $f = \dfrac{v}{\lambda}$.

48. **The correct answer is (B).** The heat content of a substance is dependent on three different things, the specific heat of the substance, the mass of the substance, and the temperature of the substance. The specific heat can be disregarded since the substance is the same for both containers. The mass of the water in the cup is less than the mass of the water in the bucket, therefore the cup of water has less heat content than the bucket of water even though they are at the same temperature.

49. **The correct answer is (A).** To find the capacitance for a group of capacitors in parallel with each other you add their capacitances together to find their sum. $10\mu f + 15\mu f + 35\mu f = 60\mu f$.

50. **The correct answer is (D).** The electron releases energy when it falls to the $n=1$ level from the $n=3$ level. $\Delta E = E_3 - E_1$, yielding a positive $+12.21\ eV$.

51. **The correct answer is (B).** The resistors can be combined in the following ways:
    4 resistors in series = 24Ω
    4 resistors in parallel = 15Ω
    3 resistors in parallel together with one resistor in series with the parallel resistors = 8Ω
    2 resistors in parallel together that are in series with 2 more resistors that are in parallel together = 6Ω
    2 resistors in parallel together that are in series with 2 resistors in series together = 15Ω

52. **The correct answer is (C).** The problem can be solved as a combination work-energy theorem problem. KE = Work is restated as $1/2\ mv^2 = (F_f)(s)(\cos\theta)$. The F_f is found by using the equation for frictional force, $F_f = \mu N$. Put it all together and solve

$$s = \frac{(m)(v^2)}{2(\mu)(N)}$$

in this manner $\qquad s = \dfrac{(7.25\text{kg})(10\ \text{m/s})^2}{2(.0025)(7.25\text{kg})(9.8\ \text{m/s}^2)}$

$$2040\text{m} \simeq 2\text{km}$$

53. **The correct answer is (B).** The binding energy is the result of the conversion of the mass defect into the energy that holds the protons in the nucleus in spite of their repulsion for each other.

54. **The correct answer is (A).** During the time when the substance is at the part of the graph, it can either evaporate or condense. This entails a phase change, which is accomplished by the substance gaining energy.

55. **The correct answer is (A).** The temperature can only increase when no phase change occurs. The first rise on the graph is where the solid phase exists and its temperature changes.

56. **The correct answer is (E).** The higher the frequency of a photon, the more energy it has, therefore the more energy it can impart to the electron.

57. **The correct answer is (E).** When the light is incident to the surface of the second material, a small amount of reflection occurs even though most of the light passes through the surface interface and into the second substance. This means the law of reflection is in effect for the reflected part of the light ray, the angle of reflection equals the angle of incidence.

58. **The correct answer is (D).** The material with the higher index of refraction has a greater optical density to the light. The ray bends toward the normal when it slows down in the optically more dense material

59. **The correct answer is (A).** The pressure he feels is equal to force per unit area. His partner's heel is a tiny area, which bears most of her weight. This gives a large local force at the small end of her heel.

60. **The correct answer is (D).** This is a calorimetry problem $(cm\Delta T)_{cold} = (cm\Delta T)_{hot}$. The specific heats are the same for both hot and cold water, which may be factored out of the problem, leaving $(m\Delta T)_{cold} = (m\Delta T)_{hot}$. The answer is $86°C$.

61. **The correct answer is (D).** Take the count rate of 62.5 counts/sec and divide by 500 counts/sec. The result is the decimal number of .125, which is $(1/2)^3$. The 3 half-lives occur during the two-hour period. We have 120 min ÷ 3 = 40 min per half-life.

62. **The correct answer is (A).** Subtract the momentum of the ball from its original momentum to find the momentum of the ball as it bounces away from the floor.

63. **The correct answer is (C).** The time an object moves along the x-axis while it is also moving in free fall on the y-axis is restricted to the time the object is in free fall. The water from the fireman's hose must be in free fall at least long enough to reach the height at which the window is located above ground and cross the distance from the hose to the burning building, too. This means that at the very least, the time the water rises (t_y) must equal the time the water takes to move from the hose and cross the street on the x-axis (t_x).

64. **The correct answer is (C).** The heat in the water and any heat added to the water is used by the system to melt the ice. This constitutes a phase change, too.

65. **The correct answer is (D).** The impulse impressed onto the cart is the same as the momentum the cart achieves. The momentum is given as $P = mv$, which was given to the cart in a time of .8 sec. The impulse an object receives in a given time is $Ft = \Delta P$. The solution is found by replacing the P (momentum), yielding the equation $Ft = mv$, which is rearranged to find the force. $F = \dfrac{(m)(v)}{t}$.

66. **The correct answer is (D).** The highly polished interior surface of the thermos bottle reflects radiated heat from the substance back into the substance it is keeping hot.

67. **The correct answer is (A).** Charge builds across a capacitor at a high rate when voltage is initially applied. The rate of charge on the capacitor decreases with time as the capacitor builds charge.

68. **The correct answer is (A).** Current flows in the circuit when the switch is first closed. As time passes and the charge builds on the capacitor, the current flow decreases inversely in relation to the charge on the capacitor. When the capacitor is fully charged, the capacitor blocks the circuit as if it was an open and no current is able to flow.

69. **The correct answer is (C).** The problem may be solved in several ways. Perhaps the best solution is a little thought. E.g., the potential energy and the kinetic energy are equal to each other when the object has fallen half the distance to the ground, or 10 m. We now treat it as a free fall problem by restating the situation a little. What is the velocity of an object that starts from rest and free falls a distance of 10 m? The solution is found by

$$V_f = \sqrt{2(a)(s)}$$
$$\sqrt{2(9.8 \text{ m/s})(10\text{m})} = 14 \text{ m/s}$$

70. **The correct answer is (C).** The rocket sled is already moving. The two rocket engines apply *two* (different pairs) of forces of equal magnitude to the same object but in different directions. There is therefore no unbalanced force and the sled continues in its state of motion.

71. **The correct answer is (D).** The particle is completely unaffected by the field, which eliminates the charge-carrying particles. Thus the electron, the positron (a positive electron), and the proton are not the correct choice. The gamma ray is also unaffected by a magnetic field, but it is not a particle and would not be seen, so it, too, is eliminated from consideration. The only particle that is unaffected by the magnetic field is the neutron.

72. **The correct answer is (E).** Sound waves are propagated in a manner that is parallel to their direction of movement. They are composed of a series of compressions and rarefactions.

73. **The correct answer is (D).** When the string breaks, the object travels in a straight-line tangent to the circular pathway it had followed.

74. **The correct answer is (A).** The refrigerator is essentially a heat engine that is being run in reverse. The refrigerator "heats" the room outside by removing heat energy from the enclosed and insulated refrigerator box. The process produces the cooling effect.

75. **The correct answer is (B).** When the object leaves the hand of the person who throws it out of the vehicle, the object is in free fall. The acceleration of any object in free fall is a constant 9.8 m/s^2, therefore the acceleration does not change. Since there is acceleration, however, the velocity will change.

Practice Test 3

PHYSICS TEST

PRACTICE TEST 3

PHYSICS TEST

While you have taken many standardized tests and know to blacken completely the ovals on the answer sheets and to erase completely any errors, the instructions for the SAT II Physics Test differ in an important way from the directions for other standardized tests. You need to indicate on the answer key which test you are taking. The instructions on the answer sheet will tell you to fill out the top portion of the answer sheet exactly as shown.

1. Print PHYSICS on the line under the words *Subject Test (print)*.
2. In the shaded box labeled *Test Code* fill in four ovals:

       —Fill in oval 1 in the row labeled V.
       —Fill in oval 6 in the row labeled W.
       —Fill in oval 3 in the row labeled X.
       —Fill in oval C in the row labeled Y.
       —Leave the ovals in row Q blank.

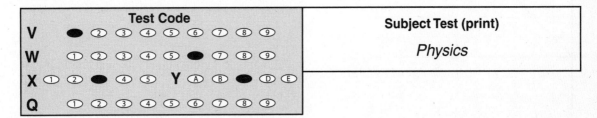

There are two additional questions that you will be asked to answer. One is "How many semesters of physics have you taken in high school?" The other question lists courses and asks you to mark those that you have taken. You will be told which ovals to fill in for each question. The College Board is collecting statistical information. If you choose to answer, you will use the key that is provided and blacken the appropriate ovals in row Q. You may also choose not to answer, and that will not affect your grade.

When everyone has completed filling in this portion of the answer sheet, the supervisor will tell you to turn the page and begin. The answer sheet has 100 numbered ovals, but there are only approximately 75 multiple-choice questions on the test, so be sure to use only ovals 1 to 75 (or however many questions there are) to record your answers.

PHYSICS TEST

Part A

Directions: Each of the sets of lettered choices below refers to the questions and/or statements that follow. Select the lettered choice that is the best answer to each question and fill in the corresponding oval on the answer sheet. In each set, each choice may be used once, more than once, or not at all.

Questions 1–3 relate to the velocity time graph shown below. Select the answer that is most representative of the physical quantity named.

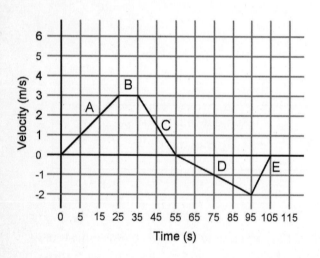

1. At which point on the graph is no net force applied?

2. At which point on the graph is the acceleration greatest?

3. At which point on the graph does the object move the greatest distance?

PHYSICS TEST—*Continued*

Questions 4-6 relate to the DC circuit shown below.

Questions 7-9

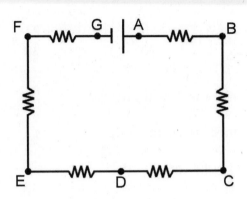

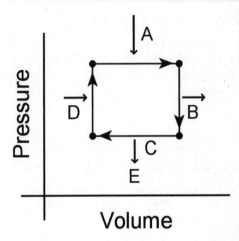

The values for current, voltage, and resistance in the circuit are graphed from point A through point G in the graphs directly below.

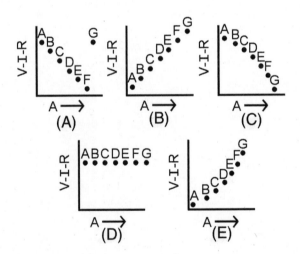

The idealized *P-V* diagram above shows a complete cycle through compression and expansion of a gas. The questions below relate to the processes within the cycle.

7. Which letter shows isothermal compression?

8. Which letter shows work done?

9. Which letter shows an adiabatic expansion?

4. Which of the graphs shows the current from point A to point G?

5. Which of the graphs shows the resistance from point A to point G?

6. Which of the graphs shows the voltage from point A to point G?

GO ON TO THE NEXT PAGE

PHYSICS TEST

PHYSICS TEST—*Continued*

<u>Questions 10–12</u> relate to the diagram below.

<u>Questions 13–15</u> relate to the nuclear equation shown below.

$$\begin{array}{ccccc} (A) & (B) & (C) & (D) & (E) \\ {}^{235}_{92}U \rightarrow & {}^{4}_{2}He + & {}^{234}_{90}Th \rightarrow & {}^{0}_{-1}e + & {}^{234}_{91}Pa \end{array}$$

13. Identify the parent nucleus.

14. Identify the alpha particle.

15. Identify the beta particle.

A 50 kg object slides to a stop over a period of time. Which of the graphs represents each of the described factors?

10. The frictional force on the object

11. Velocity of the object

12. Displacement of the object

Peterson's SAT II Success: Physics

PHYSICS TEST—*Continued*

Part B

> <u>Directions:</u> Each question or statement below is followed by five possible answers. In each case, select the best possible answer and fill in the corresponding oval on the answer sheet.

16. The processes of constructive interference and destructive interference occur in
    (A) cosmic rays.
    (B) light rays.
    (C) sound waves.
    (D) water waves.
    (E) all of these.

17. A positively charged rod is brought near an uncharged pith ball that is being touched by a copper wire. Both the rod and the copper wire are simultaneously removed, and the pith ball is tested to find if any electrostatic charge is present. What is the result?
    (A) The pith ball has been positively charged by conduction.
    (B) The pith ball has been positively charged by induction.
    (C) The pith ball has been negatively charged by conduction.
    (D) The pith ball has been negatively charged by induction.
    (E) The pith ball has not been charged in any way.

18. Two point charges are separated by a small distance. When the distance between the two particles is halved, which of the following descriptions is true?
    (A) The particles attract one another.
    (B) The particles repel one another.
    (C) The particles exert the same force on one another.
    (D) The particles exert twice as much force on one another.
    (E) The particles exert four times as much force on one another.

19. A photon of light from which of the following electromagnetic radiations carries the greater amount of energy?
    (A) Blue
    (B) Green
    (C) Orange
    (D) Red
    (E) Yellow

GO ON TO THE NEXT PAGE

20. A person standing in an elevator watches a spider hanging from a thread attached to the ceiling. Suddenly the elevator accelerates downward. The person watching the spider on the thread will see

   (A) the spider thread snap and the spider slowly fall.

   (B) the spider thread and spider float upward.

   (C) the spider thread snap and the spider slowly float upward.

   (D) the spider thread and the spider remain as they were before the acceleration began.

   (E) the spider thread begin to swing back and forth like a pendulum.

21. Three ice cubes are placed into three equal beakers filled with water. One ice cube has a mass of 50 g, the second ice cube has a mass of 75 g, and the third ice cube has a mass of 100 g. After the ice cubes are added, each beaker is filled to the brim with water at a temperature of $1°C$. After a period of time passes and all three ice cubes melt, which of the following situations is most likely?

   (A) All three beakers have overflowed.

   (B) None of the beakers have overflowed.

   (C) The beaker with the 100 g ice cube has overflowed.

   (D) The beakers with the 100 g and the 75 g ice cube in them have overflowed.

   (E) The beaker with the 50 g ice cube has overflowed.

22. One mole of helium gas and one mole of neon gas are both at *STP.* Which of the following statements about the gases is correct?

   (A) Their pressure is the same.

   (B) Their temperature is the same.

   (C) Their volume is the same.

   (D) Their number of particles is the same.

   (E) The pressure, temperature, volume, and number of particles is the same.

23. A step down transformer changes the high input voltage used in our houses ($120V$) into the low voltage used to charge an electric razor ($24V$). What must be the ratio of the turns of wire from the primary side of the transformer to the secondary side?

   (A) 1:5

   (B) 2:7

   (C) 1:8

   (D) 2:9

   (E) 1:10

Equilibrant

24. The equilibrant vector of a resultant vector is shown above. Which of the choices below represents the *y* component of the equilibrant vector?

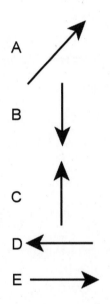

(A) Line A
(B) Line B
(C) Line C
(D) Line D
(E) Line E

25. Object A (which is cold) is placed on top of object B (which is hot) in a closed system. Which of the following is the best description of what occurs in the system?

 I. Both A and B eventually reach the same temperature.
 II. Gravity stops heat from moving up into A.
 III. Heat flows from A to B.

(A) I only
(B) II only
(C) I and III only
(D) II and III only
(E) I, II, and III

26. Look at the image above produced by the convex mirror shown and choose the correct description of the image.
(A) Erect and real
(B) Real and enlarged
(C) Enlarged and virtual
(D) Virtual and reduced
(E) Reduced and real

GO ON TO THE NEXT PAGE

27. An object is moving in a circular path with a constant velocity (v). If the radius of the circle in which the object is moving is decreased by one half and the velocity remains the same, what will happen to the centripetal force?

    (A) It will be $4F$.
    (B) It will be $2F$.
    (C) It will be F.
    (D) It will be $F/2$.
    (E) It will be $F/4$.

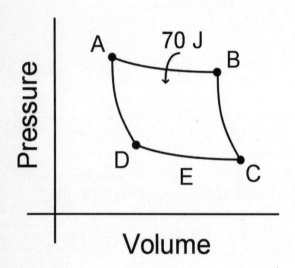

28. For the gas shown below, 70 Joules of energy is added between AB. The gas does 35 Joules of work. How much heat is exhausted between CD?

    (A) .5J
    (B) 2J
    (C) 35J
    (D) 105J
    (E) 2,450J

29. Which wave characteristic describes the number of wave crests passing a given point per unit time?

    (A) Frequency
    (B) Amplitude
    (C) Wavelength
    (D) Velocity
    (E) Period

30. What is the centripetal acceleration on the rim of a wagon wheel of 44 cm diameter if the wagon is being pulled at a constant 2.5 m/s?

    (A) 10.8 m/s
    (B) 18.6 m/s
    (C) 28.4 m/s
    (D) 32.7 m/s
    (E) 36.3 m/s

31. The specific heat for substance A is twice the specific heat of substance B. The same mass of each substance is allowed to gain 50 Joules of heat energy. As a result of the heating process

    (A) the temperature of A rises twice as much as B.
    (B) the temperature of A rises four times as much as B.
    (C) the temperature of B rises twice as much as A.
    (D) the temperature of B rises four times as much as A.
    (E) the temperature of both B and A rise the same amount.

PHYSICS TEST—*Continued*

32. A golf ball is placed inside an unmounted tire, which is then rolled down a long hill. Identify the statement(s) that best describe the situation while the tire and golf ball are rolling down the hill.

    I. The centripetal force on the tire operates in the same direction as the centripetal force on the golf ball.

    II. The centripetal force acting on the tire is opposite the centripetal force acting on the golf ball.

    III. The centripetal force acting on the golf ball is equal to the centripetal force on the tire.

    (A) I only
    (B) II only
    (C) I and III only
    (D) II and III only
    (E) I, II, and III

33. A 50 kg block slides down a plane that has been raised to an angle of 30° above the horizontal at a constant rate. After the block slides completely to the bottom of the plane, a rope is attached to the block. The rope pulls parallel to the surface of the plane as the block is pulled up the plane at a constant rate. Which statement about the tension in the rope is correct?

    (A) The tension in the rope is greater than the frictional force but less than the weight of the block.
    (B) The tension in the rope is greater than the frictional force plus the weight of the block.
    (C) The tension in the rope is equal to the weight of the block minus the frictional force.
    (D) The tension in the rope is equal to the weight of the block.
    (E) The tension in the rope is equal to the frictional force.

34. The length of time a satellite takes to orbit the earth depends on its

    (A) launch speed.
    (B) mass.
    (C) distance from the earth.
    (D) weight.
    (E) orbital direction.

35. An object falls with constant acceleration near the earth. Which statement best describes the velocity of the object?

    (A) The velocity is constant.
    (B) The velocity is decreasing.
    (C) The velocity constantly changes in proportion to its weight.
    (D) The velocity is not related to its acceleration.
    (E) The velocity changes by the same amount each second.

36. The normal force between two surfaces is increased by four times. The coefficient of static friction will

    (A) be cut in half.
    (B) be doubled.
    (C) remain the same.
    (D) be quadrupled.
    (E) be undetermined.

37. Which of the following methods can be used to induce a voltage into a coil of wire?

    (A) Rotating a magnet around the coils of wire
    (B) Passing a magnet through the center of the coils of wire
    (C) Rotating the coil of wire in a magnetic field
    (D) Changing the strength of the magnetic field applied to the wire
    (E) All of the methods listed can be used to induce current into a coil of wire.

GO ON TO THE NEXT PAGE

38. Scientists identify the elements that are burning in the stars by using which of the following devices?
    (A) Refractive telescopes
    (B) Reflective telescopes
    (C) Spectroscopes
    (D) Polarimeters
    (E) Photoelectric microscopes

39. The discrete spectral lines of line spectra occur when excitation of electrons takes place in
    (A) solids.
    (B) liquids.
    (C) gases.
    (D) plastics.
    (E) all of these.

40. A proton and an electron are each placed in an electric field between a pair of parallel plates. The electron is placed exactly halfway between the two plates, and the proton is placed midway between the electron and the negative plate. Which of the following statements is correct about the forces the particles experience?
    (A) The force on the electron is larger because it has less mass.
    (B) The force on the proton is larger because it has greater mass
    (C) The force on the electron is larger because it is in the strongest part of the electric field.
    (D) The force on the proton is larger because it is closer to the negative plate.
    (E) They both experience the same force.

41. A light ray that enters a glass block from the air is refracted because
    (A) the light travels faster in the glass than in the air.
    (B) the light travels slower in the glass than in the air.
    (C) the light waves invert as they enter the glass.
    (D) the light waves increase their amplitudes in the glass.
    (E) the light intensity is greater in the glass than in the air.

42. Each and every person on earth is made of atoms that originated in
    (A) the food we eat.
    (B) the ancient stars.
    (C) our mother's body.
    (D) the oceans.
    (E) the earth.

43. A toy rocket is launched straight up. At the exact top of its flight path, which of the following is true?
    (A) Its velocity and acceleration are zero.
    (B) Its velocity is zero and acceleration is $9.8 \ m/s^2$.
    (C) Its velocity is 9.8 m/s and acceleration is $9.8 \ m/s^2$.
    (D) Its velocity is 9.8 m/s and acceleration is zero.
    (E) Its velocity is 9.8 m/s and displacement is 9.8 m.

44. Sir Isaac Newton's third law of motion is called the action-reaction law. Which of the following statements appropriately describes the action-reaction forces?
    - (A) They act on different objects.
    - (B) They act on the same object.
    - (C) They are unequal in magnitude.
    - (D) They act at right angles to one another.
    - (E) They act in the same direction.

45. When a gas undergoes an adiabatic compression its
    - (A) temperature decreases.
    - (B) temperature increases.
    - (C) volume increases.
    - (D) pressure decreases.
    - (E) energy decreases.

46. A clothesline is strung between two posts, and wet clothing weighing 200 N is hung on the line, which sags under the weight of the clothes. If one end of the line is pulled to straighten the line, which of the following would be true?

    I. The tension in the rope undergoes a large increase.
    II. The tension in the rope undergoes a large decrease.
    III. The weight in the rope undergoes a large increase.

    - (A) I only
    - (B) II only
    - (C) I and III only
    - (D) II and III only
    - (E) I, II, and III

47. The current through a 20Ω resistor connected to a 12V battery is
    - (A) .3 amperes.
    - (B) .6 amperes.
    - (C) .9 amperes.
    - (D) 1.6 amperes.
    - (E) 1.9 amperes.

48. When *U*-235 is fissioned in a nuclear reactor, the nuclear reaction is maintained by
    - (A) heat produced in the reactor.
    - (B) the moderator rods.
    - (C) radioactive decay products.
    - (D) vibrations induced in the *U*-235.
    - (E) neutrons produced in the reaction.

49. The force a magnetic field exerts on an electron is largest when the path of the electron is oriented
    - (A) in the opposite direction from the magnetic field's direction.
    - (B) in the same direction as the magnetic field's direction.
    - (C) up through the magnetic field at a 45° angle.
    - (D) down through the magnetic field at a 45° angle.
    - (E) at a right angle to the magnetic field.

50. When a light ray strikes a perfectly reflective mirror at an angle, which of the following happens?
    - (A) The frequency of the light ray changes.
    - (B) The wavelength of the light ray changes.
    - (C) The velocity of the light ray changes.
    - (D) The period of the light ray changes.
    - (E) The direction of motion of the light ray changes.

GO ON TO THE NEXT PAGE

Peterson's: www.petersons.com   317

PHYSICS TEST—*Continued*

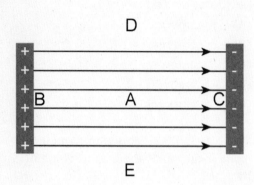

51. An electron, a proton, and a neutron are located at point (A) above in an electric field. A short period of time passes. At which position as indicated by the letter on the diagram will the proton be located?

   (A) Point A
   (B) Point B
   (C) Point C
   (D) Point D
   (E) Point E

52. If the pressure acting on an ideal gas that is kept at constant temperature is multiplied by four, its volume

   (A) triples.
   (B) reduces to 1/3.
   (C) increases by four.
   (D) reduces to 1/4.
   (E) There is not enough information to tell.

53. The electron-volt (*eV*) is a unit of

   (A) power.
   (B) voltage.
   (C) current.
   (D) potential.
   (E) energy.

54. A pile driver is raised to a height of 25 m in 10 seconds. It is released and allowed to fall onto a piling. Although guided by a set of rails, the pile driver essentially is in free fall after its release. Which of the following is/are correct?

   I.   The power input equals the power output.
   II. The PE in equals the KE out.
   III. The KE in equals the work out.

   (A) I only
   (B) II only
   (C) I and III only
   (D) II and III only
   (E) I, II, and III only

55. A dog walks 120 m due east, then turns and runs 60 m west. An interesting smell attracts the dog, and it trots 40 m due north. At this point the dog is 85 m north-east of his home. The dog hears his master call him and he runs directly home. Which part of the trip is the largest vector?

   (A) The eastward leg
   (B) The westward leg
   (C) The northward leg
   (D) The distance from home
   (E) The distance to home

PHYSICS TEST—*Continued*

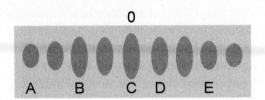

56. Which letter above represents a 3λ difference in path length?

    (A) Position A
    (B) Position B
    (C) Position C
    (D) Position D
    (E) Position E

57. A 1,000 kg car rolls without friction down a hill that is 20 m long and inclined at 15°C from the horizontal. What is the velocity of the car at the bottom of the hill?

    (A) 2 m/s
    (B) 5 m/s
    (C) 10 m/s
    (D) 20 m/s
    (E) 30 m/s

58. Sound waves cannot travel in

    (A) air.
    (B) metal.
    (C) vacuum.
    (D) water.
    (E) wood.

Questions 59-60 refer to the situation described below.

Consider a light wave that passes from air into a very thick clear glass block that has its opposite internal side mirrored (facing into the glass). The light ray passes into the glass block at an angle greater than 0° and less than 90°, strikes the mirrored surface and reflects back through the glass into the air.

59. What happens while the light ray is in the glass block but before it strikes the mirrored surface?

    (A) The frequency of the waves increases.
    (B) The frequency of the waves decreases.
    (C) The wavelength of the waves decreases.
    (D) The velocity of the waves decreases.
    (E) The period of the waves increases.

60. What happens when the light ray leaves the glass block after it has struck the mirrored surface?

    (A) The waves reflect back on the glass.
    (B) The waves increase velocity.
    (C) The waves leave the glass at the same angle at which they entered the glass.
    (D) The angle of refraction is greater than the angle of incidence.
    (E) The angle of reflection from the mirror is equal to the incident angle at which the light struck the glass block.

GO ON TO THE NEXT PAGE

PHYSICS TEST—*Continued*

61. The most notable difference between a radio wave and a light wave is
    (A) speed.
    (B) refractive index.
    (C) reflectivity.
    (D) amplitude.
    (E) frequency.

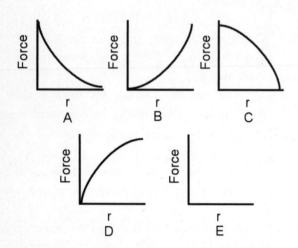

62. Which of the graphs above shows two electrons as they separate from one another?
    (A) Graph A
    (B) Graph B
    (C) Graph C
    (D) Graph D
    (E) Graph E

63. During a pool game the cue ball is shot at the red ball. When the cue ball strikes the red ball, the cue ball stops dead, and the red ball moves away at the same velocity the cue ball had before the collision. The type of collision represented in this example is
    (A) an elastic collision.
    (B) a perfectly inelastic collision.
    (C) an inelastic collision.
    (D) all of the above.
    (E) none of the above.

64. The images formed by convex mirrors
    (A) are always real.
    (B) are always virtual.
    (C) are only real when the object is placed outside the radius of curvature.
    (D) are only virtual when the object is placed inside the focal point.
    (E) None of the above describes the images formed by convex mirrors.

65. Two different light bulbs are in a DC circuit powered by an 18 V battery as its power source. The two bulbs are rated at 4.5 watts (B_1) and 6.75 watts (B_2) each. What are the resistances of the two light bulbs (B_1) and (B_2)?
    (A) B_1 is 48 Ω, and B_2 is 72 Ω.
    (B) B_1 is 72 Ω, and B_2 is 48 Ω.
    (C) B_1 is 2.67 Ω, and B_2 is 4 Ω.
    (D) B_1 is 4 Ω, and B_2 is 2.67 Ω.
    (E) B_1 is 20.25 Ω, and B_2 is 45.56 Ω.

66. Scientists can determine whether a star is approaching the earth by looking at its
    (A) red shift.
    (B) blue shift.
    (C) rate of shimmer.
    (D) brightness.
    (E) absolute magnitude.

PHYSICS TEST—*Continued*

67. The volt is a measure of electrical potential and may be defined as
    (A) opposition to electrical motion.
    (B) number of particles in motion.
    (C) work per unit charge.
    (D) field strength per unit of force.
    (E) electrostatic discharge.

68. A laboratory centrifuge starts from rest and reaches a rotational speed of 8,000 radians/sec in a time of 25 seconds. What is the angular acceleration of the centrifuge?
    (A) 160 radians/sec²
    (B) 320 radians/sec²
    (C) 640 radians/sec²
    (D) 10,000 radians/sec²
    (E) 20,000 radians/sec²

69. An object at rest is placed into free fall at a height of 20 m. What is the velocity of the object when the *PE* equals the *KE*?
    (A) 8 m/s
    (B) 11 m/s
    (C) 14 m/s
    (D) 17 m/s
    (E) Velocity cannot be determined.

70. A battery and a variable resistor are in series with a small fan. A switch is closed, and the fan runs. When the variable resistor is moved slightly to the left, the fan slows down a little. When the variable resistor is moved slightly to the right, the fan speeds up a little. The following question is about the operation of the circuit described. If the variable resistor in the circuit is set all the way to the right, what happens in the circuit?

    I. The fan runs faster.
    II. The voltage decreases.
    III. The current increases.

    (A) I only
    (B) II only
    (C) I and III only
    (D) II and III only
    (E) I, II, and III

GO ON TO THE NEXT PAGE

PHYSICS TEST—*Continued*

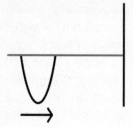

71. A pulse on a string moves toward and strikes a fixed end as shown. The pulse is
    - (A) reflected and transmitted.
    - (B) reflected and refracted.
    - (C) reflected and reduced.
    - (D) reflected and magnified.
    - (E) reflected and inverted.

72. A thrown baseball hits and breaks a glass window and ends up inside the house. Which of the following is correct about the ball?
    - (A) The force the ball exerted on the window was larger than the force the window exerted on the ball.
    - (B) The force the ball exerted on the window was smaller than the force the window exerted on the ball.
    - (C) The force the ball exerted on the window was the same as the force the window exerted on the ball.
    - (D) Since the ball broke the window, it didn't lose any momentum.
    - (E) The kinetic energy the ball had before it broke the window equaled the kinetic energy the ball had after it broke the window.

73. When a voltage source that is inducing voltage into a large number of coils is disconnected, and a switch that is in series with the coils of wire is also opened, a spark is observed to jump across the switch terminals as the switch begins to open up. What is the cause of this spark?
    - (A) Free electrons from the voltage source
    - (B) Free electrons from the coils of wire
    - (C) Collapse of the magnetic field in the coils of wire
    - (D) Secondary electron flow from the source
    - (E) Stored voltage in the coils of wire

74. Electrical energy is changed into mechanical energy in a device called a/an
    - (A) electromagnet.
    - (B) generator.
    - (C) magnetron.
    - (D) motor.
    - (E) transformer.

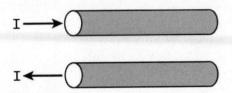

75. Two wires are aligned side by side as shown above. They are both hooked into different circuits in which the current is off. A switch is closed, allowing current to flow into each circuit. Which of the following statements is correct?

    (A) The two currents destructively interfere with one another.
    (B) The two currents constructively interfere with one another.
    (C) The two wires attract and move closer.
    (D) The two wires repel and move away.
    (E) The two wires remain still.

STOP

IF YOU FINISH BEFORE THE TEST SESSION ENDS, YOU MAY REVIEW YOUR WORK ON THIS TEST ONLY. YOU MAY NOT TURN TO ANY OTHER TEST IN THIS BOOK.

ANSWER SHEET

Leave any unused answer spaces blank.

	Test Code	Subject Test (print)

Test Code

V ① ② ③ ④ ⑤ ⑥ ⑦ ⑧ ⑨
W ① ② ③ ④ ⑤ ⑥ ⑦ ⑧ ⑨
X ① ② ③ ④ ⑤   Y Ⓐ Ⓑ Ⓒ Ⓓ Ⓔ
Q ① ② ③ ④ ⑤ ⑥ ⑦ ⑧ ⑨

Subject Test (print)

FOR ETS USE ONLY	R/C	W/S1	FS/S2	CS/S3	WS

1 Ⓐ Ⓑ Ⓒ Ⓓ Ⓔ   21 Ⓐ Ⓑ Ⓒ Ⓓ Ⓔ   41 Ⓐ Ⓑ Ⓒ Ⓓ Ⓔ   61 Ⓐ Ⓑ Ⓒ Ⓓ Ⓔ   81 Ⓐ Ⓑ Ⓒ Ⓓ Ⓔ
2 Ⓐ Ⓑ Ⓒ Ⓓ Ⓔ   22 Ⓐ Ⓑ Ⓒ Ⓓ Ⓔ   42 Ⓐ Ⓑ Ⓒ Ⓓ Ⓔ   62 Ⓐ Ⓑ Ⓒ Ⓓ Ⓔ   82 Ⓐ Ⓑ Ⓒ Ⓓ Ⓔ
3 Ⓐ Ⓑ Ⓒ Ⓓ Ⓔ   23 Ⓐ Ⓑ Ⓒ Ⓓ Ⓔ   43 Ⓐ Ⓑ Ⓒ Ⓓ Ⓔ   63 Ⓐ Ⓑ Ⓒ Ⓓ Ⓔ   83 Ⓐ Ⓑ Ⓒ Ⓓ Ⓔ
4 Ⓐ Ⓑ Ⓒ Ⓓ Ⓔ   24 Ⓐ Ⓑ Ⓒ Ⓓ Ⓔ   44 Ⓐ Ⓑ Ⓒ Ⓓ Ⓔ   64 Ⓐ Ⓑ Ⓒ Ⓓ Ⓔ   84 Ⓐ Ⓑ Ⓒ Ⓓ Ⓔ
5 Ⓐ Ⓑ Ⓒ Ⓓ Ⓔ   25 Ⓐ Ⓑ Ⓒ Ⓓ Ⓔ   45 Ⓐ Ⓑ Ⓒ Ⓓ Ⓔ   65 Ⓐ Ⓑ Ⓒ Ⓓ Ⓔ   85 Ⓐ Ⓑ Ⓒ Ⓓ Ⓔ
6 Ⓐ Ⓑ Ⓒ Ⓓ Ⓔ   26 Ⓐ Ⓑ Ⓒ Ⓓ Ⓔ   46 Ⓐ Ⓑ Ⓒ Ⓓ Ⓔ   66 Ⓐ Ⓑ Ⓒ Ⓓ Ⓔ   86 Ⓐ Ⓑ Ⓒ Ⓓ Ⓔ
7 Ⓐ Ⓑ Ⓒ Ⓓ Ⓔ   27 Ⓐ Ⓑ Ⓒ Ⓓ Ⓔ   47 Ⓐ Ⓑ Ⓒ Ⓓ Ⓔ   67 Ⓐ Ⓑ Ⓒ Ⓓ Ⓔ   87 Ⓐ Ⓑ Ⓒ Ⓓ Ⓔ
8 Ⓐ Ⓑ Ⓒ Ⓓ Ⓔ   28 Ⓐ Ⓑ Ⓒ Ⓓ Ⓔ   48 Ⓐ Ⓑ Ⓒ Ⓓ Ⓔ   68 Ⓐ Ⓑ Ⓒ Ⓓ Ⓔ   88 Ⓐ Ⓑ Ⓒ Ⓓ Ⓔ
9 Ⓐ Ⓑ Ⓒ Ⓓ Ⓔ   29 Ⓐ Ⓑ Ⓒ Ⓓ Ⓔ   49 Ⓐ Ⓑ Ⓒ Ⓓ Ⓔ   69 Ⓐ Ⓑ Ⓒ Ⓓ Ⓔ   89 Ⓐ Ⓑ Ⓒ Ⓓ Ⓔ
10 Ⓐ Ⓑ Ⓒ Ⓓ Ⓔ   30 Ⓐ Ⓑ Ⓒ Ⓓ Ⓔ   50 Ⓐ Ⓑ Ⓒ Ⓓ Ⓔ   70 Ⓐ Ⓑ Ⓒ Ⓓ Ⓔ   90 Ⓐ Ⓑ Ⓒ Ⓓ Ⓔ
11 Ⓐ Ⓑ Ⓒ Ⓓ Ⓔ   31 Ⓐ Ⓑ Ⓒ Ⓓ Ⓔ   51 Ⓐ Ⓑ Ⓒ Ⓓ Ⓔ   71 Ⓐ Ⓑ Ⓒ Ⓓ Ⓔ   91 Ⓐ Ⓑ Ⓒ Ⓓ Ⓔ
12 Ⓐ Ⓑ Ⓒ Ⓓ Ⓔ   32 Ⓐ Ⓑ Ⓒ Ⓓ Ⓔ   52 Ⓐ Ⓑ Ⓒ Ⓓ Ⓔ   72 Ⓐ Ⓑ Ⓒ Ⓓ Ⓔ   92 Ⓐ Ⓑ Ⓒ Ⓓ Ⓔ
13 Ⓐ Ⓑ Ⓒ Ⓓ Ⓔ   33 Ⓐ Ⓑ Ⓒ Ⓓ Ⓔ   53 Ⓐ Ⓑ Ⓒ Ⓓ Ⓔ   73 Ⓐ Ⓑ Ⓒ Ⓓ Ⓔ   93 Ⓐ Ⓑ Ⓒ Ⓓ Ⓔ
14 Ⓐ Ⓑ Ⓒ Ⓓ Ⓔ   34 Ⓐ Ⓑ Ⓒ Ⓓ Ⓔ   54 Ⓐ Ⓑ Ⓒ Ⓓ Ⓔ   74 Ⓐ Ⓑ Ⓒ Ⓓ Ⓔ   94 Ⓐ Ⓑ Ⓒ Ⓓ Ⓔ
15 Ⓐ Ⓑ Ⓒ Ⓓ Ⓔ   35 Ⓐ Ⓑ Ⓒ Ⓓ Ⓔ   55 Ⓐ Ⓑ Ⓒ Ⓓ Ⓔ   75 Ⓐ Ⓑ Ⓒ Ⓓ Ⓔ   95 Ⓐ Ⓑ Ⓒ Ⓓ Ⓔ
16 Ⓐ Ⓑ Ⓒ Ⓓ Ⓔ   36 Ⓐ Ⓑ Ⓒ Ⓓ Ⓔ   56 Ⓐ Ⓑ Ⓒ Ⓓ Ⓔ   76 Ⓐ Ⓑ Ⓒ Ⓓ Ⓔ   96 Ⓐ Ⓑ Ⓒ Ⓓ Ⓔ
17 Ⓐ Ⓑ Ⓒ Ⓓ Ⓔ   37 Ⓐ Ⓑ Ⓒ Ⓓ Ⓔ   57 Ⓐ Ⓑ Ⓒ Ⓓ Ⓔ   77 Ⓐ Ⓑ Ⓒ Ⓓ Ⓔ   97 Ⓐ Ⓑ Ⓒ Ⓓ Ⓔ
18 Ⓐ Ⓑ Ⓒ Ⓓ Ⓔ   38 Ⓐ Ⓑ Ⓒ Ⓓ Ⓔ   58 Ⓐ Ⓑ Ⓒ Ⓓ Ⓔ   78 Ⓐ Ⓑ Ⓒ Ⓓ Ⓔ   98 Ⓐ Ⓑ Ⓒ Ⓓ Ⓔ
19 Ⓐ Ⓑ Ⓒ Ⓓ Ⓔ   39 Ⓐ Ⓑ Ⓒ Ⓓ Ⓔ   59 Ⓐ Ⓑ Ⓒ Ⓓ Ⓔ   79 Ⓐ Ⓑ Ⓒ Ⓓ Ⓔ   99 Ⓐ Ⓑ Ⓒ Ⓓ Ⓔ
20 Ⓐ Ⓑ Ⓒ Ⓓ Ⓔ   40 Ⓐ Ⓑ Ⓒ Ⓓ Ⓔ   60 Ⓐ Ⓑ Ⓒ Ⓓ Ⓔ   80 Ⓐ Ⓑ Ⓒ Ⓓ Ⓔ   100 Ⓐ Ⓑ Ⓒ Ⓓ Ⓔ

PRACTICE TEST 3

ANSWERS AND EXPLANATIONS

QUICK-SCORE ANSWERS

1. B	9. A	17. D	25. A	33. D	41. B	48. E	55. A	62. A	69. C
2. E	10. D	18. E	26. D	34. C	42. B	49. E	56. E	63. A	70. C
3. D	11. C	19. A	27. B	35. E	43. B	50. E	57. C	64. B	71. E
4. D	12. A	20. D	28. C	36. C	44. A	51. C	58. C	65. B	72. C
5. B	13. A	21. B	29. A	37. E	45. B	52. D	59. D	66. B	73. C
6. A	14. B	22. E	30. C	38. C	46. A	53. E	60. C	67. C	74. D
7. C	15. D	23. A	31. C	39. C	47. B	54. D	61. E	68. B	75. C
8. E	16. E	24. B	32. A	40. E					

ANSWERS AND EXPLANATIONS

ANSWERS TO PART A, QUESTIONS 1–14

1. **The correct answer is (B).** The velocity of the object is constant between the 3rd and 4th seconds. An acceleration is defined as the time rate change in velocity, $a = \dfrac{\Delta v}{\Delta t}$. If there is no change in velocity, there is no acceleration.

2. **The correct answer is (E).** The magnitude of the acceleration is greatest between $t = 10s$ and $t = 11s$. The slope of the graph is steeper between these two times than anywhere else on the graph.

3. **The correct answer is (D).** The distance the object travels is the product of the average velocity multiplied by the time.

4. **The correct answer is (D).** The current in a series circuit remains the same throughout the entire circuit. Graph D shows a constant value of current from point A through point G.

5. **The correct answer is (B).** The resistance through the circuit is cumulative. At each point the resistance has increased by the same amount. Remember that the resistors are all the same value. Graph B shows the resistance increase by the same value from point to point.

6. **The correct answer is (A).** The voltage measurement throughout the circuit decreases as the distance from point A increases and the number of resistors the current has passed through increases. Each increase in the resistance produces a corresponding decrease in voltage.

7. **The correct answer is (C).** The part of the cycle represented by the letter C is compression. During compression, the system heat is kept constant by allowing heat to escape from the system.

8. **The correct answer is (E).** The work done by a heat engine is the area under the pressure-volume curve. The work done under the A part of the diagram is positive work, but the negative work done under the C part of the diagram must be subtracted, leaving the work as E.

9. **The correct answer is (A).** The volume of the enclosed gas increases during phase A.

10. **The correct answer is (D).** As long as the object is moving, the frictional force is a constant force that opposes motion. This is shown in graph D.

11. **The correct answer is (C).** The object is subjected to a constant negative acceleration (it is slowing down). The velocity time graph for an object that is subjected to a constant acceleration is a linear curve, as in the graph shown in C.

12. **The correct answer is (A).** The object increases its displacement from the origin until it stops moving. Then the object remains in its position where its motion ceased.

13. **The correct answer is (A).** The parent nucleus is the nucleus with which the nuclear reaction begins. In this case $^{235}_{92}U$ is the parent nucleus.

14. **The correct answer is (B).** An alpha particle is a helium nucleus. That is, it is $^{4}_{2}He$.

15. **The correct answer is (D).** The beta particle is a high-energy electron. It has the symbol $^{0}_{-1}e$, or β.

ANSWERS TO PART B, QUESTIONS 16–75

16. **The correct answer is (E).** All of the choices exhibit a wave nature at some time. All waves can interfere with one another, either constructively or destructively.

17. **The correct answer is (D).** Objects that are touched by the charging body are charged by *conduction*. Objects that are not touched by the charging body are charged by *induction*. The negative charge is placed on the pith ball when a positively charged rod is brought near the pith ball. The pith ball is touched by a body other than the charging rod, which provides a path for electrons to flow onto the pith ball and charges the pith ball oppositely from the charge on the rod.

18. **The correct answer is (E).** The force the particles exert on one another increases as the inverse of the square of the distance between the two particles.

19. **The correct answer is (A).** The higher the frequency of the light waves, the higher the energy of the photons. Of the choices presented, blue light has the highest frequency.

20. **The correct answer is (D).** The acceleration affects the spider in the same way that it affects the observer. If the elevator were in free fall, everything in the elevator would free fall together, including the spider. If the elevator accelerates upward, the spider experiences an apparent gain in weight, just as a person riding in the elevator does.

21. **The correct answer is (B).** When water freezes, it becomes less dense. Therefore, when ice cubes are placed into liquid water, they displace a volume of water equal to their weight. When the ice melts no further, volume is added to the container.

22. **The correct answer is (E).** At *STP* the molar volume of any gas is 22.4 *L*. Standard pressure and volume are also the same for all gases, and of course a mole of any substance is the same number of particles.

23. **The correct answer is (A).** The ratio between the number of turns in the primary and the number of turns in the secondary is equal to the ratio of the secondary voltage and the primary voltage $\dfrac{24V}{120V} = .2$, or 1:5.

24. **The correct answer is (B).** The equilibrant vector is pointed into the third quadrant. The y component for a vector in the third quadrant also points into the third quadrant.

25. **The correct answer is (A).** Gravity has nothing to do with heat transfer. Both objects will reach the same temperature when they have reached equilibrium.

26. **The correct answer is (D).** The image produced when the object is placed inside the focal distance of a convex mirror is virtual and reduced.

27. **The correct answer is (B).** Since the centripetal force is found with the equation $F_c = \dfrac{(m)(v^2)}{r}$ we can change the r value to $.5r$ and substitute it into the equation and solve to find the relative force. $F_c = \dfrac{(m)(v^2)}{.5r}$. Clearly the force will be double when the radius is halved and the velocity remains the same.

28. **The correct answer is (C).** The heat added to the system minus the work done by the system yields the heat that is exhausted between points CD.

29. **The correct answer is (A).** The definition of the frequency of a wave system is the number of waves per unit time, which is the same as saying the number of crests that pass a given point over a given time.

30. **The correct answer is (C).** The centripetal acceleration is found with the following equation: $\dfrac{v^2}{r} = \dfrac{(2.5\text{m/s})^2}{.22\text{m}} = 28.4\text{m/s}^2$.

31. **The correct answer is (C).** The specific heat capacity of a substance is defined as the amount of heat required to raise 1 g of the substance by $1°C$. If substance A has a specific heat capacity that is twice the specific heat capacity of substance B, that means twice as much heat is required to raise the temperature of substance A as is required for substance B. The converse is also true—the heat required to raise the temperature of substance A by $1°C$ will raise the temperature of substance B by $2°C$.

32. **The correct answer is (A).** Centripetal force is also called the center-seeking force. Both the tire and the golf ball roll about their centers of mass, which are located in the center of the objects. The centripetal force for the two cannot be equal because the radii of the two objects are different, yet they roll with the same tangential velocity.

33. **The correct answer is (D).** The block slides down the incline at a constant rate. This tells us that the frictional force (F_f) is equal to the force down the plane (F_{11}). When the block is pulled up the plane at a constant rate, the force down the plane and the frictional force add together. The tension in the rope therefore equals the two of them. The inclined plane is at an angle of 30°, and the sine of 30° is .5, which when multiplied times the weight is equal to one half the weight of the block. The frictional force

is also equal to half the weight of the block ($F_f = F_{11}$), so the tension in the rope is equal to the sum of the two forces, which is equal to the weight of the block.

34. **The correct answer is (C).** The closer a satellite orbits the earth, the faster its period of rotation. The farther a satellite orbits from the earth, the longer its period of rotation.

35. **The correct answer is (E).** Look at the graph of velocity. It is a straight line. The velocity increases by the same amount each second, additional proof that $V = at$.

Time	Acceleration	Velocity	Increase
1 sec	9.8 m/s^2	9.8 m/s	+9.8m/s
2 sec	9.8 m/s^2	19.6 m/s	+9.8m/s
3 sec	9.8 m/s^2	29.4 m/s	+9.8m/s
4 sec	9.8 m/s^2	39.2 m/s	+9.8m/s

36. **The correct answer is (C).** The frictional force between two surfaces will increase when the normal force increases, but the coefficient of friction between two surfaces is constant.

37. **The correct answer is (E).** All of the methods listed cause the wire to move through the magnetic field or lines of force, which induces a voltage into the wire.

38. **The correct answer is (C).** Scientists look at the light from a star by passing the light through a spectometer, which separates the starlight into the individual line spectra of the elements that are burning in the star.

39. **The correct answer is (C).** Gases provide electron sources that can be excited by the photons of light that strike them.

40. **The correct answer is (E).** The electric field between a pair of parallel plates is uniform in nature. Therefore any charged particle within the field experiences the same force no matter where it is located in the field.

41. **The correct answer is (B).** When a light ray enters an optically denser material, it bends toward the normal because the light slows down in the material.

42. **The correct answer is (B).** All the elements on the periodic table were combined in the fusion furnace of some past star. In

fact all substances in existence were formed from elements which were formed in stars.

43. **The correct answer is (B).** The toy rocket achieves zero velocity at the exact top of its flight when it is not moving upward nor is it moving downward. It is constantly accelerated toward the earth while it is in free fall.

44. **The correct answer is (A).** The force pairs discussed in the third law are equal in magnitude, oppositely directed, and operate on differing bodies.

45. **The correct answer is (B).** As the gas undergoes air adiabatic compression, its temperature increases.

46. **The correct answer is (A).** The tension in the rope increases as the angle decreases because the sum of the four forces leads to the following: $\sum F = 2T = \dfrac{Wt}{\sin\theta}$. Note that as the angle becomes smaller, its sine also becomes smaller. This causes the tension in the line to increase drastically.

47. **The correct answer is (B).** According to Ohm's Law, the current is equal to $I = \dfrac{V}{r}$. Solving for the current, we have

$$\frac{12V}{20\Omega} = .6 \text{ ampere.}$$

48. **The correct answer is (E).** A chain reaction (industrial fission is a chain reaction) continues because of the neutrons that are emitted in the fissioning of each U-235 atom.

49. **The correct answer is (E).** The largest force a magnetic field exerts on a moving charged particle occurs when the particle crosses the most lines of force. This occurs when the particle enters a magnetic field at right angles to the field.

50. **The correct answer is (E).** The process of reflection occurs when the direction of a wave is changed because the wave strikes a barrier (which in this occasion is a mirror).

51. **The correct answer is (C).** The proton carries a positive charge, and it will be repelled by the positive plate and attracted to the negative plate.

52. **The correct answer is (D).** An ideal gas follows Boyle's law. If the pressure increases by a factor of four, the volume decreases by a factor of four. Whatever the change in one, the other is indirectly related by the same factor.

53. **The correct answer is (E).** The electron carries a negative charge of $1.6 \times 10^{-19}C$, which is a tiny amount of energy. The electron volt is the energy required to move 1 electron through an electric potential of 1 volt.

54. **The correct answer is (D).** The potential energy transforms into kinetic energy, or the pile driver falls. At the end of the fall, all the kinetic energy the pile driver has is converted into frictional work to drive the post into the ground.

55. **The correct answer is (A).** The longest leg the dog walked is the eastward vector. The fact that some of the length of the vector was later cancelled when the dog walked in the opposite direction does not change the length of the individual vector.

56. **The correct answer is (E).** After the zeroth fringe, each bright spot represents a position of convergence for the two light beams. The bright spots represent the number of whole wavelengths difference in the path length taken by one of the light beams compared to the other light beam.

57. **The correct answer is (C).** The car rolls down a 20 m long incline that is raised at 15° from the horizontal. Using trigonometry (sin 15°)(20 m) we find the car "falls" 5.125 m. Using the PE = KE relationship, we have $mgh = \frac{1}{2}mv^2$. The masses factor out, leaving $gh = \frac{1}{2}v^2$, leading to $v = \sqrt{2gh}$. The answer is 10 m/s.

58. **The correct answer is (C).** Sound waves are compressional waves; thus they need a medium through which they can move. A vacuum does not provide a way for the compressions to move along.

59. **The correct answer is (D).** While the light ray is moving through an optically denser material, its velocity decreases.

60. **The correct answer is (C).** The light ray is refracted toward the normal passes through the glass and is incident on the mirrored surface. The angle of incidence equals the angle of reflection, and the light ray reflects toward the same surface it entered. At

the surface the light ray refracts away from the normal, producing a larger angle than the approach (incident) angle. The angle at which the ray leaves the glass block is the same angle at which it originally approached the glass block.

61. **The correct answer is (E).** Both light and radio waves are electromagnetic radiation. The difference between the two is their frequency.

62. **The correct answer is (A).** The force the two electrons exert on each other decreases when the distance between the two particles increases. A variation of a parabolic curve that is shown is graph A.

63. **The correct answer is (A).** This is an example of an elastic collision. The momentum of the cue ball transfers to the red ball.

64. **The correct answer is (B).** Convex mirrors only produce virtual images. That is because the light rays are diverged when they are incident to the surface of the mirror

65. **The correct answer is (B).** The resistance is calculated by using the power equation, $R = \dfrac{V^2}{P}$. The solutions are:

$$\frac{18V^2}{4.5\,\text{Watts}} = 72\Omega \text{ and } \frac{18V^2}{6.75\,\text{Watts}} = 48\Omega.$$

66. **The correct answer is (B).** The Doppler Shift is useful for all kinds of waves, including light. When a star or any object that is producing waves approaches, the individual wave fronts are contacted at a higher rate. In the case of stars, the higher rate at which the wave fronts are contacted causes the starlight to move toward the blue range.

67. **The correct answer is (C).** The volt is defined as the force required to move a unit charge through a distance, or the work done per unit charge.

68. **The correct answer is (B).** The angular acceleration is found by dividing the change in angular velocity by the change in time:

$$\frac{8000\dfrac{\text{rad}}{\text{s}}}{25\text{s}} = 320\frac{\text{rad}}{\text{s}^2}.$$

69. **The correct answer is (C).** The problem may be solved in several ways. Perhaps the best solution is a little thought. The potential energy and the kinetic energy are equal to one another when the object has fallen half the distance to the ground, or 10 m. All we have to do now is treat the problem as a free fall problem by restating the situation a little. The velocity of an object that starts from rest and free falls 10 m? The solution is found by $v_f = \sqrt{2gs}$.

70. **The correct answer is (C).** When the variable resistor is moved toward the right, more of the resistance value of the variable resistor is bypassed which means there is less resistance in the circuit. A decrease in the resistance of a circuit allows more current to flow (Ohm's Law). Since there is more current flowing in the circuit the fan has more current flowing through it too, and the fan runs faster.

71. **The correct answer is (E).** The pulse shown strikes a fixed barrier. The wave is reflected and inverted.

72. **The correct answer is (C).** All forces occur in pairs, are equal in magnitude and oppositely directed. The pairs of forces are the ball on the window, and the window on the ball, which are equal and opposite.

73. **The correct answer is (C).** When the voltage is disconnected there is a small lag time between the disconnection of the current and the ceasing of the flow because the magnetic field, which is induced into the wires, collapses. This produces a current flow that causes the spark.

74. **The correct answer is (D).** An electric current is passed through an electromagnet or rotor, which causes it to spin within an applied magnetic field. The spinning rotor is the source of mechanical energy that is derived from electrical energy.

75. **The correct answer is (C).** The two wires have a magnetic field around them that is caused by the current in the wires. The two fields are in opposition, which weakens them on the sides closest to one another. This allows the unweakened field on the other (outside) of the wires to push the two wires together.

Practice Test 4

PHYSICS TEST

PRACTICE TEST 4

PHYSICS TEST

While you have taken many standardized tests and know to blacken completely the ovals on the answer sheets and to erase completely any errors, the instructions for the SAT II Physics Test differ in an important way from the directions for other standardized tests. You need to indicate on the answer key which test you are taking. The instructions on the answer sheet will tell you to fill out the top portion of the answer sheet exactly as shown.

1. Print PHYSICS on the line under the words *Subject Test (print)*.
2. In the shaded box labeled *Test Code* fill in four ovals:

    —Fill in oval 1 in the row labeled V.
    —Fill in oval 6 in the row labeled W.
    —Fill in oval 3 in the row labeled X.
    —Fill in oval C in the row labeled Y.
    —Leave the ovals in row Q blank.

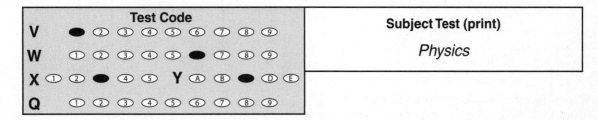

There are two additional questions that you will be asked to answer. One is "How many semesters of physics have you taken in high school?" The other question lists courses and asks you to mark those that you have taken. You will be told which ovals to fill in for each question. The College Board is collecting statistical information. If you choose to answer, you will use the key that is provided and blacken the appropriate ovals in row Q. You may also choose not to answer, and that will not affect your grade.

When everyone has completed filling in this portion of the answer sheet, the supervisor will tell you to turn the page and begin. The answer sheet has 100 numbered ovals, but there are only approximately 75 multiple-choice questions on the test, so be sure to use only ovals 1 to 75 (or however many questions there are) to record your answers.

PHYSICS TEST

Part A

Questions 1–3 relate to the diagram shown below.

Questions 4–6 relate to the information shown below.

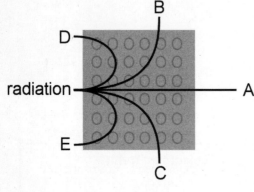

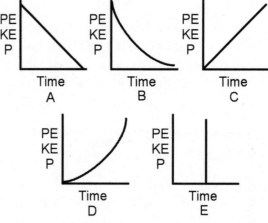

1. Which line shows the path of alpha radiation in a magnetic field?

2. Which line shows the path of beta radiation in a magnetic field?

3. Which line shows the path of gamma radiation in a magnetic field?

An object free falls 15m from the top of a ladder. Select the graph that best describes the following quantities during the fall.

4. The potential energy of the object

5. The kinetic energy of the object

6. The momentum of the object

PHYSICS TEST—*Continued*

Questions 7-9 relate to particles placed in the electric field shown below.

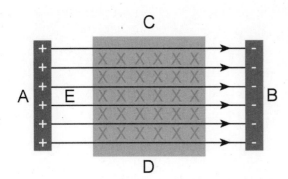

A particle is placed into the electric field (E), which has a magnetic field superimposed on it as shown. Where in the electric field will the three particles named below be located after a short period of time if they start at Point E?

7. The particle is a proton.

8. The particle is a neutron.

9. The particle is an electron.

Questions 10-13 relate to the electron energy level diagram below. The questions are about a hydrogen electron located at E_3.

$-.38eV$	_____	$n=6$
$-.54ev$	_____	$n=5$
$-.85eV$	_____	$n=4$
$-1.52eV$	_____	$n=3$
$-3.39eV$	_____	$n=2$
$-13.6eV$	_____	$n=1$

(A) $+66eV$

(B) $+.98eV$

(C) $-1.87eV$

(D) $-10.2eV$

(E) $+12.08eV$

10. What is the emission energy when it moves to E_2?

11. What is the absorbed energy when it moves to E_5?

12. What is the emission energy when it moves to E_1?

GO ON TO THE NEXT PAGE

<u>Questions 13-15</u> relate to the electric circuit below.

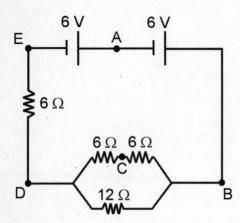

13. Through which point does half the total current pass?

14. At which point is all the voltage in the circuit dropped to zero?

15. At which point is the voltage halved?

PHYSICS TEST—*Continued*

Part B

> **Directions:** Each question or statement below is followed by five possible answers. In each case, select the best possible answer and fill in the corresponding oval on the answer sheet.

16. An electron is allowed to freely move between a pair of parallel plates that have a 1.5 volt potential difference. The electron starts at the negative plate. The velocity of the electron as it strikes the positive plate is most nearly
    (A) 7.3×10^{-8} m/s
    (B) 7.3×10^{-5} m/s
    (C) 7.3×10^{5} m/s
    (D) 7.3×10^{8} m/s
    (E) 7.3×10^{11} m/s

17. The half-life of a radioisotope is one week. How much of the substance is left after a 28-day period?

    (A) $\dfrac{1}{2}$
    (B) $\dfrac{1}{4}$
    (C) $\dfrac{1}{8}$
    (D) $\dfrac{1}{16}$
    (E) $\dfrac{1}{32}$

18. All of the following are examples of electromagnetic waves EXCEPT
    (A) X-rays.
    (B) gamma rays.
    (C) sound waves.
    (D) radio waves.
    (E) light waves.

19. A batter hits a long fly ball. Neglecting air resistance, the baseball's horizontal component of speed is constant because it
    (A) is not acted upon by any forces.
    (B) is not acted upon by gravitational sources.
    (C) is not acted upon by any vertical forces.
    (D) is not acted upon by any horizontal forces.
    (E) the net forces acting on the baseball are zero.

20. Two spheres are placed into free fall from rest. Sphere B has a mass three times larger than sphere A. Which statement(s) correctly explains the situation?

    I.   Sphere B falls faster.
    II.   Sphere B has more momentum when the two reach the ground.
    III. Both spheres reach the ground with the same kinetic energy.

    (A) I only
    (B) II only
    (C) I and III only
    (D) II and II only
    (E) I, II, and III

GO ON TO THE NEXT PAGE

21. When Johannes Kepler developed his laws for the movement of planetary bodies, one of the laws stated that the orbits of the planets about the sun are
    (A) circular.
    (B) elliptical.
    (C) parabolic.
    (D) sinusoidal.
    (E) straight lines.

22. The purpose of a transformer is to do which of the following?
    (A) Change voltage
    (B) Reduce resistance
    (C) Decrease heat transfer
    (D) Increase magnetic fields
    (E) Reverse current flow

23. Astronomers can tell whether a star is approaching or receding from the earth by the
    (A) absorption spectra of the star.
    (B) Doppler shift of the starlight.
    (C) temperature of the star.
    (D) brightness of the starlight.
    (E) thermal signature of the star.

24. A batter hits a long fly ball. Neglecting friction, which of the following statements is/are true?

    I. The time the ball is in free fall determines the horizontal distance it travels.
    II. The ball reaches its maximum velocity at the highest point of its flight.
    III. The upward velocity can never be greater than the horizontal velocity.

    (A) I only
    (B) II only
    (C) I and III only
    (D) II and III only
    (E) I, II, and III

25. Electromagnetic induction occurs in a wire when a change occurs in the
    (A) current in the wire.
    (B) intensity of the electric field of the wire.
    (C) voltage applied to the wire.
    (D) magnetic field intensity applied to the wire.
    (E) resistance is added to the wire.

26. Whether a substance is a solid, liquid or gas is determined by
    (A) conductivity.
    (B) number of protons.
    (C) temperature.
    (D) number of neutrons.
    (E) resistively.

344

Peterson's SAT II Success: Physics

PHYSICS TEST—*Continued*

27. A pile of 11 books weighing 2 N each is sitting on a table. With what total force does the table push back on the books?
    - (A) 2N
    - (B) 11N
    - (C) 22N
    - (D) 33N
    - (E) 44N

28. Which of the following statements best describes the relationship between two objects that are in thermal equilibrium?
    - (A) Their masses are equal.
    - (B) Their volumes are equal.
    - (C) Their density is equal.
    - (D) Their heat content is equal.
    - (E) Their temperatures are equal.

29. Two vectors X and Y are added together. Which of the following statements could be true?

    - I. The resultant magnitude is smaller than X.
    - II. The resultant magnitude is larger than Y.
    - III. The resultant direction is the same as either X or Y.

    - (A) I only
    - (B) II only
    - (C) I and III only
    - (D) II and III only
    - (E) I, II, and III

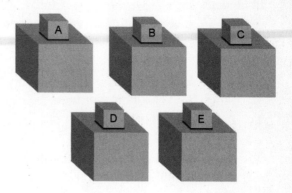

30. Five blocks having equal mass but made of different substances, as shown above, are heated to 100°C and placed on separate 10 kg blocks of ice that are at a temperature of 0°C. Which substance melts the greatest amount of ice?
    - (A) The substance with the lowest specific heat.
    - (B) The substance with the highest specific heat.
    - (C) The substance with the greatest surface area.
    - (D) The substance with the smallest surface area.
    - (E) The substance that started with the highest temperature.

GO ON TO THE NEXT PAGE

31. When can the instantaneous velocity of an object be equal to the average velocity of an object?
    (A) It can never equal the average velocity.
    (B) It can only equal the average velocity during acceleration.
    (C) It can only equal the average velocity when the velocity is constant.
    (D) It is always equal at the end of a displacement.
    (E) They are equal at the end of a displacement

32. How does one use the right hand rule to determine the direction of the force applied to a current carrying wire?
    (A) Point the fingers of the right hand in the same direction as the magnetic lines of force.
    (B) Point the thumb at right angles to the lines of force.
    (C) Point the fingers of the right hand along the wire in the direction of the current.
    (D) Point the thumb in the direction of the magnetic lines of force.
    (E) Point the fingers of the right hand against the direction of the magnetic lines of force.

33. When blue light is shined onto a certain metal, no electrons are ejected. Which of the following lights might eject electrons from the metal?
    (A) Red
    (B) Yellow
    (C) Green
    (D) Infrared
    (E) Ultraviolet

34. An astronaut visits the planet Mars, which has less of a gravitational acceleration than the earth. While on Mars, the astronaut will notice that his
    (A) weight is less and his mass is greater.
    (B) weight is the same and his mass is the same.
    (C) weight is less and his mass is the same.
    (D) weight is the same and his mass is less.
    (E) weight is less and his mass is less.

35. A negative ion is an object that has
    (A) more electrons than neutrons.
    (B) more electrons than protons.
    (C) more protons that neutrons.
    (D) more protons than electrons.
    (E) more neutrons than electrons or protons.

PHYSICS TEST—Continued

36. When it is known that a net force is operating on an object, it is known that the object is
    (A) moving with constant velocity.
    (B) losing mass.
    (C) at rest.
    (D) being accelerated.
    (E) gaining weight.

37. Which wave characteristic describes the product of the frequency and the wavelength?
    (A) Frequency
    (B) Amplitude
    (C) Wavelength
    (D) Velocity
    (E) Period

38. Einstein's theory of relativity states that all the laws of nature are the same in
    (A) accelerating reference frames.
    (B) constant velocity reference frames.
    (C) oscillating reference frames.
    (D) vibrating reference frames.
    (E) circling reference frames.

39. A 24 *V* battery supplies a total current of .75 amperes to a circuit. How much power does the battery supply to the circuit?
    (A) .04 watts
    (B) 13.5 watts
    (C) 18 watts
    (D) 32 watts
    (E) 32 watts

40. Two children are riding a merry-go-round. Child (*P*) rides on a pony on the outside rim of the merry-go-round, while Child (*L*) rides a lion on the inside rim of the merry-go-round. At the end of the ride, which of the following statements is true?
    (A) Child (*P*) had the largest angular displacement.
    (B) Child (*L*) had the largest tangential displacement.
    (C) Child (*P*) had the largest tangential velocity.
    (D) Child (*L*) had the largest angular velocity.
    (E) Child (*L*) had the largest linear acceleration.

GO ON TO THE NEXT PAGE

41. Two high school students attempt to push a car uphill. The car rolls downhill against them for a distance of 10 m before they can bring it to a stop. If both students pushed on the car with a force of 1000N while it rolled downhill, how much work did they do?

    (A)   0
    (B)   1000 J
    (C)   −1000 J
    (D)   10,000 J
    (E)   −10,000 J

42. During a collision between two objects, the kinetic energy is conserved. Which statement best describes the momentum after the collision?

    (A) The momentum equals the kinetic energy.
    (B) The momentum may be conserved.
    (C) The momentum must be conserved.
    (D) The momentum decreases by half.
    (E) The momentum increases to double the original value.

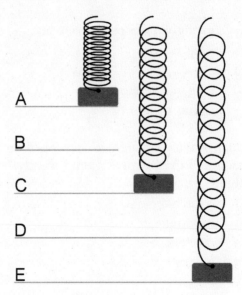

43. The hanging spring shown above has a mass attached to it. The spring is set in motion by displacing the mass downward and releasing it. At which point is the kinetic energy of the mass the greatest value? (Point A is the maximum compression of the spring, and Point E is the maximum expansion of the spring.)

    (A) Point A
    (B) Point B
    (C) Point C
    (D) Point D
    (E) Point E

Peterson's SAT II Success: Physics

PHYSICS TEST—*Continued*

44. A gamma ray is emitted from the nucleus of an unstable atom. What is the result?
    (A) The number of electrons decreases.
    (B) The number of electrons increases.
    (C) The mass of the nucleus increases.
    (D) The mass of the nucleus decreases.
    (E) The mass of the nucleus remains the same.

45. Which of the following statements is true about an ideal gas contained at a fixed volume when its temperature is raised?
    (A) The density of the gas decreases.
    (B) The average velocity of the gas particles increases.
    (C) The density of the gas increases.
    (D) The pressure remains constant.
    (E) The pressure decreases.

46. Two objects have the same mass and are located near each other at a distance (r). If the mass of one of the objects is doubled and the mass of the other object is tripled, what would be the change in gravitational attraction between them?
    (A) Decrease by 1/6
    (B) Decrease by 2/3
    (C) Increase by 3/2
    (D) Increase by 5
    (E) Increase by 6

47. The critical angle for a beam of light passing from a diamond into the air is 24.4°. This means that any light rays that strike the surface interface between the diamond and the air with an angle less than 24.4° are
    (A) completely reflected.
    (B) partially reflected and partially refracted.
    (C) completely absorbed.
    (D) partially absorbed and partially transmitted.
    (E) completely transmitted.

48. A pendulum has a 1 second period of vibration. At what period in time would the string have to break for the pendulum bob to fly away the maximum possible distance from, but not below, the rest position of the pendulum bob? (The zero point for the pendulum at $t = 0$ is at the maximum displacement)
    (A) $t = .125$ sec
    (B) $t = .25$ sec
    (C) $t = .375$ sec
    (D) $t = .5$ sec
    (E) $t = .625$ sec

GO ON TO THE NEXT PAGE

49. A 400N box is suspended motionless from a steel frame by two ropes, A and B, which hang straight up and down. Which of the following statements about the tension in the two ropes is correct?

   (A) The tension in rope A is larger than in rope B.

   (B) The tension in rope B is larger than in rope A.

   (C) The tension in the two ropes is greater than 400N.

   (D) The tension in the two ropes is less than 400N.

   (E) The tension in the two ropes is equal to 400N.

50. When a skydiver jumps from an airplane, he eventually reaches terminal velocity. At that time the force of the air resistance is

   (A) equal to his mass.

   (B) equal to twice his mass.

   (C) equal to his weight.

   (D) equal to twice his weight.

   (E) equal to 1/2 his weight.

51. During an electrostatics experiment a student touches an electroscope with a negatively charged rod, and the leaves of the electroscope separate. What will be the result when a second positively charged rod is brought near, but *does not touch*, the electroscope?

   (A) The leaves will begin to flutter.

   (B) The leaves will separate further.

   (C) The leaves will move closer together.

   (D) The leaves will be unaffected.

   (E) None of the above will happen.

52. An object is placed inside the focal point of a concave mirror. Which of the following describes the image?

   (A) Virtual, erect, and reduced

   (B) Virtual, erect, and magnified

   (C) Virtual, inverted, and reduced

   (D) Real, erect, and reduced

   (E) Real, inverted, and magnified

53. Two separate 10L containers each contain a different gas. One gas is at a temperature of 400K; the other gas is at a temperature of 200K. When both gases are added to the same 10L container, which statement is correct?

   I.   The hotter gas loses heat to the cooler gas.

   II. The hotter gas increases in temperature when the two are squeezed together.

   III. The cooler gas decreases in temperature when placed into the second container.

   (A) I only

   (B) II only

   (C) I and III only

   (D) II and III only

   (E) I, II, and III

PHYSICS TEST—*Continued*

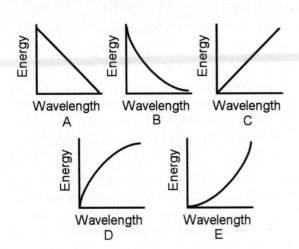

54. Select the graph shown above that most correctly represents the relationship between the energy of the photon and its wavelength.
    (A) Graph A
    (B) Graph B
    (C) Graph C
    (D) Graph D
    (E) Graph E

55. Water drips from a leaky rainspout that is located at the top of a high building. The droplets of water fall at an interval of 1/2 second. As time passes, the distance between two consecutive drops of water
    (A) decreases in a linear manner.
    (B) increases in a linear manner.
    (C) remains the same.
    (D) decreases in a parabolic manner.
    (E) increases in a parabolic manner.

56. A pendulum swings at a rate of .75 vibration/sec. Which of the following changes could be made to the pendulum to cause the period of the pendulum to increase?
    (A) Mass of the bob was increased
    (B) Length of the pendulum was increased
    (C) Mass of the bob was decreased
    (D) Length of the pendulum was decreased
    (E) The material from which the pendulum bob was made

57. A constant voltage power source is in a circuit where the resistance is increased by four. The voltage in the circuit
    (A) increases by two.
    (B) increases by four.
    (C) decreases by two.
    (D) decreases by four.
    (E) remains the same.

GO ON TO THE NEXT PAGE

58. Materials called dielectrics are placed between the plates of capacitors to
    (A) speed the current flow.
    (B) slow the current flow.
    (C) reduce change leakage from the capacitor.
    (D) increase capacitance of the capacitor.
    (E) decrease capacitance of the capacitor.

59. Water waves strike a solid barrier in which there is a single small opening. Waves that pass through the opening
    (A) converge.
    (B) fan out.
    (C) invert.
    (D) interfere.
    (E) polarize.

60. A mass is suspended by a rubber band. The rubber band is stretched by the weight of the mass, but it is not moving. The action force that causes the rubber band to stretch comes from the earth. What is the reaction force of the force pair?
    (A) The rubber band pulling on the mass
    (B) The rubber band pulling on the earth
    (C) The mass pulling on the rubber band
    (D) The mass pulling on the earth
    (E) The earth pulling on the rubber band

61. What is the one factor that distinguishes each element from every other element?
    (A) The number of protons in the nucleus
    (B) The number of neutrons in the nucleus
    (C) The number of electrons about the nucleus
    (D) The total mass of the nucleus (protons plus neutrons)
    (E) Its position on the periodic table

62. When a switch is closed to operate a DC circuit, the electrons that cause the current
    (A) travel from the negative plate of the battery to the positive plate.
    (B) travel from the positive plate of the battery to the negative plate.
    (C) travel from one resistance to the next resistance.
    (D) travel from the negative plate of the battery to the positive plate inside the battery.
    (E) travel from one atom in the circuit to the next atom.

63. A car skids a distance of 54 m on a dry road. What was the velocity of the car when the skid began if the coefficient of friction between the tires and the road is .46?
    (A) 16 m/s
    (B) 22 m/s
    (C) 28 m/s
    (D) 34 m/s
    (E) Velocity cannot be determined with the information given.

64. A force of 53N is applied to a 176.4N object that is at rest. A frictional force of 8N must be overcome to move the object. What is the acceleration of the object?

    (A)   .3 m/s²
    (B)   2.5 m/s²
    (C)   2.9 m/s²
    (D)   4.24 m/s²
    (E)   6.625 m/s²

65. Two objects A and B are placed into free fall 14.7 m above the ground at exactly the same time. Object A reaches the ground in exactly 1 second, and object B reaches the ground in exactly 3 seconds. Which of the following is/are true?

    I.   Object B was thrown horizontally.
    II.   Both objects were thrown.
    III. Neither object was thrown.

    (A) I only
    (B) II only
    (C) I and III only
    (D) II and III only
    (E) I, II, and III

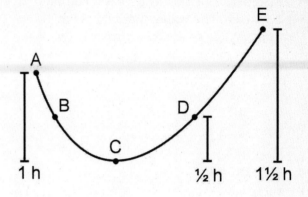

66. A 50 gram bead slides on a frictionless wire as shown above. At what point on the wire will the bead come to a complete stop?

    (A) Point A
    (B) Point B
    (C) Point C
    (D) Point D
    (E) Point E

67. A container holds 1 mole of an ideal gas. If the temperature of the gas is held constant and the volume of the gas is halved, the pressure of the gas will double. This happens because

    (A) the gas particles have gained energy.
    (B) the gas particles collide with one another more often.
    (C) the gas particles move more slowly.
    (D) the gas particles collide with the container walls less often.
    (E) the gas particles collide with the container walls more often.

PHYSICS TEST—*Continued*

68. A step-down transformer has a coil ratio of 1.5 to 17. The voltage applied at the primary side of the transformer is 136 *V*. What is the output voltage of the transformer?
    (A) 1.2 *V*
    (B) 1.5 *V*
    (C) 5.25 *V*
    (D) 12 *V*
    (E) 18.75 *V*

69. A car is driving along a level road at a constant 60 km/hr. The force acting on the car from the tires of the car is
    (A) equal to the power of the engine.
    (B) the normal force times the coefficient of friction.
    (C) larger than the normal force times the coefficient of friction.
    (D) less than the normal force times the coefficient of friction.
    (E) zero.

70. The mass of the atom is
    (A) equally dispersed throughout the entire atom cloud.
    (B) equally divided between all its parts: the electrons, neutrons, and protons.
    (C) concentrated in the orbital cloud.
    (D) concentrated in the nucleus.
    (E) determined by spectroscopic analysis.

71. The reason an observer cannot detect the wave nature of a fast moving truck is
    (A) the momentum of the truck is too large.
    (B) the velocity of the wave is too large.
    (C) there are no waves to be detected.
    (D) the frequency is too low.
    (E) the wavelengths are too small.

72. A large object is placed at exactly 55% of the distance to the moon from the earth. Eventually the object will
    (A) fall to the sun.
    (B) fall to the moon.
    (C) fall to the earth.
    (D) remain in the same place.
    (E) drift out of the solar system.

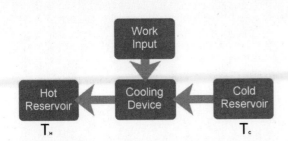

73. The diagrammatic representation of the cooling process above shows which of the following?

    I.   Negative work
    II. An isothermal process
    III. Increasing energy

    (A) I only
    (B) II only
    (C) I and III only
    (D) II and III only
    (E) I, II, and III

74. A heat engine receives 150 Joules of heat energy and performs 70 Joules of work. If heat cannot be removed from the heat engine in any other way, by what value does the internal energy of the system change?

    (A)   0 J
    (B)   40 J
    (C)   80 J
    (D) 120 J
    (E) 150 J

75. What information is learned from looking at the curve of an acceleration time graph?

    (A) The position of the object
    (B) The displacement of the object
    (C) The velocity of the object
    (D) The acceleration of the object
    (E) None of the above

STOP

IF YOU FINISH BEFORE THE TEST SESSION ENDS, YOU MAY REVIEW YOUR WORK ON THIS TEST ONLY. YOU MAY NOT TURN TO ANY OTHER TEST IN THIS BOOK.

ANSWER SHEET

Leave any unused answer spaces blank.

	Test Code										Subject Test (print)					
V	①	②	③	④	⑤	⑥	⑦	⑧	⑨							
W		①	②	③	④	⑤	⑥	⑦		⑧	⑨					
X	①	②	③	④	⑤	Y	Ⓐ	Ⓑ	Ⓒ	Ⓓ	Ⓔ	FOR ETS USE ONLY	R/C	W/S1	FS/S2	CS/S3	WS
Q		①	②	③	④	⑤	⑥	⑦	⑧	⑨							

1 Ⓐ Ⓑ Ⓒ Ⓓ Ⓔ   21 Ⓐ Ⓑ Ⓒ Ⓓ Ⓔ   41 Ⓐ Ⓑ Ⓒ Ⓓ Ⓔ   61 Ⓐ Ⓑ Ⓒ Ⓓ Ⓔ   81 Ⓐ Ⓑ Ⓒ Ⓓ Ⓔ
2 Ⓐ Ⓑ Ⓒ Ⓓ Ⓔ   22 Ⓐ Ⓑ Ⓒ Ⓓ Ⓔ   42 Ⓐ Ⓑ Ⓒ Ⓓ Ⓔ   62 Ⓐ Ⓑ Ⓒ Ⓓ Ⓔ   82 Ⓐ Ⓑ Ⓒ Ⓓ Ⓔ
3 Ⓐ Ⓑ Ⓒ Ⓓ Ⓔ   23 Ⓐ Ⓑ Ⓒ Ⓓ Ⓔ   43 Ⓐ Ⓑ Ⓒ Ⓓ Ⓔ   63 Ⓐ Ⓑ Ⓒ Ⓓ Ⓔ   83 Ⓐ Ⓑ Ⓒ Ⓓ Ⓔ
4 Ⓐ Ⓑ Ⓒ Ⓓ Ⓔ   24 Ⓐ Ⓑ Ⓒ Ⓓ Ⓔ   44 Ⓐ Ⓑ Ⓒ Ⓓ Ⓔ   64 Ⓐ Ⓑ Ⓒ Ⓓ Ⓔ   84 Ⓐ Ⓑ Ⓒ Ⓓ Ⓔ
5 Ⓐ Ⓑ Ⓒ Ⓓ Ⓔ   25 Ⓐ Ⓑ Ⓒ Ⓓ Ⓔ   45 Ⓐ Ⓑ Ⓒ Ⓓ Ⓔ   65 Ⓐ Ⓑ Ⓒ Ⓓ Ⓔ   85 Ⓐ Ⓑ Ⓒ Ⓓ Ⓔ
6 Ⓐ Ⓑ Ⓒ Ⓓ Ⓔ   26 Ⓐ Ⓑ Ⓒ Ⓓ Ⓔ   46 Ⓐ Ⓑ Ⓒ Ⓓ Ⓔ   66 Ⓐ Ⓑ Ⓒ Ⓓ Ⓔ   86 Ⓐ Ⓑ Ⓒ Ⓓ Ⓔ
7 Ⓐ Ⓑ Ⓒ Ⓓ Ⓔ   27 Ⓐ Ⓑ Ⓒ Ⓓ Ⓔ   47 Ⓐ Ⓑ Ⓒ Ⓓ Ⓔ   67 Ⓐ Ⓑ Ⓒ Ⓓ Ⓔ   87 Ⓐ Ⓑ Ⓒ Ⓓ Ⓔ
8 Ⓐ Ⓑ Ⓒ Ⓓ Ⓔ   28 Ⓐ Ⓑ Ⓒ Ⓓ Ⓔ   48 Ⓐ Ⓑ Ⓒ Ⓓ Ⓔ   68 Ⓐ Ⓑ Ⓒ Ⓓ Ⓔ   88 Ⓐ Ⓑ Ⓒ Ⓓ Ⓔ
9 Ⓐ Ⓑ Ⓒ Ⓓ Ⓔ   29 Ⓐ Ⓑ Ⓒ Ⓓ Ⓔ   49 Ⓐ Ⓑ Ⓒ Ⓓ Ⓔ   69 Ⓐ Ⓑ Ⓒ Ⓓ Ⓔ   89 Ⓐ Ⓑ Ⓒ Ⓓ Ⓔ
10 Ⓐ Ⓑ Ⓒ Ⓓ Ⓔ   30 Ⓐ Ⓑ Ⓒ Ⓓ Ⓔ   50 Ⓐ Ⓑ Ⓒ Ⓓ Ⓔ   70 Ⓐ Ⓑ Ⓒ Ⓓ Ⓔ   90 Ⓐ Ⓑ Ⓒ Ⓓ Ⓔ
11 Ⓐ Ⓑ Ⓒ Ⓓ Ⓔ   31 Ⓐ Ⓑ Ⓒ Ⓓ Ⓔ   51 Ⓐ Ⓑ Ⓒ Ⓓ Ⓔ   71 Ⓐ Ⓑ Ⓒ Ⓓ Ⓔ   91 Ⓐ Ⓑ Ⓒ Ⓓ Ⓔ
12 Ⓐ Ⓑ Ⓒ Ⓓ Ⓔ   32 Ⓐ Ⓑ Ⓒ Ⓓ Ⓔ   52 Ⓐ Ⓑ Ⓒ Ⓓ Ⓔ   72 Ⓐ Ⓑ Ⓒ Ⓓ Ⓔ   92 Ⓐ Ⓑ Ⓒ Ⓓ Ⓔ
13 Ⓐ Ⓑ Ⓒ Ⓓ Ⓔ   33 Ⓐ Ⓑ Ⓒ Ⓓ Ⓔ   53 Ⓐ Ⓑ Ⓒ Ⓓ Ⓔ   73 Ⓐ Ⓑ Ⓒ Ⓓ Ⓔ   93 Ⓐ Ⓑ Ⓒ Ⓓ Ⓔ
14 Ⓐ Ⓑ Ⓒ Ⓓ Ⓔ   34 Ⓐ Ⓑ Ⓒ Ⓓ Ⓔ   54 Ⓐ Ⓑ Ⓒ Ⓓ Ⓔ   74 Ⓐ Ⓑ Ⓒ Ⓓ Ⓔ   94 Ⓐ Ⓑ Ⓒ Ⓓ Ⓔ
15 Ⓐ Ⓑ Ⓒ Ⓓ Ⓔ   35 Ⓐ Ⓑ Ⓒ Ⓓ Ⓔ   55 Ⓐ Ⓑ Ⓒ Ⓓ Ⓔ   75 Ⓐ Ⓑ Ⓒ Ⓓ Ⓔ   95 Ⓐ Ⓑ Ⓒ Ⓓ Ⓔ
16 Ⓐ Ⓑ Ⓒ Ⓓ Ⓔ   36 Ⓐ Ⓑ Ⓒ Ⓓ Ⓔ   56 Ⓐ Ⓑ Ⓒ Ⓓ Ⓔ   76 Ⓐ Ⓑ Ⓒ Ⓓ Ⓔ   96 Ⓐ Ⓑ Ⓒ Ⓓ Ⓔ
17 Ⓐ Ⓑ Ⓒ Ⓓ Ⓔ   37 Ⓐ Ⓑ Ⓒ Ⓓ Ⓔ   57 Ⓐ Ⓑ Ⓒ Ⓓ Ⓔ   77 Ⓐ Ⓑ Ⓒ Ⓓ Ⓔ   97 Ⓐ Ⓑ Ⓒ Ⓓ Ⓔ
18 Ⓐ Ⓑ Ⓒ Ⓓ Ⓔ   38 Ⓐ Ⓑ Ⓒ Ⓓ Ⓔ   58 Ⓐ Ⓑ Ⓒ Ⓓ Ⓔ   78 Ⓐ Ⓑ Ⓒ Ⓓ Ⓔ   98 Ⓐ Ⓑ Ⓒ Ⓓ Ⓔ
19 Ⓐ Ⓑ Ⓒ Ⓓ Ⓔ   39 Ⓐ Ⓑ Ⓒ Ⓓ Ⓔ   59 Ⓐ Ⓑ Ⓒ Ⓓ Ⓔ   79 Ⓐ Ⓑ Ⓒ Ⓓ Ⓔ   99 Ⓐ Ⓑ Ⓒ Ⓓ Ⓔ
20 Ⓐ Ⓑ Ⓒ Ⓓ Ⓔ   40 Ⓐ Ⓑ Ⓒ Ⓓ Ⓔ   60 Ⓐ Ⓑ Ⓒ Ⓓ Ⓔ   80 Ⓐ Ⓑ Ⓒ Ⓓ Ⓔ   100 Ⓐ Ⓑ Ⓒ Ⓓ Ⓔ

PRACTICE TEST 4

ANSWERS AND EXPLANATIONS

QUICK-SCORE ANSWERS

1. E	9. A	17. D	25. D	33. E	41. E	48. C	55. E	62. E	69. E
2. D	10. C	18. C	26. C	34. C	42. C	49. E	56. B	63. B	70. D
3. A	11. B	19. D	27. C	35. B	43. C	50. C	57. E	64. B	71. D
4. A	12. E	20. B	28. E	36. D	44. E	51. C	58. D	65. B	72. C
5. D	13. C	21. B	29. E	37. D	45. D	52. A	59. B	66. A	73. A
6. C	14. E	22. A	30. B	38. B	46. E	53. A	60. D	67. E	74. C
7. C	15. D	23. B	31. C	39. C	47. A	54. A	61. A	68. D	75. C
8. E	16. C	24. A	32. A	40. C					

ANSWERS AND EXPLANATIONS

ANSWERS TO PART A, QUESTIONS 1–14

1. **The correct answer is (E).** Use the right-hand rule to find the direction of the force applied to the alpha particle. The field is oriented out of the page, meaning you point your fingers at yourself and your thumb in the direction of the motion of the particle. Your palm points down toward the letter C, but remember the force exerted on the particle is constant. The pathway will *not* straighten. The particle continues in a circular path until it exits the magnetic field at E.

2. **The correct answer is (D).** Again, we use the right-hand rule as we did in the previous question. Point your finger toward yourself and your thumb in the direction of motion of the particle. Now is the time you must remember the right-hand rule is used for positive particles. Your palm points down but the electron is negative. It moves in the opposite direction from the proton. This means the electron curves toward Point B, but to reach Point B it must travel in a partially straight pathway. The correct pathway is one where the electron (particle B) curves continuously until it leaves the magnetic field.

3. **The correct answer is (A).** The gamma ray is completely unaffected by the magnetic field. It travels in a straight line through the magnetic field.

4. **The correct answer is (A).** The gravitational potential energy of an object located above the earth's surface decreases as it nears the earth's surface

5. **The correct answer is (D).** The kinetic energy rises as the square of the velocity, which is a parabolic curve.

6. **The correct answer is (C).** The momentum of an object is the product of the mass of the object and its velocity. In this situation, the velocity is increasing in a linear manner, as shown in Graph C.

7. **The correct answer is (C).** The proton moves toward the negative plate of the electric field. When it enters the magnetic field, it is deflected (right-hand rule) toward C.

8. **The correct answer is (E)**. A neutron is completely unaffected by the electric field into which it is placed. Consequently, it will not move.

9. **The correct answer is (A)**. The electron moves toward the positive plate in the electric field. It does not enter the magnetic field, so the magnetic field has no affect on it.

10. **The correct answer is (C)**. The electron emits +1.87 *eV* of energy, which is equal to the difference between $E_3 - E_2$. The energy is positive because it is emitted as the electron falls closer to the nucleus.

11. **The correct answer is (B)**. The electron absorbs -.98 *eV* of energy to jump from level 3 to level 5 ($E_3 - E_5$) The energy is negative because it is absorbed by the electron as it rises closer to zero potential and a possible escape from the nucleus.

12. **The correct answer is (E)**. The electron emits +12.08 *eV* of energy, which is equal to the difference between $E_3 - E_1$. The energy is positive because it is emitted as the electron falls closer to the nucleus

13. **The correct answer is (C)**. Point C is located in a parallel circuit, which contains two pathways. Both of the parallel legs offer the same resistance to the current, therefore the two equal legs receive half of the current each.

14. **The correct answer is (E)**. At point E, all of the electromotive force has been used to push the current through the circuit elements.

15. **The correct answer is (D)**. At point D, exactly one-half the resistance in the circuit has been passed by the current.

ANSWERS TO PART B, QUESTIONS 16–75

16. **The correct answer is (C)**. The voltage of the battery is equal to electrical potential energy, and the kinetic energy is $1/2\ mv^2$. Setting the two equal to each other, $1/2\ mv^2 = (1.5\ V)(q)$. Solving the equation yields 7.3×10^5 m/s, which is the velocity of the electron just as it reaches the positive plate of the battery.

17. **The correct answer is (D).** During a period of 28 days, the sample has 4 half-lives. This means $(1/2)^4 = .0625$, or 1/16 of the substance is left.

18. **The correct answer is (C).** All of the waves are electromagnetic waves except for sound waves.

19. **The correct answer is (D).** According to Newton's first law, an object in motion remains in motion and an object at rest remains at rest unless a net force acts on the object. The ball is in free fall. Even though it is accelerating on the y axis (up and down), nothing is affecting the ball on the x axis (horizontal)

20. **The correct answer is (B).** Both spheres fall from the same height. This means the objects are in free fall, so their accelerations are the same. Sphere B has more mass than sphere A, which gives sphere B more momentum and more kinetic energy when the two spheres reach the ground.

21. **The correct answer is (B).** One of Kepler's observations in his laws of planetary motion was that the planets orbit the sun in elliptical orbits.

22. **The correct answer is (A).** Transformers are used to change voltages to a form that is usable for specific applications. For example, an electrical line voltage of 1800 V is reduced by a transformer to the voltage we use in our homes.

23. **The correct answer is (B).** Stars are a source of light waves. As such, the waves approach the earth as fronts. When a star is approaching the earth the wave fronts reach us at an increasing rate. When a star is receding from us, the wave fronts reach us at a lower rate. In both cases a frequency change (Doppler shift) can be detected.

24. **The correct answer is (A).** In this problem the object has both horizontal and vertical motion. The original velocity of the object can be of large magnitude on either the x axis or the y axis. It is absolutely true, however, that the object can only travel along the x (horizontal) axis as long as it is in free fall.

25. **The correct answer is (D).** Current is induced into a wire when the wire is placed in a changing magnetic field because of the moving line of flux crossing the wire. This is one of the ways a current is magnetically induced into a wire.

26. **The correct answer is (C).** The physical characteristics of melting and boiling are directly related to how much thermal energy a substance contains. The measure of the thermal energy is temperature.

27. **The correct answer is (C).** This is an example of the first condition of equilibrium.

$$\Sigma F = 0$$
$$\Sigma F_y = [F_{table} = 2\text{N} \times 11 \ \text{books}]$$
$$F_{table} = 22\text{N}$$

28. **The correct answer is (E).** Two different objects that are in thermal equilibrium must be at the same temperature.

29. **The correct answer is (E).** If the two vectors are exactly 180° apart, in each case all of the choices are a possibility.

30. **The correct answer is (B).** The substance that has the largest specific heat contains the most heat at a given temperature for an equal mass of the substance. Since the substance with the largest specific heat contains the most heat, it will have the most heat content to transfer to the melting of the ice.

31. **The correct answer is (C).** The only time the instantaneous velocity of an object equals the average velocity of an object is when the object moves with constant velocity.

32. **The correct answer is (A).** The second step of the right-hand rule is appropriate to answer the question. The entire right-hand rule is restated below
    i.   Point the thumb of the right hand in the direction of the current or the motion of the particle.
    ii. Point the fingers of the right hand in the direction of the magnetic field (toward the south pole).
    iii. The palm of the right hand points in the direction of the applied force.

33. **The correct answer is (E).** Of the choices listed, the only electromagnetic radiation that carries more energy than the blue light is ultraviolet.

34. **The correct answer is (C).** The weight of the astronaut is dependent upon the gravitational attraction of the planetary body. Mars has a lower gravitational attraction than the earth, so

the astronaut weighs less on Mars. The mass of an object, or a person, is an intrinsic quality of a body that does not change.

35. **The correct answer is (B).** A negative ion is an object that has an excess of electrons. Electrons are the negatively charged part of the atom, therefore they give an object that carries excess of electrons a negative charge.

36. **The correct answer is (D).** Any time a net or unbalanced force is applied to an object, the object is accelerated.

37. **The correct answer is (D).** Wavelength has the units $\dfrac{\text{meters}}{\text{wave}}$ and frequency has the units $\dfrac{\text{waves}}{\text{second}}$. The product of the two produces a velocity unit $\left(\dfrac{\text{meters}}{\text{wave}}\right)\left(\dfrac{\text{waves}}{\text{second}}\right)=\left(\dfrac{\text{meters}}{\text{second}}\right)$.

38. **The correct answer is (B).** This statement is one of Einstein's postulates to the theory of relativity.

39. **The correct answer is (C).** The power developed in a circuit element is equal to $(V)(I)$. Solve by substituting the correct values into the equation: $(24V)(.75A) = 18$ watts.

40. **The correct answer is (C).** The tangential velocity is the product of the angular velocity and the radius of the object or the person from the center of the rotating device. Both children have the same angular velocity, but the child on the pony is farther from the center of the merry-go-round.

41. **The correct answer is (E).** Work can be either a positive quantity or a negative quantity. When a force is applied in one direction and the displacement is in the opposite direction, the work equation becomes $F \cdot s \cdot \text{cosine } 180°$. The cosine of $180°$ is -1, therefore any work done under those conditions is negative work. $W = -F \cdot S = -(1000N)(10 \text{ m}) = -10,000 \text{ J}$

42. **The correct answer is (C).** This answer is a statement of the law of conservation of momentum. Momentum before an event equals the momentum after an event.

43. **The correct answer is (C).** The vibrating spring stores energy when it is compressed or stretched. The potential energy stored in the spring is converted into kinetic energy in between the two

end points. The maximum kinetic energy of the mass is directly between the two high potential energy points.

44. **The correct answer is (E)**. Gamma radiation has no mass. It is emitted from an unstable nucleus, which changes to a lower energy state. There is no mass change involved, so the nucleus remains essentially the same minus the emitted energy.

45. **The correct answer is (D)**. The temperature of a gas is directly related to the rate at which gas particles strike the sides of the container in which the gas is contained. The measure of the number of times gas particles strike the sides of the container is pressure. Charles Law shows the direct relationship between the two. When the temperature increases, the pressure increases. This means the velocity of the gas particles increases, too.

46. **The correct answer is (E)**. The radius between the two masses does not change. That means in the gravitational equation

$$F = G\frac{m_1 m_2}{r^2}$$ the only thing that changes is the mass of the two

bodies. Multiply them together to find the magnitude of the change in force they exert on each other.

47. **The correct answer is (A)**. Light rays leaving an optically more dense material and striking the surface interface between the two substances are totally reflected back into the material when the angle of incidence is equal to or less than the critical angle.

48. **The correct answer is (C)**. When the time equals .375 seconds, the pendulum is 3/4 of the way through the first half of its period. At that time, if the pendulum string breaks, the pendulum will fly off at a 45° angle, which is the angle that gives the pendulum bob maximum time of flight.

49. **The correct answer is (E)**. According to the first condition of equilibrium, the sum of all the applied forces must equal zero if an object is not to move.

50. **The correct answer is (C)**. The skydiver accelerates after he jumps until the friction from the air is equal to his downward force, which is his weight.

51. **The correct answer is (C)**. The positively charged rod attracts the excess electrons that were deposited by the negatively charged rod. The movement of the electrons toward the positive rod reduces the repulsive force applied to the leaves, and the leaves are able to move closer to one another.

52. **The correct answer is (A).** An object that is placed inside the focal point of a concave mirror produces a virtual image, which is erect and reduced.

53. **The correct answer is (A).** The first law of thermodynamics makes it clear that a hot object loses heat to a cold object. If no heat is added or subtracted from a system, the heat in the system remains constant in the system.

54. **The correct answer is (A).** The energy of a photon is indirectly related to the wavelength of the light. Consequently, as the wavelength of the light increases, the energy of the photon decreases

55. **The correct answer is (E).** Each droplet of water falls at an increasing velocity with the passage of time. The distance between the droplets increases as the square of the time increases.

$$s = \frac{1}{2}at^2$$

56. **The correct answer is (B).** An increase in the length of the pendulum causes the period of the pendulum to increase too.

$T = 2\pi\sqrt{\dfrac{\ell}{g}}$. Notice the ℓ in the period equation.

57. **The correct answer is (E).** A constant voltage source does not change, regardless of the value of the resistance added to the circuit.

58. **The correct answer is (D).** A dielectric is used in a capacitor to increase the capacitance of the capacitor.

59. **The correct answer is (B).** This is an example of Hyugen's principle, which states that a point on a wave front can act as a source of waves. The waves fan out from the point at the barrier as new waves are formed.

60. **The correct answer is (D).** According to Newton's Third Law, the action-reaction force pair must be equal in magnitude and oppositely directed. The earth pulls on the mass, and the mass pulls on the earth (the pair) with the same force.

61. **The correct answer is (A).** The only single factor that makes each element unique is the number of protons the element has in its nucleus.

Peterson's SAT II Success: Physics

62. **The correct answer is (E).** The battery that provides the force to push electrons through the circuit causes the electrons to jump from atom to atom, a process that causes the current to flow. The process is similar to water flowing in a hose. Water enters one end of the hose and leaves the other end, but they are not the same water molecules.

63. **The correct answer is (B).** The problem is a work energy conversion. Set the kinetic energy of the car equal to the frictional work to be done by the tires. $1/2\ mv^2 = Fs$. The mass of the car is not given, but if we expand the equation a little more we find it is not necessary. $1/2\ mv^2 = \mu Ns$, which leads to $1/2\ mv^2 = \mu mgs$. At this point the mass cancels out on both sides, which leaves $1/2\ v^2 = \mu gs$. The working equation becomes $v = \sqrt{2(\mu)(g)(s)}$. The solution to the problem is

$$v = \sqrt{2(.46)(9.8\text{m/s})(54\text{m})} = 22\text{m/s}.$$

64. **The correct answer is (B).** Use $F=ma$ to solve the problem. Don't forget to subtract the frictional force from the applied force. Also don't forget to convert the weight of the object into mass. Set the problem up in this manner:

$$F = m * a$$

$$53\text{N} - 8\text{N} = \frac{176.4\text{N}}{9.8\text{m/s}} * a$$

$$a = 2.5\text{m/s}^2$$

65. **The correct answer is (B).** Neither object could reach the ground in 1 second unless it was *thrown* downward. Therefore one of the objects, A, was thrown downward. The other object, B could not have been placed into free fall from rest and taken 3 seconds to reach the ground from a height of 14.7 m because it only takes 1.73 seconds to reach the ground for an object starting from rest. The object that takes 3 seconds to reach the ground must therefore have been thrown upward. This means both objects were thrown.

66. **The correct answer is (A).** The bead slides on a frictionless wire to the other side, where it stops and slides back to A, where it again stops to repeat the process over again.

67. **The correct answer is (E).** Pressure is the measure of the rate at which the gas particles collide with the sides of the containers. The more often the gas particles collide with the container walls, the higher the pressure.

68. **The correct answer is (D).** The transformer reduces the voltage when the number of coils of wire on the secondary side is less than the number of coils of wire on the secondary side. The voltage output is found: $\frac{1.5}{17} = \frac{x}{136V} = 12V$.

69. **The correct answer is (E).** An object that is not being accelerated cannot have any unbalanced forces acting upon it. The car is moving at a constant velocity, which means there are no forces exerted on the car anywhere.

70. **The correct answer is (D).** Rutherford found that most of the mass of an atom is concentrated in the nucleus of the atom.

71. **The correct answer is (D).** The de Broglia wavelength cannot be detected because the objects in question have velocities that are too small for the waves they create to be detectable.

72. **The correct answer is (C).** The moon is only 1/6 the size of the earth, so at a distance 55% of the way to the moon, the object is still under the influence of the earth's gravitational field. That means the object will eventually fall back to the earth.

73. **The correct answer is (A).** The diagram shows a heat diagram operating in reverse. The system shown is a cooling system, such as a refrigerator.

74. **The correct answer is (C).** The first law of thermodynamics is the answer here. $\Delta Q = \Delta U + \Delta W$. The work done by the system is 70 *Joules*, but 150 *Joules* of heat was added. Rearrange the first law equation and subtract the work from the input heat to find the increase in internal energy. $\Delta Q - \Delta W = \Delta U$ leads us to $150J - 70J = 80J$.

75. **The correct answer is (C).** The acceleration-time graph shows a time rate change in velocity. This is the definition of acceleration.

Answer Sheets

ANSWER SHEET

Leave any unused answer spaces blank.

Test Code											
V		①	②	③	④	⑤	⑥	⑦	⑧	⑨	
W		①	②	③	④	⑤	⑥	⑦	⑧	⑨	
X	①	②	③	④	⑤		Y	Ⓐ	Ⓑ	Ⓒ	Ⓓ Ⓔ
Q		①	②	③	④	⑤	⑥	⑦	⑧	⑨	

Subject Test (print)

FOR ETS USE ONLY	R/C	W/S1	FS/S2	CS/S3	WS

1 Ⓐ Ⓑ Ⓒ Ⓓ Ⓔ   21 Ⓐ Ⓑ Ⓒ Ⓓ Ⓔ   41 Ⓐ Ⓑ Ⓒ Ⓓ Ⓔ   61 Ⓐ Ⓑ Ⓒ Ⓓ Ⓔ   81 Ⓐ Ⓑ Ⓒ Ⓓ Ⓔ
2 Ⓐ Ⓑ Ⓒ Ⓓ Ⓔ   22 Ⓐ Ⓑ Ⓒ Ⓓ Ⓔ   42 Ⓐ Ⓑ Ⓒ Ⓓ Ⓔ   62 Ⓐ Ⓑ Ⓒ Ⓓ Ⓔ   82 Ⓐ Ⓑ Ⓒ Ⓓ Ⓔ
3 Ⓐ Ⓑ Ⓒ Ⓓ Ⓔ   23 Ⓐ Ⓑ Ⓒ Ⓓ Ⓔ   43 Ⓐ Ⓑ Ⓒ Ⓓ Ⓔ   63 Ⓐ Ⓑ Ⓒ Ⓓ Ⓔ   83 Ⓐ Ⓑ Ⓒ Ⓓ Ⓔ
4 Ⓐ Ⓑ Ⓒ Ⓓ Ⓔ   24 Ⓐ Ⓑ Ⓒ Ⓓ Ⓔ   44 Ⓐ Ⓑ Ⓒ Ⓓ Ⓔ   64 Ⓐ Ⓑ Ⓒ Ⓓ Ⓔ   84 Ⓐ Ⓑ Ⓒ Ⓓ Ⓔ
5 Ⓐ Ⓑ Ⓒ Ⓓ Ⓔ   25 Ⓐ Ⓑ Ⓒ Ⓓ Ⓔ   45 Ⓐ Ⓑ Ⓒ Ⓓ Ⓔ   65 Ⓐ Ⓑ Ⓒ Ⓓ Ⓔ   85 Ⓐ Ⓑ Ⓒ Ⓓ Ⓔ
6 Ⓐ Ⓑ Ⓒ Ⓓ Ⓔ   26 Ⓐ Ⓑ Ⓒ Ⓓ Ⓔ   46 Ⓐ Ⓑ Ⓒ Ⓓ Ⓔ   66 Ⓐ Ⓑ Ⓒ Ⓓ Ⓔ   86 Ⓐ Ⓑ Ⓒ Ⓓ Ⓔ
7 Ⓐ Ⓑ Ⓒ Ⓓ Ⓔ   27 Ⓐ Ⓑ Ⓒ Ⓓ Ⓔ   47 Ⓐ Ⓑ Ⓒ Ⓓ Ⓔ   67 Ⓐ Ⓑ Ⓒ Ⓓ Ⓔ   87 Ⓐ Ⓑ Ⓒ Ⓓ Ⓔ
8 Ⓐ Ⓑ Ⓒ Ⓓ Ⓔ   28 Ⓐ Ⓑ Ⓒ Ⓓ Ⓔ   48 Ⓐ Ⓑ Ⓒ Ⓓ Ⓔ   68 Ⓐ Ⓑ Ⓒ Ⓓ Ⓔ   88 Ⓐ Ⓑ Ⓒ Ⓓ Ⓔ
9 Ⓐ Ⓑ Ⓒ Ⓓ Ⓔ   29 Ⓐ Ⓑ Ⓒ Ⓓ Ⓔ   49 Ⓐ Ⓑ Ⓒ Ⓓ Ⓔ   69 Ⓐ Ⓑ Ⓒ Ⓓ Ⓔ   89 Ⓐ Ⓑ Ⓒ Ⓓ Ⓔ
10 Ⓐ Ⓑ Ⓒ Ⓓ Ⓔ   30 Ⓐ Ⓑ Ⓒ Ⓓ Ⓔ   50 Ⓐ Ⓑ Ⓒ Ⓓ Ⓔ   70 Ⓐ Ⓑ Ⓒ Ⓓ Ⓔ   90 Ⓐ Ⓑ Ⓒ Ⓓ Ⓔ
11 Ⓐ Ⓑ Ⓒ Ⓓ Ⓔ   31 Ⓐ Ⓑ Ⓒ Ⓓ Ⓔ   51 Ⓐ Ⓑ Ⓒ Ⓓ Ⓔ   71 Ⓐ Ⓑ Ⓒ Ⓓ Ⓔ   91 Ⓐ Ⓑ Ⓒ Ⓓ Ⓔ
12 Ⓐ Ⓑ Ⓒ Ⓓ Ⓔ   32 Ⓐ Ⓑ Ⓒ Ⓓ Ⓔ   52 Ⓐ Ⓑ Ⓒ Ⓓ Ⓔ   72 Ⓐ Ⓑ Ⓒ Ⓓ Ⓔ   92 Ⓐ Ⓑ Ⓒ Ⓓ Ⓔ
13 Ⓐ Ⓑ Ⓒ Ⓓ Ⓔ   33 Ⓐ Ⓑ Ⓒ Ⓓ Ⓔ   53 Ⓐ Ⓑ Ⓒ Ⓓ Ⓔ   73 Ⓐ Ⓑ Ⓒ Ⓓ Ⓔ   93 Ⓐ Ⓑ Ⓒ Ⓓ Ⓔ
14 Ⓐ Ⓑ Ⓒ Ⓓ Ⓔ   34 Ⓐ Ⓑ Ⓒ Ⓓ Ⓔ   54 Ⓐ Ⓑ Ⓒ Ⓓ Ⓔ   74 Ⓐ Ⓑ Ⓒ Ⓓ Ⓔ   94 Ⓐ Ⓑ Ⓒ Ⓓ Ⓔ
15 Ⓐ Ⓑ Ⓒ Ⓓ Ⓔ   35 Ⓐ Ⓑ Ⓒ Ⓓ Ⓔ   55 Ⓐ Ⓑ Ⓒ Ⓓ Ⓔ   75 Ⓐ Ⓑ Ⓒ Ⓓ Ⓔ   95 Ⓐ Ⓑ Ⓒ Ⓓ Ⓔ
16 Ⓐ Ⓑ Ⓒ Ⓓ Ⓔ   36 Ⓐ Ⓑ Ⓒ Ⓓ Ⓔ   56 Ⓐ Ⓑ Ⓒ Ⓓ Ⓔ   76 Ⓐ Ⓑ Ⓒ Ⓓ Ⓔ   96 Ⓐ Ⓑ Ⓒ Ⓓ Ⓔ
17 Ⓐ Ⓑ Ⓒ Ⓓ Ⓔ   37 Ⓐ Ⓑ Ⓒ Ⓓ Ⓔ   57 Ⓐ Ⓑ Ⓒ Ⓓ Ⓔ   77 Ⓐ Ⓑ Ⓒ Ⓓ Ⓔ   97 Ⓐ Ⓑ Ⓒ Ⓓ Ⓔ
18 Ⓐ Ⓑ Ⓒ Ⓓ Ⓔ   38 Ⓐ Ⓑ Ⓒ Ⓓ Ⓔ   58 Ⓐ Ⓑ Ⓒ Ⓓ Ⓔ   78 Ⓐ Ⓑ Ⓒ Ⓓ Ⓔ   98 Ⓐ Ⓑ Ⓒ Ⓓ Ⓔ
19 Ⓐ Ⓑ Ⓒ Ⓓ Ⓔ   39 Ⓐ Ⓑ Ⓒ Ⓓ Ⓔ   59 Ⓐ Ⓑ Ⓒ Ⓓ Ⓔ   79 Ⓐ Ⓑ Ⓒ Ⓓ Ⓔ   99 Ⓐ Ⓑ Ⓒ Ⓓ Ⓔ
20 Ⓐ Ⓑ Ⓒ Ⓓ Ⓔ   40 Ⓐ Ⓑ Ⓒ Ⓓ Ⓔ   60 Ⓐ Ⓑ Ⓒ Ⓓ Ⓔ   80 Ⓐ Ⓑ Ⓒ Ⓓ Ⓔ   100 Ⓐ Ⓑ Ⓒ Ⓓ Ⓔ

Leave any unused
answer spaces blank.

Test Code

V ① ② ③ ④ ⑤ ⑥ ⑦ ⑧ ⑨
W ① ② ③ ④ ⑤ ⑥ ⑦ ⑧ ⑨
X ① ② ③ ④ ⑤   Y Ⓐ Ⓑ Ⓒ Ⓓ Ⓔ
Q ① ② ③ ④ ⑤ ⑥ ⑦ ⑧ ⑨

Subject Test (print)

FOR ETS USE ONLY	R/C	W/S1	FS/S2	CS/S3	WS

1 Ⓐ Ⓑ Ⓒ Ⓓ Ⓔ   21 Ⓐ Ⓑ Ⓒ Ⓓ Ⓔ   41 Ⓐ Ⓑ Ⓒ Ⓓ Ⓔ   61 Ⓐ Ⓑ Ⓒ Ⓓ Ⓔ   81 Ⓐ Ⓑ Ⓒ Ⓓ Ⓔ
2 Ⓐ Ⓑ Ⓒ Ⓓ Ⓔ   22 Ⓐ Ⓑ Ⓒ Ⓓ Ⓔ   42 Ⓐ Ⓑ Ⓒ Ⓓ Ⓔ   62 Ⓐ Ⓑ Ⓒ Ⓓ Ⓔ   82 Ⓐ Ⓑ Ⓒ Ⓓ Ⓔ
3 Ⓐ Ⓑ Ⓒ Ⓓ Ⓔ   23 Ⓐ Ⓑ Ⓒ Ⓓ Ⓔ   43 Ⓐ Ⓑ Ⓒ Ⓓ Ⓔ   63 Ⓐ Ⓑ Ⓒ Ⓓ Ⓔ   83 Ⓐ Ⓑ Ⓒ Ⓓ Ⓔ
4 Ⓐ Ⓑ Ⓒ Ⓓ Ⓔ   24 Ⓐ Ⓑ Ⓒ Ⓓ Ⓔ   44 Ⓐ Ⓑ Ⓒ Ⓓ Ⓔ   64 Ⓐ Ⓑ Ⓒ Ⓓ Ⓔ   84 Ⓐ Ⓑ Ⓒ Ⓓ Ⓔ
5 Ⓐ Ⓑ Ⓒ Ⓓ Ⓔ   25 Ⓐ Ⓑ Ⓒ Ⓓ Ⓔ   45 Ⓐ Ⓑ Ⓒ Ⓓ Ⓔ   65 Ⓐ Ⓑ Ⓒ Ⓓ Ⓔ   85 Ⓐ Ⓑ Ⓒ Ⓓ Ⓔ
6 Ⓐ Ⓑ Ⓒ Ⓓ Ⓔ   26 Ⓐ Ⓑ Ⓒ Ⓓ Ⓔ   46 Ⓐ Ⓑ Ⓒ Ⓓ Ⓔ   66 Ⓐ Ⓑ Ⓒ Ⓓ Ⓔ   86 Ⓐ Ⓑ Ⓒ Ⓓ Ⓔ
7 Ⓐ Ⓑ Ⓒ Ⓓ Ⓔ   27 Ⓐ Ⓑ Ⓒ Ⓓ Ⓔ   47 Ⓐ Ⓑ Ⓒ Ⓓ Ⓔ   67 Ⓐ Ⓑ Ⓒ Ⓓ Ⓔ   87 Ⓐ Ⓑ Ⓒ Ⓓ Ⓔ
8 Ⓐ Ⓑ Ⓒ Ⓓ Ⓔ   28 Ⓐ Ⓑ Ⓒ Ⓓ Ⓔ   48 Ⓐ Ⓑ Ⓒ Ⓓ Ⓔ   68 Ⓐ Ⓑ Ⓒ Ⓓ Ⓔ   88 Ⓐ Ⓑ Ⓒ Ⓓ Ⓔ
9 Ⓐ Ⓑ Ⓒ Ⓓ Ⓔ   29 Ⓐ Ⓑ Ⓒ Ⓓ Ⓔ   49 Ⓐ Ⓑ Ⓒ Ⓓ Ⓔ   69 Ⓐ Ⓑ Ⓒ Ⓓ Ⓔ   89 Ⓐ Ⓑ Ⓒ Ⓓ Ⓔ
10 Ⓐ Ⓑ Ⓒ Ⓓ Ⓔ   30 Ⓐ Ⓑ Ⓒ Ⓓ Ⓔ   50 Ⓐ Ⓑ Ⓒ Ⓓ Ⓔ   70 Ⓐ Ⓑ Ⓒ Ⓓ Ⓔ   90 Ⓐ Ⓑ Ⓒ Ⓓ Ⓔ
11 Ⓐ Ⓑ Ⓒ Ⓓ Ⓔ   31 Ⓐ Ⓑ Ⓒ Ⓓ Ⓔ   51 Ⓐ Ⓑ Ⓒ Ⓓ Ⓔ   71 Ⓐ Ⓑ Ⓒ Ⓓ Ⓔ   91 Ⓐ Ⓑ Ⓒ Ⓓ Ⓔ
12 Ⓐ Ⓑ Ⓒ Ⓓ Ⓔ   32 Ⓐ Ⓑ Ⓒ Ⓓ Ⓔ   52 Ⓐ Ⓑ Ⓒ Ⓓ Ⓔ   72 Ⓐ Ⓑ Ⓒ Ⓓ Ⓔ   92 Ⓐ Ⓑ Ⓒ Ⓓ Ⓔ
13 Ⓐ Ⓑ Ⓒ Ⓓ Ⓔ   33 Ⓐ Ⓑ Ⓒ Ⓓ Ⓔ   53 Ⓐ Ⓑ Ⓒ Ⓓ Ⓔ   73 Ⓐ Ⓑ Ⓒ Ⓓ Ⓔ   93 Ⓐ Ⓑ Ⓒ Ⓓ Ⓔ
14 Ⓐ Ⓑ Ⓒ Ⓓ Ⓔ   34 Ⓐ Ⓑ Ⓒ Ⓓ Ⓔ   54 Ⓐ Ⓑ Ⓒ Ⓓ Ⓔ   74 Ⓐ Ⓑ Ⓒ Ⓓ Ⓔ   94 Ⓐ Ⓑ Ⓒ Ⓓ Ⓔ
15 Ⓐ Ⓑ Ⓒ Ⓓ Ⓔ   35 Ⓐ Ⓑ Ⓒ Ⓓ Ⓔ   55 Ⓐ Ⓑ Ⓒ Ⓓ Ⓔ   75 Ⓐ Ⓑ Ⓒ Ⓓ Ⓔ   95 Ⓐ Ⓑ Ⓒ Ⓓ Ⓔ
16 Ⓐ Ⓑ Ⓒ Ⓓ Ⓔ   36 Ⓐ Ⓑ Ⓒ Ⓓ Ⓔ   56 Ⓐ Ⓑ Ⓒ Ⓓ Ⓔ   76 Ⓐ Ⓑ Ⓒ Ⓓ Ⓔ   96 Ⓐ Ⓑ Ⓒ Ⓓ Ⓔ
17 Ⓐ Ⓑ Ⓒ Ⓓ Ⓔ   37 Ⓐ Ⓑ Ⓒ Ⓓ Ⓔ   57 Ⓐ Ⓑ Ⓒ Ⓓ Ⓔ   77 Ⓐ Ⓑ Ⓒ Ⓓ Ⓔ   97 Ⓐ Ⓑ Ⓒ Ⓓ Ⓔ
18 Ⓐ Ⓑ Ⓒ Ⓓ Ⓔ   38 Ⓐ Ⓑ Ⓒ Ⓓ Ⓔ   58 Ⓐ Ⓑ Ⓒ Ⓓ Ⓔ   78 Ⓐ Ⓑ Ⓒ Ⓓ Ⓔ   98 Ⓐ Ⓑ Ⓒ Ⓓ Ⓔ
19 Ⓐ Ⓑ Ⓒ Ⓓ Ⓔ   39 Ⓐ Ⓑ Ⓒ Ⓓ Ⓔ   59 Ⓐ Ⓑ Ⓒ Ⓓ Ⓔ   79 Ⓐ Ⓑ Ⓒ Ⓓ Ⓔ   99 Ⓐ Ⓑ Ⓒ Ⓓ Ⓔ
20 Ⓐ Ⓑ Ⓒ Ⓓ Ⓔ   40 Ⓐ Ⓑ Ⓒ Ⓓ Ⓔ   60 Ⓐ Ⓑ Ⓒ Ⓓ Ⓔ   80 Ⓐ Ⓑ Ⓒ Ⓓ Ⓔ   100 Ⓐ Ⓑ Ⓒ Ⓓ Ⓔ

Leave any unused
answer spaces blank.

Test Code

V ① ② ③ ④ ⑤ ⑥ ⑦ ⑧ ⑨
W ① ② ③ ④ ⑤ ⑥ ⑦ ⑧ ⑨
X ① ② ③ ④ ⑤   Y Ⓐ Ⓑ Ⓒ Ⓓ Ⓔ
Q ① ② ③ ④ ⑤ ⑥ ⑦ ⑧ ⑨

Subject Test (print)

FOR ETS USE ONLY	R/C	W/S1	FS/S2	CS/S3	WS

1 Ⓐ Ⓑ Ⓒ Ⓓ Ⓔ   21 Ⓐ Ⓑ Ⓒ Ⓓ Ⓔ   41 Ⓐ Ⓑ Ⓒ Ⓓ Ⓔ   61 Ⓐ Ⓑ Ⓒ Ⓓ Ⓔ   81 Ⓐ Ⓑ Ⓒ Ⓓ Ⓔ
2 Ⓐ Ⓑ Ⓒ Ⓓ Ⓔ   22 Ⓐ Ⓑ Ⓒ Ⓓ Ⓔ   42 Ⓐ Ⓑ Ⓒ Ⓓ Ⓔ   62 Ⓐ Ⓑ Ⓒ Ⓓ Ⓔ   82 Ⓐ Ⓑ Ⓒ Ⓓ Ⓔ
3 Ⓐ Ⓑ Ⓒ Ⓓ Ⓔ   23 Ⓐ Ⓑ Ⓒ Ⓓ Ⓔ   43 Ⓐ Ⓑ Ⓒ Ⓓ Ⓔ   63 Ⓐ Ⓑ Ⓒ Ⓓ Ⓔ   83 Ⓐ Ⓑ Ⓒ Ⓓ Ⓔ
4 Ⓐ Ⓑ Ⓒ Ⓓ Ⓔ   24 Ⓐ Ⓑ Ⓒ Ⓓ Ⓔ   44 Ⓐ Ⓑ Ⓒ Ⓓ Ⓔ   64 Ⓐ Ⓑ Ⓒ Ⓓ Ⓔ   84 Ⓐ Ⓑ Ⓒ Ⓓ Ⓔ
5 Ⓐ Ⓑ Ⓒ Ⓓ Ⓔ   25 Ⓐ Ⓑ Ⓒ Ⓓ Ⓔ   45 Ⓐ Ⓑ Ⓒ Ⓓ Ⓔ   65 Ⓐ Ⓑ Ⓒ Ⓓ Ⓔ   85 Ⓐ Ⓑ Ⓒ Ⓓ Ⓔ
6 Ⓐ Ⓑ Ⓒ Ⓓ Ⓔ   26 Ⓐ Ⓑ Ⓒ Ⓓ Ⓔ   46 Ⓐ Ⓑ Ⓒ Ⓓ Ⓔ   66 Ⓐ Ⓑ Ⓒ Ⓓ Ⓔ   86 Ⓐ Ⓑ Ⓒ Ⓓ Ⓔ
7 Ⓐ Ⓑ Ⓒ Ⓓ Ⓔ   27 Ⓐ Ⓑ Ⓒ Ⓓ Ⓔ   47 Ⓐ Ⓑ Ⓒ Ⓓ Ⓔ   67 Ⓐ Ⓑ Ⓒ Ⓓ Ⓔ   87 Ⓐ Ⓑ Ⓒ Ⓓ Ⓔ
8 Ⓐ Ⓑ Ⓒ Ⓓ Ⓔ   28 Ⓐ Ⓑ Ⓒ Ⓓ Ⓔ   48 Ⓐ Ⓑ Ⓒ Ⓓ Ⓔ   68 Ⓐ Ⓑ Ⓒ Ⓓ Ⓔ   88 Ⓐ Ⓑ Ⓒ Ⓓ Ⓔ
9 Ⓐ Ⓑ Ⓒ Ⓓ Ⓔ   29 Ⓐ Ⓑ Ⓒ Ⓓ Ⓔ   49 Ⓐ Ⓑ Ⓒ Ⓓ Ⓔ   69 Ⓐ Ⓑ Ⓒ Ⓓ Ⓔ   89 Ⓐ Ⓑ Ⓒ Ⓓ Ⓔ
10 Ⓐ Ⓑ Ⓒ Ⓓ Ⓔ   30 Ⓐ Ⓑ Ⓒ Ⓓ Ⓔ   50 Ⓐ Ⓑ Ⓒ Ⓓ Ⓔ   70 Ⓐ Ⓑ Ⓒ Ⓓ Ⓔ   90 Ⓐ Ⓑ Ⓒ Ⓓ Ⓔ
11 Ⓐ Ⓑ Ⓒ Ⓓ Ⓔ   31 Ⓐ Ⓑ Ⓒ Ⓓ Ⓔ   51 Ⓐ Ⓑ Ⓒ Ⓓ Ⓔ   71 Ⓐ Ⓑ Ⓒ Ⓓ Ⓔ   91 Ⓐ Ⓑ Ⓒ Ⓓ Ⓔ
12 Ⓐ Ⓑ Ⓒ Ⓓ Ⓔ   32 Ⓐ Ⓑ Ⓒ Ⓓ Ⓔ   52 Ⓐ Ⓑ Ⓒ Ⓓ Ⓔ   72 Ⓐ Ⓑ Ⓒ Ⓓ Ⓔ   92 Ⓐ Ⓑ Ⓒ Ⓓ Ⓔ
13 Ⓐ Ⓑ Ⓒ Ⓓ Ⓔ   33 Ⓐ Ⓑ Ⓒ Ⓓ Ⓔ   53 Ⓐ Ⓑ Ⓒ Ⓓ Ⓔ   73 Ⓐ Ⓑ Ⓒ Ⓓ Ⓔ   93 Ⓐ Ⓑ Ⓒ Ⓓ Ⓔ
14 Ⓐ Ⓑ Ⓒ Ⓓ Ⓔ   34 Ⓐ Ⓑ Ⓒ Ⓓ Ⓔ   54 Ⓐ Ⓑ Ⓒ Ⓓ Ⓔ   74 Ⓐ Ⓑ Ⓒ Ⓓ Ⓔ   94 Ⓐ Ⓑ Ⓒ Ⓓ Ⓔ
15 Ⓐ Ⓑ Ⓒ Ⓓ Ⓔ   35 Ⓐ Ⓑ Ⓒ Ⓓ Ⓔ   55 Ⓐ Ⓑ Ⓒ Ⓓ Ⓔ   75 Ⓐ Ⓑ Ⓒ Ⓓ Ⓔ   95 Ⓐ Ⓑ Ⓒ Ⓓ Ⓔ
16 Ⓐ Ⓑ Ⓒ Ⓓ Ⓔ   36 Ⓐ Ⓑ Ⓒ Ⓓ Ⓔ   56 Ⓐ Ⓑ Ⓒ Ⓓ Ⓔ   76 Ⓐ Ⓑ Ⓒ Ⓓ Ⓔ   96 Ⓐ Ⓑ Ⓒ Ⓓ Ⓔ
17 Ⓐ Ⓑ Ⓒ Ⓓ Ⓔ   37 Ⓐ Ⓑ Ⓒ Ⓓ Ⓔ   57 Ⓐ Ⓑ Ⓒ Ⓓ Ⓔ   77 Ⓐ Ⓑ Ⓒ Ⓓ Ⓔ   97 Ⓐ Ⓑ Ⓒ Ⓓ Ⓔ
18 Ⓐ Ⓑ Ⓒ Ⓓ Ⓔ   38 Ⓐ Ⓑ Ⓒ Ⓓ Ⓔ   58 Ⓐ Ⓑ Ⓒ Ⓓ Ⓔ   78 Ⓐ Ⓑ Ⓒ Ⓓ Ⓔ   98 Ⓐ Ⓑ Ⓒ Ⓓ Ⓔ
19 Ⓐ Ⓑ Ⓒ Ⓓ Ⓔ   39 Ⓐ Ⓑ Ⓒ Ⓓ Ⓔ   59 Ⓐ Ⓑ Ⓒ Ⓓ Ⓔ   79 Ⓐ Ⓑ Ⓒ Ⓓ Ⓔ   99 Ⓐ Ⓑ Ⓒ Ⓓ Ⓔ
20 Ⓐ Ⓑ Ⓒ Ⓓ Ⓔ   40 Ⓐ Ⓑ Ⓒ Ⓓ Ⓔ   60 Ⓐ Ⓑ Ⓒ Ⓓ Ⓔ   80 Ⓐ Ⓑ Ⓒ Ⓓ Ⓔ   100 Ⓐ Ⓑ Ⓒ Ⓓ Ⓔ

Leave any unused answer spaces blank.

Subject Test (print)

FOR ETS USE ONLY	R/C	W/S1	FS/S2	CS/S3	WS

1 Ⓐ Ⓑ Ⓒ Ⓓ Ⓔ 21 Ⓐ Ⓑ Ⓒ Ⓓ Ⓔ 41 Ⓐ Ⓑ Ⓒ Ⓓ Ⓔ 61 Ⓐ Ⓑ Ⓒ Ⓓ Ⓔ 81 Ⓐ Ⓑ Ⓒ Ⓓ Ⓔ
2 Ⓐ Ⓑ Ⓒ Ⓓ Ⓔ 22 Ⓐ Ⓑ Ⓒ Ⓓ Ⓔ 42 Ⓐ Ⓑ Ⓒ Ⓓ Ⓔ 62 Ⓐ Ⓑ Ⓒ Ⓓ Ⓔ 82 Ⓐ Ⓑ Ⓒ Ⓓ Ⓔ
3 Ⓐ Ⓑ Ⓒ Ⓓ Ⓔ 23 Ⓐ Ⓑ Ⓒ Ⓓ Ⓔ 43 Ⓐ Ⓑ Ⓒ Ⓓ Ⓔ 63 Ⓐ Ⓑ Ⓒ Ⓓ Ⓔ 83 Ⓐ Ⓑ Ⓒ Ⓓ Ⓔ
4 Ⓐ Ⓑ Ⓒ Ⓓ Ⓔ 24 Ⓐ Ⓑ Ⓒ Ⓓ Ⓔ 44 Ⓐ Ⓑ Ⓒ Ⓓ Ⓔ 64 Ⓐ Ⓑ Ⓒ Ⓓ Ⓔ 84 Ⓐ Ⓑ Ⓒ Ⓓ Ⓔ
5 Ⓐ Ⓑ Ⓒ Ⓓ Ⓔ 25 Ⓐ Ⓑ Ⓒ Ⓓ Ⓔ 45 Ⓐ Ⓑ Ⓒ Ⓓ Ⓔ 65 Ⓐ Ⓑ Ⓒ Ⓓ Ⓔ 85 Ⓐ Ⓑ Ⓒ Ⓓ Ⓔ
6 Ⓐ Ⓑ Ⓒ Ⓓ Ⓔ 26 Ⓐ Ⓑ Ⓒ Ⓓ Ⓔ 46 Ⓐ Ⓑ Ⓒ Ⓓ Ⓔ 66 Ⓐ Ⓑ Ⓒ Ⓓ Ⓔ 86 Ⓐ Ⓑ Ⓒ Ⓓ Ⓔ
7 Ⓐ Ⓑ Ⓒ Ⓓ Ⓔ 27 Ⓐ Ⓑ Ⓒ Ⓓ Ⓔ 47 Ⓐ Ⓑ Ⓒ Ⓓ Ⓔ 67 Ⓐ Ⓑ Ⓒ Ⓓ Ⓔ 87 Ⓐ Ⓑ Ⓒ Ⓓ Ⓔ
8 Ⓐ Ⓑ Ⓒ Ⓓ Ⓔ 28 Ⓐ Ⓑ Ⓒ Ⓓ Ⓔ 48 Ⓐ Ⓑ Ⓒ Ⓓ Ⓔ 68 Ⓐ Ⓑ Ⓒ Ⓓ Ⓔ 88 Ⓐ Ⓑ Ⓒ Ⓓ Ⓔ
9 Ⓐ Ⓑ Ⓒ Ⓓ Ⓔ 29 Ⓐ Ⓑ Ⓒ Ⓓ Ⓔ 49 Ⓐ Ⓑ Ⓒ Ⓓ Ⓔ 69 Ⓐ Ⓑ Ⓒ Ⓓ Ⓔ 89 Ⓐ Ⓑ Ⓒ Ⓓ Ⓔ
10 Ⓐ Ⓑ Ⓒ Ⓓ Ⓔ 30 Ⓐ Ⓑ Ⓒ Ⓓ Ⓔ 50 Ⓐ Ⓑ Ⓒ Ⓓ Ⓔ 70 Ⓐ Ⓑ Ⓒ Ⓓ Ⓔ 90 Ⓐ Ⓑ Ⓒ Ⓓ Ⓔ
11 Ⓐ Ⓑ Ⓒ Ⓓ Ⓔ 31 Ⓐ Ⓑ Ⓒ Ⓓ Ⓔ 51 Ⓐ Ⓑ Ⓒ Ⓓ Ⓔ 71 Ⓐ Ⓑ Ⓒ Ⓓ Ⓔ 91 Ⓐ Ⓑ Ⓒ Ⓓ Ⓔ
12 Ⓐ Ⓑ Ⓒ Ⓓ Ⓔ 32 Ⓐ Ⓑ Ⓒ Ⓓ Ⓔ 52 Ⓐ Ⓑ Ⓒ Ⓓ Ⓔ 72 Ⓐ Ⓑ Ⓒ Ⓓ Ⓔ 92 Ⓐ Ⓑ Ⓒ Ⓓ Ⓔ
13 Ⓐ Ⓑ Ⓒ Ⓓ Ⓔ 33 Ⓐ Ⓑ Ⓒ Ⓓ Ⓔ 53 Ⓐ Ⓑ Ⓒ Ⓓ Ⓔ 73 Ⓐ Ⓑ Ⓒ Ⓓ Ⓔ 93 Ⓐ Ⓑ Ⓒ Ⓓ Ⓔ
14 Ⓐ Ⓑ Ⓒ Ⓓ Ⓔ 34 Ⓐ Ⓑ Ⓒ Ⓓ Ⓔ 54 Ⓐ Ⓑ Ⓒ Ⓓ Ⓔ 74 Ⓐ Ⓑ Ⓒ Ⓓ Ⓔ 94 Ⓐ Ⓑ Ⓒ Ⓓ Ⓔ
15 Ⓐ Ⓑ Ⓒ Ⓓ Ⓔ 35 Ⓐ Ⓑ Ⓒ Ⓓ Ⓔ 55 Ⓐ Ⓑ Ⓒ Ⓓ Ⓔ 75 Ⓐ Ⓑ Ⓒ Ⓓ Ⓔ 95 Ⓐ Ⓑ Ⓒ Ⓓ Ⓔ
16 Ⓐ Ⓑ Ⓒ Ⓓ Ⓔ 36 Ⓐ Ⓑ Ⓒ Ⓓ Ⓔ 56 Ⓐ Ⓑ Ⓒ Ⓓ Ⓔ 76 Ⓐ Ⓑ Ⓒ Ⓓ Ⓔ 96 Ⓐ Ⓑ Ⓒ Ⓓ Ⓔ
17 Ⓐ Ⓑ Ⓒ Ⓓ Ⓔ 37 Ⓐ Ⓑ Ⓒ Ⓓ Ⓔ 57 Ⓐ Ⓑ Ⓒ Ⓓ Ⓔ 77 Ⓐ Ⓑ Ⓒ Ⓓ Ⓔ 97 Ⓐ Ⓑ Ⓒ Ⓓ Ⓔ
18 Ⓐ Ⓑ Ⓒ Ⓓ Ⓔ 38 Ⓐ Ⓑ Ⓒ Ⓓ Ⓔ 58 Ⓐ Ⓑ Ⓒ Ⓓ Ⓔ 78 Ⓐ Ⓑ Ⓒ Ⓓ Ⓔ 98 Ⓐ Ⓑ Ⓒ Ⓓ Ⓔ
19 Ⓐ Ⓑ Ⓒ Ⓓ Ⓔ 39 Ⓐ Ⓑ Ⓒ Ⓓ Ⓔ 59 Ⓐ Ⓑ Ⓒ Ⓓ Ⓔ 79 Ⓐ Ⓑ Ⓒ Ⓓ Ⓔ 99 Ⓐ Ⓑ Ⓒ Ⓓ Ⓔ
20 Ⓐ Ⓑ Ⓒ Ⓓ Ⓔ 40 Ⓐ Ⓑ Ⓒ Ⓓ Ⓔ 60 Ⓐ Ⓑ Ⓒ Ⓓ Ⓔ 80 Ⓐ Ⓑ Ⓒ Ⓓ Ⓔ 100 Ⓐ Ⓑ Ⓒ Ⓓ Ⓔ

Leave any unused answer spaces blank.

Test Code

V ① ② ③ ④ ⑤ ⑥ ⑦ ⑧ ⑨
W ① ② ③ ④ ⑤ ⑥ ⑦ ⑧ ⑨
X ① ② ③ ④ ⑤ Y Ⓐ Ⓑ Ⓒ Ⓓ Ⓔ
Q ① ② ③ ④ ⑤ ⑥ ⑦ ⑧ ⑨

Subject Test (print)

FOR ETS USE ONLY	R/C	W/S1	FS/S2	CS/S3	WS

1 Ⓐ Ⓑ Ⓒ Ⓓ Ⓔ 21 Ⓐ Ⓑ Ⓒ Ⓓ Ⓔ 41 Ⓐ Ⓑ Ⓒ Ⓓ Ⓔ 61 Ⓐ Ⓑ Ⓒ Ⓓ Ⓔ 81 Ⓐ Ⓑ Ⓒ Ⓓ Ⓔ
2 Ⓐ Ⓑ Ⓒ Ⓓ Ⓔ 22 Ⓐ Ⓑ Ⓒ Ⓓ Ⓔ 42 Ⓐ Ⓑ Ⓒ Ⓓ Ⓔ 62 Ⓐ Ⓑ Ⓒ Ⓓ Ⓔ 82 Ⓐ Ⓑ Ⓒ Ⓓ Ⓔ
3 Ⓐ Ⓑ Ⓒ Ⓓ Ⓔ 23 Ⓐ Ⓑ Ⓒ Ⓓ Ⓔ 43 Ⓐ Ⓑ Ⓒ Ⓓ Ⓔ 63 Ⓐ Ⓑ Ⓒ Ⓓ Ⓔ 83 Ⓐ Ⓑ Ⓒ Ⓓ Ⓔ
4 Ⓐ Ⓑ Ⓒ Ⓓ Ⓔ 24 Ⓐ Ⓑ Ⓒ Ⓓ Ⓔ 44 Ⓐ Ⓑ Ⓒ Ⓓ Ⓔ 64 Ⓐ Ⓑ Ⓒ Ⓓ Ⓔ 84 Ⓐ Ⓑ Ⓒ Ⓓ Ⓔ
5 Ⓐ Ⓑ Ⓒ Ⓓ Ⓔ 25 Ⓐ Ⓑ Ⓒ Ⓓ Ⓔ 45 Ⓐ Ⓑ Ⓒ Ⓓ Ⓔ 65 Ⓐ Ⓑ Ⓒ Ⓓ Ⓔ 85 Ⓐ Ⓑ Ⓒ Ⓓ Ⓔ
6 Ⓐ Ⓑ Ⓒ Ⓓ Ⓔ 26 Ⓐ Ⓑ Ⓒ Ⓓ Ⓔ 46 Ⓐ Ⓑ Ⓒ Ⓓ Ⓔ 66 Ⓐ Ⓑ Ⓒ Ⓓ Ⓔ 86 Ⓐ Ⓑ Ⓒ Ⓓ Ⓔ
7 Ⓐ Ⓑ Ⓒ Ⓓ Ⓔ 27 Ⓐ Ⓑ Ⓒ Ⓓ Ⓔ 47 Ⓐ Ⓑ Ⓒ Ⓓ Ⓔ 67 Ⓐ Ⓑ Ⓒ Ⓓ Ⓔ 87 Ⓐ Ⓑ Ⓒ Ⓓ Ⓔ
8 Ⓐ Ⓑ Ⓒ Ⓓ Ⓔ 28 Ⓐ Ⓑ Ⓒ Ⓓ Ⓔ 48 Ⓐ Ⓑ Ⓒ Ⓓ Ⓔ 68 Ⓐ Ⓑ Ⓒ Ⓓ Ⓔ 88 Ⓐ Ⓑ Ⓒ Ⓓ Ⓔ
9 Ⓐ Ⓑ Ⓒ Ⓓ Ⓔ 29 Ⓐ Ⓑ Ⓒ Ⓓ Ⓔ 49 Ⓐ Ⓑ Ⓒ Ⓓ Ⓔ 69 Ⓐ Ⓑ Ⓒ Ⓓ Ⓔ 89 Ⓐ Ⓑ Ⓒ Ⓓ Ⓔ
10 Ⓐ Ⓑ Ⓒ Ⓓ Ⓔ 30 Ⓐ Ⓑ Ⓒ Ⓓ Ⓔ 50 Ⓐ Ⓑ Ⓒ Ⓓ Ⓔ 70 Ⓐ Ⓑ Ⓒ Ⓓ Ⓔ 90 Ⓐ Ⓑ Ⓒ Ⓓ Ⓔ
11 Ⓐ Ⓑ Ⓒ Ⓓ Ⓔ 31 Ⓐ Ⓑ Ⓒ Ⓓ Ⓔ 51 Ⓐ Ⓑ Ⓒ Ⓓ Ⓔ 71 Ⓐ Ⓑ Ⓒ Ⓓ Ⓔ 91 Ⓐ Ⓑ Ⓒ Ⓓ Ⓔ
12 Ⓐ Ⓑ Ⓒ Ⓓ Ⓔ 32 Ⓐ Ⓑ Ⓒ Ⓓ Ⓔ 52 Ⓐ Ⓑ Ⓒ Ⓓ Ⓔ 72 Ⓐ Ⓑ Ⓒ Ⓓ Ⓔ 92 Ⓐ Ⓑ Ⓒ Ⓓ Ⓔ
13 Ⓐ Ⓑ Ⓒ Ⓓ Ⓔ 33 Ⓐ Ⓑ Ⓒ Ⓓ Ⓔ 53 Ⓐ Ⓑ Ⓒ Ⓓ Ⓔ 73 Ⓐ Ⓑ Ⓒ Ⓓ Ⓔ 93 Ⓐ Ⓑ Ⓒ Ⓓ Ⓔ
14 Ⓐ Ⓑ Ⓒ Ⓓ Ⓔ 34 Ⓐ Ⓑ Ⓒ Ⓓ Ⓔ 54 Ⓐ Ⓑ Ⓒ Ⓓ Ⓔ 74 Ⓐ Ⓑ Ⓒ Ⓓ Ⓔ 94 Ⓐ Ⓑ Ⓒ Ⓓ Ⓔ
15 Ⓐ Ⓑ Ⓒ Ⓓ Ⓔ 35 Ⓐ Ⓑ Ⓒ Ⓓ Ⓔ 55 Ⓐ Ⓑ Ⓒ Ⓓ Ⓔ 75 Ⓐ Ⓑ Ⓒ Ⓓ Ⓔ 95 Ⓐ Ⓑ Ⓒ Ⓓ Ⓔ
16 Ⓐ Ⓑ Ⓒ Ⓓ Ⓔ 36 Ⓐ Ⓑ Ⓒ Ⓓ Ⓔ 56 Ⓐ Ⓑ Ⓒ Ⓓ Ⓔ 76 Ⓐ Ⓑ Ⓒ Ⓓ Ⓔ 96 Ⓐ Ⓑ Ⓒ Ⓓ Ⓔ
17 Ⓐ Ⓑ Ⓒ Ⓓ Ⓔ 37 Ⓐ Ⓑ Ⓒ Ⓓ Ⓔ 57 Ⓐ Ⓑ Ⓒ Ⓓ Ⓔ 77 Ⓐ Ⓑ Ⓒ Ⓓ Ⓔ 97 Ⓐ Ⓑ Ⓒ Ⓓ Ⓔ
18 Ⓐ Ⓑ Ⓒ Ⓓ Ⓔ 38 Ⓐ Ⓑ Ⓒ Ⓓ Ⓔ 58 Ⓐ Ⓑ Ⓒ Ⓓ Ⓔ 78 Ⓐ Ⓑ Ⓒ Ⓓ Ⓔ 98 Ⓐ Ⓑ Ⓒ Ⓓ Ⓔ
19 Ⓐ Ⓑ Ⓒ Ⓓ Ⓔ 39 Ⓐ Ⓑ Ⓒ Ⓓ Ⓔ 59 Ⓐ Ⓑ Ⓒ Ⓓ Ⓔ 79 Ⓐ Ⓑ Ⓒ Ⓓ Ⓔ 99 Ⓐ Ⓑ Ⓒ Ⓓ Ⓔ
20 Ⓐ Ⓑ Ⓒ Ⓓ Ⓔ 40 Ⓐ Ⓑ Ⓒ Ⓓ Ⓔ 60 Ⓐ Ⓑ Ⓒ Ⓓ Ⓔ 80 Ⓐ Ⓑ Ⓒ Ⓓ Ⓔ 100 Ⓐ Ⓑ Ⓒ Ⓓ Ⓔ

Leave any unused answer spaces blank.

	Test Code										Subject Test (print)				
V		①	②	③	④	⑤	⑥	⑦	⑧	⑨					
W		①	②	③	④	⑤	⑥	⑦	⑧	⑨					
X	①	②	③	④	⑤	Y	Ⓐ	Ⓑ	Ⓒ	Ⓓ	Ⓔ					
Q		①	②	③	④	⑤	⑥	⑦	⑧	⑨					

FOR ETS USE ONLY	R/C	W/S1	FS/S2	CS/S3	WS

1 Ⓐ Ⓑ Ⓒ Ⓓ Ⓔ   21 Ⓐ Ⓑ Ⓒ Ⓓ Ⓔ   41 Ⓐ Ⓑ Ⓒ Ⓓ Ⓔ   61 Ⓐ Ⓑ Ⓒ Ⓓ Ⓔ   81 Ⓐ Ⓑ Ⓒ Ⓓ Ⓔ
2 Ⓐ Ⓑ Ⓒ Ⓓ Ⓔ   22 Ⓐ Ⓑ Ⓒ Ⓓ Ⓔ   42 Ⓐ Ⓑ Ⓒ Ⓓ Ⓔ   62 Ⓐ Ⓑ Ⓒ Ⓓ Ⓔ   82 Ⓐ Ⓑ Ⓒ Ⓓ Ⓔ
3 Ⓐ Ⓑ Ⓒ Ⓓ Ⓔ   23 Ⓐ Ⓑ Ⓒ Ⓓ Ⓔ   43 Ⓐ Ⓑ Ⓒ Ⓓ Ⓔ   63 Ⓐ Ⓑ Ⓒ Ⓓ Ⓔ   83 Ⓐ Ⓑ Ⓒ Ⓓ Ⓔ
4 Ⓐ Ⓑ Ⓒ Ⓓ Ⓔ   24 Ⓐ Ⓑ Ⓒ Ⓓ Ⓔ   44 Ⓐ Ⓑ Ⓒ Ⓓ Ⓔ   64 Ⓐ Ⓑ Ⓒ Ⓓ Ⓔ   84 Ⓐ Ⓑ Ⓒ Ⓓ Ⓔ
5 Ⓐ Ⓑ Ⓒ Ⓓ Ⓔ   25 Ⓐ Ⓑ Ⓒ Ⓓ Ⓔ   45 Ⓐ Ⓑ Ⓒ Ⓓ Ⓔ   65 Ⓐ Ⓑ Ⓒ Ⓓ Ⓔ   85 Ⓐ Ⓑ Ⓒ Ⓓ Ⓔ
6 Ⓐ Ⓑ Ⓒ Ⓓ Ⓔ   26 Ⓐ Ⓑ Ⓒ Ⓓ Ⓔ   46 Ⓐ Ⓑ Ⓒ Ⓓ Ⓔ   66 Ⓐ Ⓑ Ⓒ Ⓓ Ⓔ   86 Ⓐ Ⓑ Ⓒ Ⓓ Ⓔ
7 Ⓐ Ⓑ Ⓒ Ⓓ Ⓔ   27 Ⓐ Ⓑ Ⓒ Ⓓ Ⓔ   47 Ⓐ Ⓑ Ⓒ Ⓓ Ⓔ   67 Ⓐ Ⓑ Ⓒ Ⓓ Ⓔ   87 Ⓐ Ⓑ Ⓒ Ⓓ Ⓔ
8 Ⓐ Ⓑ Ⓒ Ⓓ Ⓔ   28 Ⓐ Ⓑ Ⓒ Ⓓ Ⓔ   48 Ⓐ Ⓑ Ⓒ Ⓓ Ⓔ   68 Ⓐ Ⓑ Ⓒ Ⓓ Ⓔ   88 Ⓐ Ⓑ Ⓒ Ⓓ Ⓔ
9 Ⓐ Ⓑ Ⓒ Ⓓ Ⓔ   29 Ⓐ Ⓑ Ⓒ Ⓓ Ⓔ   49 Ⓐ Ⓑ Ⓒ Ⓓ Ⓔ   69 Ⓐ Ⓑ Ⓒ Ⓓ Ⓔ   89 Ⓐ Ⓑ Ⓒ Ⓓ Ⓔ
10 Ⓐ Ⓑ Ⓒ Ⓓ Ⓔ   30 Ⓐ Ⓑ Ⓒ Ⓓ Ⓔ   50 Ⓐ Ⓑ Ⓒ Ⓓ Ⓔ   70 Ⓐ Ⓑ Ⓒ Ⓓ Ⓔ   90 Ⓐ Ⓑ Ⓒ Ⓓ Ⓔ
11 Ⓐ Ⓑ Ⓒ Ⓓ Ⓔ   31 Ⓐ Ⓑ Ⓒ Ⓓ Ⓔ   51 Ⓐ Ⓑ Ⓒ Ⓓ Ⓔ   71 Ⓐ Ⓑ Ⓒ Ⓓ Ⓔ   91 Ⓐ Ⓑ Ⓒ Ⓓ Ⓔ
12 Ⓐ Ⓑ Ⓒ Ⓓ Ⓔ   32 Ⓐ Ⓑ Ⓒ Ⓓ Ⓔ   52 Ⓐ Ⓑ Ⓒ Ⓓ Ⓔ   72 Ⓐ Ⓑ Ⓒ Ⓓ Ⓔ   92 Ⓐ Ⓑ Ⓒ Ⓓ Ⓔ
13 Ⓐ Ⓑ Ⓒ Ⓓ Ⓔ   33 Ⓐ Ⓑ Ⓒ Ⓓ Ⓔ   53 Ⓐ Ⓑ Ⓒ Ⓓ Ⓔ   73 Ⓐ Ⓑ Ⓒ Ⓓ Ⓔ   93 Ⓐ Ⓑ Ⓒ Ⓓ Ⓔ
14 Ⓐ Ⓑ Ⓒ Ⓓ Ⓔ   34 Ⓐ Ⓑ Ⓒ Ⓓ Ⓔ   54 Ⓐ Ⓑ Ⓒ Ⓓ Ⓔ   74 Ⓐ Ⓑ Ⓒ Ⓓ Ⓔ   94 Ⓐ Ⓑ Ⓒ Ⓓ Ⓔ
15 Ⓐ Ⓑ Ⓒ Ⓓ Ⓔ   35 Ⓐ Ⓑ Ⓒ Ⓓ Ⓔ   55 Ⓐ Ⓑ Ⓒ Ⓓ Ⓔ   75 Ⓐ Ⓑ Ⓒ Ⓓ Ⓔ   95 Ⓐ Ⓑ Ⓒ Ⓓ Ⓔ
16 Ⓐ Ⓑ Ⓒ Ⓓ Ⓔ   36 Ⓐ Ⓑ Ⓒ Ⓓ Ⓔ   56 Ⓐ Ⓑ Ⓒ Ⓓ Ⓔ   76 Ⓐ Ⓑ Ⓒ Ⓓ Ⓔ   96 Ⓐ Ⓑ Ⓒ Ⓓ Ⓔ
17 Ⓐ Ⓑ Ⓒ Ⓓ Ⓔ   37 Ⓐ Ⓑ Ⓒ Ⓓ Ⓔ   57 Ⓐ Ⓑ Ⓒ Ⓓ Ⓔ   77 Ⓐ Ⓑ Ⓒ Ⓓ Ⓔ   97 Ⓐ Ⓑ Ⓒ Ⓓ Ⓔ
18 Ⓐ Ⓑ Ⓒ Ⓓ Ⓔ   38 Ⓐ Ⓑ Ⓒ Ⓓ Ⓔ   58 Ⓐ Ⓑ Ⓒ Ⓓ Ⓔ   78 Ⓐ Ⓑ Ⓒ Ⓓ Ⓔ   98 Ⓐ Ⓑ Ⓒ Ⓓ Ⓔ
19 Ⓐ Ⓑ Ⓒ Ⓓ Ⓔ   39 Ⓐ Ⓑ Ⓒ Ⓓ Ⓔ   59 Ⓐ Ⓑ Ⓒ Ⓓ Ⓔ   79 Ⓐ Ⓑ Ⓒ Ⓓ Ⓔ   99 Ⓐ Ⓑ Ⓒ Ⓓ Ⓔ
20 Ⓐ Ⓑ Ⓒ Ⓓ Ⓔ   40 Ⓐ Ⓑ Ⓒ Ⓓ Ⓔ   60 Ⓐ Ⓑ Ⓒ Ⓓ Ⓔ   80 Ⓐ Ⓑ Ⓒ Ⓓ Ⓔ   100 Ⓐ Ⓑ Ⓒ Ⓓ Ⓔ

Leave any unused answer spaces blank.

	Test Code										Subject Test (print)				
V		①	②	③	④	⑤	⑥	⑦	⑧	⑨					
W		①	②	③	④	⑤	⑥	⑦	⑧	⑨					
X	①	②	③	④	⑤	Y	Ⓐ	Ⓑ	Ⓒ	Ⓓ	Ⓔ					
Q		①	②	③	④	⑤	⑥	⑦	⑧	⑨					

FOR ETS USE ONLY	R/C	W/S1	FS/S2	CS/S3	WS

1 Ⓐ Ⓑ Ⓒ Ⓓ Ⓔ   21 Ⓐ Ⓑ Ⓒ Ⓓ Ⓔ   41 Ⓐ Ⓑ Ⓒ Ⓓ Ⓔ   61 Ⓐ Ⓑ Ⓒ Ⓓ Ⓔ   81 Ⓐ Ⓑ Ⓒ Ⓓ Ⓔ
2 Ⓐ Ⓑ Ⓒ Ⓓ Ⓔ   22 Ⓐ Ⓑ Ⓒ Ⓓ Ⓔ   42 Ⓐ Ⓑ Ⓒ Ⓓ Ⓔ   62 Ⓐ Ⓑ Ⓒ Ⓓ Ⓔ   82 Ⓐ Ⓑ Ⓒ Ⓓ Ⓔ
3 Ⓐ Ⓑ Ⓒ Ⓓ Ⓔ   23 Ⓐ Ⓑ Ⓒ Ⓓ Ⓔ   43 Ⓐ Ⓑ Ⓒ Ⓓ Ⓔ   63 Ⓐ Ⓑ Ⓒ Ⓓ Ⓔ   83 Ⓐ Ⓑ Ⓒ Ⓓ Ⓔ
4 Ⓐ Ⓑ Ⓒ Ⓓ Ⓔ   24 Ⓐ Ⓑ Ⓒ Ⓓ Ⓔ   44 Ⓐ Ⓑ Ⓒ Ⓓ Ⓔ   64 Ⓐ Ⓑ Ⓒ Ⓓ Ⓔ   84 Ⓐ Ⓑ Ⓒ Ⓓ Ⓔ
5 Ⓐ Ⓑ Ⓒ Ⓓ Ⓔ   25 Ⓐ Ⓑ Ⓒ Ⓓ Ⓔ   45 Ⓐ Ⓑ Ⓒ Ⓓ Ⓔ   65 Ⓐ Ⓑ Ⓒ Ⓓ Ⓔ   85 Ⓐ Ⓑ Ⓒ Ⓓ Ⓔ
6 Ⓐ Ⓑ Ⓒ Ⓓ Ⓔ   26 Ⓐ Ⓑ Ⓒ Ⓓ Ⓔ   46 Ⓐ Ⓑ Ⓒ Ⓓ Ⓔ   66 Ⓐ Ⓑ Ⓒ Ⓓ Ⓔ   86 Ⓐ Ⓑ Ⓒ Ⓓ Ⓔ
7 Ⓐ Ⓑ Ⓒ Ⓓ Ⓔ   27 Ⓐ Ⓑ Ⓒ Ⓓ Ⓔ   47 Ⓐ Ⓑ Ⓒ Ⓓ Ⓔ   67 Ⓐ Ⓑ Ⓒ Ⓓ Ⓔ   87 Ⓐ Ⓑ Ⓒ Ⓓ Ⓔ
8 Ⓐ Ⓑ Ⓒ Ⓓ Ⓔ   28 Ⓐ Ⓑ Ⓒ Ⓓ Ⓔ   48 Ⓐ Ⓑ Ⓒ Ⓓ Ⓔ   68 Ⓐ Ⓑ Ⓒ Ⓓ Ⓔ   88 Ⓐ Ⓑ Ⓒ Ⓓ Ⓔ
9 Ⓐ Ⓑ Ⓒ Ⓓ Ⓔ   29 Ⓐ Ⓑ Ⓒ Ⓓ Ⓔ   49 Ⓐ Ⓑ Ⓒ Ⓓ Ⓔ   69 Ⓐ Ⓑ Ⓒ Ⓓ Ⓔ   89 Ⓐ Ⓑ Ⓒ Ⓓ Ⓔ
10 Ⓐ Ⓑ Ⓒ Ⓓ Ⓔ   30 Ⓐ Ⓑ Ⓒ Ⓓ Ⓔ   50 Ⓐ Ⓑ Ⓒ Ⓓ Ⓔ   70 Ⓐ Ⓑ Ⓒ Ⓓ Ⓔ   90 Ⓐ Ⓑ Ⓒ Ⓓ Ⓔ
11 Ⓐ Ⓑ Ⓒ Ⓓ Ⓔ   31 Ⓐ Ⓑ Ⓒ Ⓓ Ⓔ   51 Ⓐ Ⓑ Ⓒ Ⓓ Ⓔ   71 Ⓐ Ⓑ Ⓒ Ⓓ Ⓔ   91 Ⓐ Ⓑ Ⓒ Ⓓ Ⓔ
12 Ⓐ Ⓑ Ⓒ Ⓓ Ⓔ   32 Ⓐ Ⓑ Ⓒ Ⓓ Ⓔ   52 Ⓐ Ⓑ Ⓒ Ⓓ Ⓔ   72 Ⓐ Ⓑ Ⓒ Ⓓ Ⓔ   92 Ⓐ Ⓑ Ⓒ Ⓓ Ⓔ
13 Ⓐ Ⓑ Ⓒ Ⓓ Ⓔ   33 Ⓐ Ⓑ Ⓒ Ⓓ Ⓔ   53 Ⓐ Ⓑ Ⓒ Ⓓ Ⓔ   73 Ⓐ Ⓑ Ⓒ Ⓓ Ⓔ   93 Ⓐ Ⓑ Ⓒ Ⓓ Ⓔ
14 Ⓐ Ⓑ Ⓒ Ⓓ Ⓔ   34 Ⓐ Ⓑ Ⓒ Ⓓ Ⓔ   54 Ⓐ Ⓑ Ⓒ Ⓓ Ⓔ   74 Ⓐ Ⓑ Ⓒ Ⓓ Ⓔ   94 Ⓐ Ⓑ Ⓒ Ⓓ Ⓔ
15 Ⓐ Ⓑ Ⓒ Ⓓ Ⓔ   35 Ⓐ Ⓑ Ⓒ Ⓓ Ⓔ   55 Ⓐ Ⓑ Ⓒ Ⓓ Ⓔ   75 Ⓐ Ⓑ Ⓒ Ⓓ Ⓔ   95 Ⓐ Ⓑ Ⓒ Ⓓ Ⓔ
16 Ⓐ Ⓑ Ⓒ Ⓓ Ⓔ   36 Ⓐ Ⓑ Ⓒ Ⓓ Ⓔ   56 Ⓐ Ⓑ Ⓒ Ⓓ Ⓔ   76 Ⓐ Ⓑ Ⓒ Ⓓ Ⓔ   96 Ⓐ Ⓑ Ⓒ Ⓓ Ⓔ
17 Ⓐ Ⓑ Ⓒ Ⓓ Ⓔ   37 Ⓐ Ⓑ Ⓒ Ⓓ Ⓔ   57 Ⓐ Ⓑ Ⓒ Ⓓ Ⓔ   77 Ⓐ Ⓑ Ⓒ Ⓓ Ⓔ   97 Ⓐ Ⓑ Ⓒ Ⓓ Ⓔ
18 Ⓐ Ⓑ Ⓒ Ⓓ Ⓔ   38 Ⓐ Ⓑ Ⓒ Ⓓ Ⓔ   58 Ⓐ Ⓑ Ⓒ Ⓓ Ⓔ   78 Ⓐ Ⓑ Ⓒ Ⓓ Ⓔ   98 Ⓐ Ⓑ Ⓒ Ⓓ Ⓔ
19 Ⓐ Ⓑ Ⓒ Ⓓ Ⓔ   39 Ⓐ Ⓑ Ⓒ Ⓓ Ⓔ   59 Ⓐ Ⓑ Ⓒ Ⓓ Ⓔ   79 Ⓐ Ⓑ Ⓒ Ⓓ Ⓔ   99 Ⓐ Ⓑ Ⓒ Ⓓ Ⓔ
20 Ⓐ Ⓑ Ⓒ Ⓓ Ⓔ   40 Ⓐ Ⓑ Ⓒ Ⓓ Ⓔ   60 Ⓐ Ⓑ Ⓒ Ⓓ Ⓔ   80 Ⓐ Ⓑ Ⓒ Ⓓ Ⓔ   100 Ⓐ Ⓑ Ⓒ Ⓓ Ⓔ

Leave any unused answer spaces blank.

Test Code

V	①	②	③	④	⑤	⑥	⑦	⑧	⑨	
W	①	②	③	④	⑤	⑥	⑦	⑧	⑨	
X	①	②	③	④	⑤	Y Ⓐ Ⓑ Ⓒ Ⓓ Ⓔ				
Q	①	②	③	④	⑤	⑥	⑦	⑧	⑨	

Subject Test (print)

FOR ETS USE ONLY	R/C	W/S1	FS/S2	CS/S3	WS

1 Ⓐ Ⓑ Ⓒ Ⓓ Ⓔ   21 Ⓐ Ⓑ Ⓒ Ⓓ Ⓔ   41 Ⓐ Ⓑ Ⓒ Ⓓ Ⓔ   61 Ⓐ Ⓑ Ⓒ Ⓓ Ⓔ   81 Ⓐ Ⓑ Ⓒ Ⓓ Ⓔ
2 Ⓐ Ⓑ Ⓒ Ⓓ Ⓔ   22 Ⓐ Ⓑ Ⓒ Ⓓ Ⓔ   42 Ⓐ Ⓑ Ⓒ Ⓓ Ⓔ   62 Ⓐ Ⓑ Ⓒ Ⓓ Ⓔ   82 Ⓐ Ⓑ Ⓒ Ⓓ Ⓔ
3 Ⓐ Ⓑ Ⓒ Ⓓ Ⓔ   23 Ⓐ Ⓑ Ⓒ Ⓓ Ⓔ   43 Ⓐ Ⓑ Ⓒ Ⓓ Ⓔ   63 Ⓐ Ⓑ Ⓒ Ⓓ Ⓔ   83 Ⓐ Ⓑ Ⓒ Ⓓ Ⓔ
4 Ⓐ Ⓑ Ⓒ Ⓓ Ⓔ   24 Ⓐ Ⓑ Ⓒ Ⓓ Ⓔ   44 Ⓐ Ⓑ Ⓒ Ⓓ Ⓔ   64 Ⓐ Ⓑ Ⓒ Ⓓ Ⓔ   84 Ⓐ Ⓑ Ⓒ Ⓓ Ⓔ
5 Ⓐ Ⓑ Ⓒ Ⓓ Ⓔ   25 Ⓐ Ⓑ Ⓒ Ⓓ Ⓔ   45 Ⓐ Ⓑ Ⓒ Ⓓ Ⓔ   65 Ⓐ Ⓑ Ⓒ Ⓓ Ⓔ   85 Ⓐ Ⓑ Ⓒ Ⓓ Ⓔ
6 Ⓐ Ⓑ Ⓒ Ⓓ Ⓔ   26 Ⓐ Ⓑ Ⓒ Ⓓ Ⓔ   46 Ⓐ Ⓑ Ⓒ Ⓓ Ⓔ   66 Ⓐ Ⓑ Ⓒ Ⓓ Ⓔ   86 Ⓐ Ⓑ Ⓒ Ⓓ Ⓔ
7 Ⓐ Ⓑ Ⓒ Ⓓ Ⓔ   27 Ⓐ Ⓑ Ⓒ Ⓓ Ⓔ   47 Ⓐ Ⓑ Ⓒ Ⓓ Ⓔ   67 Ⓐ Ⓑ Ⓒ Ⓓ Ⓔ   87 Ⓐ Ⓑ Ⓒ Ⓓ Ⓔ
8 Ⓐ Ⓑ Ⓒ Ⓓ Ⓔ   28 Ⓐ Ⓑ Ⓒ Ⓓ Ⓔ   48 Ⓐ Ⓑ Ⓒ Ⓓ Ⓔ   68 Ⓐ Ⓑ Ⓒ Ⓓ Ⓔ   88 Ⓐ Ⓑ Ⓒ Ⓓ Ⓔ
9 Ⓐ Ⓑ Ⓒ Ⓓ Ⓔ   29 Ⓐ Ⓑ Ⓒ Ⓓ Ⓔ   49 Ⓐ Ⓑ Ⓒ Ⓓ Ⓔ   69 Ⓐ Ⓑ Ⓒ Ⓓ Ⓔ   89 Ⓐ Ⓑ Ⓒ Ⓓ Ⓔ
10 Ⓐ Ⓑ Ⓒ Ⓓ Ⓔ   30 Ⓐ Ⓑ Ⓒ Ⓓ Ⓔ   50 Ⓐ Ⓑ Ⓒ Ⓓ Ⓔ   70 Ⓐ Ⓑ Ⓒ Ⓓ Ⓔ   90 Ⓐ Ⓑ Ⓒ Ⓓ Ⓔ
11 Ⓐ Ⓑ Ⓒ Ⓓ Ⓔ   31 Ⓐ Ⓑ Ⓒ Ⓓ Ⓔ   51 Ⓐ Ⓑ Ⓒ Ⓓ Ⓔ   71 Ⓐ Ⓑ Ⓒ Ⓓ Ⓔ   91 Ⓐ Ⓑ Ⓒ Ⓓ Ⓔ
12 Ⓐ Ⓑ Ⓒ Ⓓ Ⓔ   32 Ⓐ Ⓑ Ⓒ Ⓓ Ⓔ   52 Ⓐ Ⓑ Ⓒ Ⓓ Ⓔ   72 Ⓐ Ⓑ Ⓒ Ⓓ Ⓔ   92 Ⓐ Ⓑ Ⓒ Ⓓ Ⓔ
13 Ⓐ Ⓑ Ⓒ Ⓓ Ⓔ   33 Ⓐ Ⓑ Ⓒ Ⓓ Ⓔ   53 Ⓐ Ⓑ Ⓒ Ⓓ Ⓔ   73 Ⓐ Ⓑ Ⓒ Ⓓ Ⓔ   93 Ⓐ Ⓑ Ⓒ Ⓓ Ⓔ
14 Ⓐ Ⓑ Ⓒ Ⓓ Ⓔ   34 Ⓐ Ⓑ Ⓒ Ⓓ Ⓔ   54 Ⓐ Ⓑ Ⓒ Ⓓ Ⓔ   74 Ⓐ Ⓑ Ⓒ Ⓓ Ⓔ   94 Ⓐ Ⓑ Ⓒ Ⓓ Ⓔ
15 Ⓐ Ⓑ Ⓒ Ⓓ Ⓔ   35 Ⓐ Ⓑ Ⓒ Ⓓ Ⓔ   55 Ⓐ Ⓑ Ⓒ Ⓓ Ⓔ   75 Ⓐ Ⓑ Ⓒ Ⓓ Ⓔ   95 Ⓐ Ⓑ Ⓒ Ⓓ Ⓔ
16 Ⓐ Ⓑ Ⓒ Ⓓ Ⓔ   36 Ⓐ Ⓑ Ⓒ Ⓓ Ⓔ   56 Ⓐ Ⓑ Ⓒ Ⓓ Ⓔ   76 Ⓐ Ⓑ Ⓒ Ⓓ Ⓔ   96 Ⓐ Ⓑ Ⓒ Ⓓ Ⓔ
17 Ⓐ Ⓑ Ⓒ Ⓓ Ⓔ   37 Ⓐ Ⓑ Ⓒ Ⓓ Ⓔ   57 Ⓐ Ⓑ Ⓒ Ⓓ Ⓔ   77 Ⓐ Ⓑ Ⓒ Ⓓ Ⓔ   97 Ⓐ Ⓑ Ⓒ Ⓓ Ⓔ
18 Ⓐ Ⓑ Ⓒ Ⓓ Ⓔ   38 Ⓐ Ⓑ Ⓒ Ⓓ Ⓔ   58 Ⓐ Ⓑ Ⓒ Ⓓ Ⓔ   78 Ⓐ Ⓑ Ⓒ Ⓓ Ⓔ   98 Ⓐ Ⓑ Ⓒ Ⓓ Ⓔ
19 Ⓐ Ⓑ Ⓒ Ⓓ Ⓔ   39 Ⓐ Ⓑ Ⓒ Ⓓ Ⓔ   59 Ⓐ Ⓑ Ⓒ Ⓓ Ⓔ   79 Ⓐ Ⓑ Ⓒ Ⓓ Ⓔ   99 Ⓐ Ⓑ Ⓒ Ⓓ Ⓔ
20 Ⓐ Ⓑ Ⓒ Ⓓ Ⓔ   40 Ⓐ Ⓑ Ⓒ Ⓓ Ⓔ   60 Ⓐ Ⓑ Ⓒ Ⓓ Ⓔ   80 Ⓐ Ⓑ Ⓒ Ⓓ Ⓔ   100 Ⓐ Ⓑ Ⓒ Ⓓ Ⓔ

Leave any unused answer spaces blank.

Test Code

V	①	②	③	④	⑤	⑥	⑦	⑧	⑨	
W	①	②	③	④	⑤	⑥	⑦	⑧	⑨	
X	①	②	③	④	⑤	Y Ⓐ Ⓑ Ⓒ Ⓓ Ⓔ				
Q	①	②	③	④	⑤	⑥	⑦	⑧	⑨	

Subject Test (print)

FOR ETS USE ONLY	R/C	W/S1	FS/S2	CS/S3	WS

1 Ⓐ Ⓑ Ⓒ Ⓓ Ⓔ   21 Ⓐ Ⓑ Ⓒ Ⓓ Ⓔ   41 Ⓐ Ⓑ Ⓒ Ⓓ Ⓔ   61 Ⓐ Ⓑ Ⓒ Ⓓ Ⓔ   81 Ⓐ Ⓑ Ⓒ Ⓓ Ⓔ
2 Ⓐ Ⓑ Ⓒ Ⓓ Ⓔ   22 Ⓐ Ⓑ Ⓒ Ⓓ Ⓔ   42 Ⓐ Ⓑ Ⓒ Ⓓ Ⓔ   62 Ⓐ Ⓑ Ⓒ Ⓓ Ⓔ   82 Ⓐ Ⓑ Ⓒ Ⓓ Ⓔ
3 Ⓐ Ⓑ Ⓒ Ⓓ Ⓔ   23 Ⓐ Ⓑ Ⓒ Ⓓ Ⓔ   43 Ⓐ Ⓑ Ⓒ Ⓓ Ⓔ   63 Ⓐ Ⓑ Ⓒ Ⓓ Ⓔ   83 Ⓐ Ⓑ Ⓒ Ⓓ Ⓔ
4 Ⓐ Ⓑ Ⓒ Ⓓ Ⓔ   24 Ⓐ Ⓑ Ⓒ Ⓓ Ⓔ   44 Ⓐ Ⓑ Ⓒ Ⓓ Ⓔ   64 Ⓐ Ⓑ Ⓒ Ⓓ Ⓔ   84 Ⓐ Ⓑ Ⓒ Ⓓ Ⓔ
5 Ⓐ Ⓑ Ⓒ Ⓓ Ⓔ   25 Ⓐ Ⓑ Ⓒ Ⓓ Ⓔ   45 Ⓐ Ⓑ Ⓒ Ⓓ Ⓔ   65 Ⓐ Ⓑ Ⓒ Ⓓ Ⓔ   85 Ⓐ Ⓑ Ⓒ Ⓓ Ⓔ
6 Ⓐ Ⓑ Ⓒ Ⓓ Ⓔ   26 Ⓐ Ⓑ Ⓒ Ⓓ Ⓔ   46 Ⓐ Ⓑ Ⓒ Ⓓ Ⓔ   66 Ⓐ Ⓑ Ⓒ Ⓓ Ⓔ   86 Ⓐ Ⓑ Ⓒ Ⓓ Ⓔ
7 Ⓐ Ⓑ Ⓒ Ⓓ Ⓔ   27 Ⓐ Ⓑ Ⓒ Ⓓ Ⓔ   47 Ⓐ Ⓑ Ⓒ Ⓓ Ⓔ   67 Ⓐ Ⓑ Ⓒ Ⓓ Ⓔ   87 Ⓐ Ⓑ Ⓒ Ⓓ Ⓔ
8 Ⓐ Ⓑ Ⓒ Ⓓ Ⓔ   28 Ⓐ Ⓑ Ⓒ Ⓓ Ⓔ   48 Ⓐ Ⓑ Ⓒ Ⓓ Ⓔ   68 Ⓐ Ⓑ Ⓒ Ⓓ Ⓔ   88 Ⓐ Ⓑ Ⓒ Ⓓ Ⓔ
9 Ⓐ Ⓑ Ⓒ Ⓓ Ⓔ   29 Ⓐ Ⓑ Ⓒ Ⓓ Ⓔ   49 Ⓐ Ⓑ Ⓒ Ⓓ Ⓔ   69 Ⓐ Ⓑ Ⓒ Ⓓ Ⓔ   89 Ⓐ Ⓑ Ⓒ Ⓓ Ⓔ
10 Ⓐ Ⓑ Ⓒ Ⓓ Ⓔ   30 Ⓐ Ⓑ Ⓒ Ⓓ Ⓔ   50 Ⓐ Ⓑ Ⓒ Ⓓ Ⓔ   70 Ⓐ Ⓑ Ⓒ Ⓓ Ⓔ   90 Ⓐ Ⓑ Ⓒ Ⓓ Ⓔ
11 Ⓐ Ⓑ Ⓒ Ⓓ Ⓔ   31 Ⓐ Ⓑ Ⓒ Ⓓ Ⓔ   51 Ⓐ Ⓑ Ⓒ Ⓓ Ⓔ   71 Ⓐ Ⓑ Ⓒ Ⓓ Ⓔ   91 Ⓐ Ⓑ Ⓒ Ⓓ Ⓔ
12 Ⓐ Ⓑ Ⓒ Ⓓ Ⓔ   32 Ⓐ Ⓑ Ⓒ Ⓓ Ⓔ   52 Ⓐ Ⓑ Ⓒ Ⓓ Ⓔ   72 Ⓐ Ⓑ Ⓒ Ⓓ Ⓔ   92 Ⓐ Ⓑ Ⓒ Ⓓ Ⓔ
13 Ⓐ Ⓑ Ⓒ Ⓓ Ⓔ   33 Ⓐ Ⓑ Ⓒ Ⓓ Ⓔ   53 Ⓐ Ⓑ Ⓒ Ⓓ Ⓔ   73 Ⓐ Ⓑ Ⓒ Ⓓ Ⓔ   93 Ⓐ Ⓑ Ⓒ Ⓓ Ⓔ
14 Ⓐ Ⓑ Ⓒ Ⓓ Ⓔ   34 Ⓐ Ⓑ Ⓒ Ⓓ Ⓔ   54 Ⓐ Ⓑ Ⓒ Ⓓ Ⓔ   74 Ⓐ Ⓑ Ⓒ Ⓓ Ⓔ   94 Ⓐ Ⓑ Ⓒ Ⓓ Ⓔ
15 Ⓐ Ⓑ Ⓒ Ⓓ Ⓔ   35 Ⓐ Ⓑ Ⓒ Ⓓ Ⓔ   55 Ⓐ Ⓑ Ⓒ Ⓓ Ⓔ   75 Ⓐ Ⓑ Ⓒ Ⓓ Ⓔ   95 Ⓐ Ⓑ Ⓒ Ⓓ Ⓔ
16 Ⓐ Ⓑ Ⓒ Ⓓ Ⓔ   36 Ⓐ Ⓑ Ⓒ Ⓓ Ⓔ   56 Ⓐ Ⓑ Ⓒ Ⓓ Ⓔ   76 Ⓐ Ⓑ Ⓒ Ⓓ Ⓔ   96 Ⓐ Ⓑ Ⓒ Ⓓ Ⓔ
17 Ⓐ Ⓑ Ⓒ Ⓓ Ⓔ   37 Ⓐ Ⓑ Ⓒ Ⓓ Ⓔ   57 Ⓐ Ⓑ Ⓒ Ⓓ Ⓔ   77 Ⓐ Ⓑ Ⓒ Ⓓ Ⓔ   97 Ⓐ Ⓑ Ⓒ Ⓓ Ⓔ
18 Ⓐ Ⓑ Ⓒ Ⓓ Ⓔ   38 Ⓐ Ⓑ Ⓒ Ⓓ Ⓔ   58 Ⓐ Ⓑ Ⓒ Ⓓ Ⓔ   78 Ⓐ Ⓑ Ⓒ Ⓓ Ⓔ   98 Ⓐ Ⓑ Ⓒ Ⓓ Ⓔ
19 Ⓐ Ⓑ Ⓒ Ⓓ Ⓔ   39 Ⓐ Ⓑ Ⓒ Ⓓ Ⓔ   59 Ⓐ Ⓑ Ⓒ Ⓓ Ⓔ   79 Ⓐ Ⓑ Ⓒ Ⓓ Ⓔ   99 Ⓐ Ⓑ Ⓒ Ⓓ Ⓔ
20 Ⓐ Ⓑ Ⓒ Ⓓ Ⓔ   40 Ⓐ Ⓑ Ⓒ Ⓓ Ⓔ   60 Ⓐ Ⓑ Ⓒ Ⓓ Ⓔ   80 Ⓐ Ⓑ Ⓒ Ⓓ Ⓔ   100 Ⓐ Ⓑ Ⓒ Ⓓ Ⓔ

Leave any unused
answer spaces blank.

	Test Code										Subject Test (print)					
V	①	②	③	④	⑤	⑥	⑦	⑧	⑨							
W	①	②	③	④	⑤	⑥	⑦	⑧	⑨							
X ①	②	③	④	⑤	Y Ⓐ	Ⓑ	Ⓒ	Ⓓ	Ⓔ		FOR ETS USE ONLY	R/C	W/S1	FS/S2	CS/S3	WS
Q	①	②	③	④	⑤	⑥	⑦	⑧	⑨							

1 Ⓐ Ⓑ Ⓒ Ⓓ Ⓔ   21 Ⓐ Ⓑ Ⓒ Ⓓ Ⓔ   41 Ⓐ Ⓑ Ⓒ Ⓓ Ⓔ   61 Ⓐ Ⓑ Ⓒ Ⓓ Ⓔ   81 Ⓐ Ⓑ Ⓒ Ⓓ Ⓔ
2 Ⓐ Ⓑ Ⓒ Ⓓ Ⓔ   22 Ⓐ Ⓑ Ⓒ Ⓓ Ⓔ   42 Ⓐ Ⓑ Ⓒ Ⓓ Ⓔ   62 Ⓐ Ⓑ Ⓒ Ⓓ Ⓔ   82 Ⓐ Ⓑ Ⓒ Ⓓ Ⓔ
3 Ⓐ Ⓑ Ⓒ Ⓓ Ⓔ   23 Ⓐ Ⓑ Ⓒ Ⓓ Ⓔ   43 Ⓐ Ⓑ Ⓒ Ⓓ Ⓔ   63 Ⓐ Ⓑ Ⓒ Ⓓ Ⓔ   83 Ⓐ Ⓑ Ⓒ Ⓓ Ⓔ
4 Ⓐ Ⓑ Ⓒ Ⓓ Ⓔ   24 Ⓐ Ⓑ Ⓒ Ⓓ Ⓔ   44 Ⓐ Ⓑ Ⓒ Ⓓ Ⓔ   64 Ⓐ Ⓑ Ⓒ Ⓓ Ⓔ   84 Ⓐ Ⓑ Ⓒ Ⓓ Ⓔ
5 Ⓐ Ⓑ Ⓒ Ⓓ Ⓔ   25 Ⓐ Ⓑ Ⓒ Ⓓ Ⓔ   45 Ⓐ Ⓑ Ⓒ Ⓓ Ⓔ   65 Ⓐ Ⓑ Ⓒ Ⓓ Ⓔ   85 Ⓐ Ⓑ Ⓒ Ⓓ Ⓔ
6 Ⓐ Ⓑ Ⓒ Ⓓ Ⓔ   26 Ⓐ Ⓑ Ⓒ Ⓓ Ⓔ   46 Ⓐ Ⓑ Ⓒ Ⓓ Ⓔ   66 Ⓐ Ⓑ Ⓒ Ⓓ Ⓔ   86 Ⓐ Ⓑ Ⓒ Ⓓ Ⓔ
7 Ⓐ Ⓑ Ⓒ Ⓓ Ⓔ   27 Ⓐ Ⓑ Ⓒ Ⓓ Ⓔ   47 Ⓐ Ⓑ Ⓒ Ⓓ Ⓔ   67 Ⓐ Ⓑ Ⓒ Ⓓ Ⓔ   87 Ⓐ Ⓑ Ⓒ Ⓓ Ⓔ
8 Ⓐ Ⓑ Ⓒ Ⓓ Ⓔ   28 Ⓐ Ⓑ Ⓒ Ⓓ Ⓔ   48 Ⓐ Ⓑ Ⓒ Ⓓ Ⓔ   68 Ⓐ Ⓑ Ⓒ Ⓓ Ⓔ   88 Ⓐ Ⓑ Ⓒ Ⓓ Ⓔ
9 Ⓐ Ⓑ Ⓒ Ⓓ Ⓔ   29 Ⓐ Ⓑ Ⓒ Ⓓ Ⓔ   49 Ⓐ Ⓑ Ⓒ Ⓓ Ⓔ   69 Ⓐ Ⓑ Ⓒ Ⓓ Ⓔ   89 Ⓐ Ⓑ Ⓒ Ⓓ Ⓔ
10 Ⓐ Ⓑ Ⓒ Ⓓ Ⓔ   30 Ⓐ Ⓑ Ⓒ Ⓓ Ⓔ   50 Ⓐ Ⓑ Ⓒ Ⓓ Ⓔ   70 Ⓐ Ⓑ Ⓒ Ⓓ Ⓔ   90 Ⓐ Ⓑ Ⓒ Ⓓ Ⓔ
11 Ⓐ Ⓑ Ⓒ Ⓓ Ⓔ   31 Ⓐ Ⓑ Ⓒ Ⓓ Ⓔ   51 Ⓐ Ⓑ Ⓒ Ⓓ Ⓔ   71 Ⓐ Ⓑ Ⓒ Ⓓ Ⓔ   91 Ⓐ Ⓑ Ⓒ Ⓓ Ⓔ
12 Ⓐ Ⓑ Ⓒ Ⓓ Ⓔ   32 Ⓐ Ⓑ Ⓒ Ⓓ Ⓔ   52 Ⓐ Ⓑ Ⓒ Ⓓ Ⓔ   72 Ⓐ Ⓑ Ⓒ Ⓓ Ⓔ   92 Ⓐ Ⓑ Ⓒ Ⓓ Ⓔ
13 Ⓐ Ⓑ Ⓒ Ⓓ Ⓔ   33 Ⓐ Ⓑ Ⓒ Ⓓ Ⓔ   53 Ⓐ Ⓑ Ⓒ Ⓓ Ⓔ   73 Ⓐ Ⓑ Ⓒ Ⓓ Ⓔ   93 Ⓐ Ⓑ Ⓒ Ⓓ Ⓔ
14 Ⓐ Ⓑ Ⓒ Ⓓ Ⓔ   34 Ⓐ Ⓑ Ⓒ Ⓓ Ⓔ   54 Ⓐ Ⓑ Ⓒ Ⓓ Ⓔ   74 Ⓐ Ⓑ Ⓒ Ⓓ Ⓔ   94 Ⓐ Ⓑ Ⓒ Ⓓ Ⓔ
15 Ⓐ Ⓑ Ⓒ Ⓓ Ⓔ   35 Ⓐ Ⓑ Ⓒ Ⓓ Ⓔ   55 Ⓐ Ⓑ Ⓒ Ⓓ Ⓔ   75 Ⓐ Ⓑ Ⓒ Ⓓ Ⓔ   95 Ⓐ Ⓑ Ⓒ Ⓓ Ⓔ
16 Ⓐ Ⓑ Ⓒ Ⓓ Ⓔ   36 Ⓐ Ⓑ Ⓒ Ⓓ Ⓔ   56 Ⓐ Ⓑ Ⓒ Ⓓ Ⓔ   76 Ⓐ Ⓑ Ⓒ Ⓓ Ⓔ   96 Ⓐ Ⓑ Ⓒ Ⓓ Ⓔ
17 Ⓐ Ⓑ Ⓒ Ⓓ Ⓔ   37 Ⓐ Ⓑ Ⓒ Ⓓ Ⓔ   57 Ⓐ Ⓑ Ⓒ Ⓓ Ⓔ   77 Ⓐ Ⓑ Ⓒ Ⓓ Ⓔ   97 Ⓐ Ⓑ Ⓒ Ⓓ Ⓔ
18 Ⓐ Ⓑ Ⓒ Ⓓ Ⓔ   38 Ⓐ Ⓑ Ⓒ Ⓓ Ⓔ   58 Ⓐ Ⓑ Ⓒ Ⓓ Ⓔ   78 Ⓐ Ⓑ Ⓒ Ⓓ Ⓔ   98 Ⓐ Ⓑ Ⓒ Ⓓ Ⓔ
19 Ⓐ Ⓑ Ⓒ Ⓓ Ⓔ   39 Ⓐ Ⓑ Ⓒ Ⓓ Ⓔ   59 Ⓐ Ⓑ Ⓒ Ⓓ Ⓔ   79 Ⓐ Ⓑ Ⓒ Ⓓ Ⓔ   99 Ⓐ Ⓑ Ⓒ Ⓓ Ⓔ
20 Ⓐ Ⓑ Ⓒ Ⓓ Ⓔ   40 Ⓐ Ⓑ Ⓒ Ⓓ Ⓔ   60 Ⓐ Ⓑ Ⓒ Ⓓ Ⓔ   80 Ⓐ Ⓑ Ⓒ Ⓓ Ⓔ   100 Ⓐ Ⓑ Ⓒ Ⓓ Ⓔ

Leave any unused
answer spaces blank.

	Test Code										Subject Test (print)					
V	①	②	③	④	⑤	⑥	⑦	⑧	⑨							
W	①	②	③	④	⑤	⑥	⑦	⑧	⑨							
X ①	②	③	④	⑤	Y Ⓐ	Ⓑ	Ⓒ	Ⓓ	Ⓔ		FOR ETS USE ONLY	R/C	W/S1	FS/S2	CS/S3	WS
Q	①	②	③	④	⑤	⑥	⑦	⑧	⑨							

1 Ⓐ Ⓑ Ⓒ Ⓓ Ⓔ   21 Ⓐ Ⓑ Ⓒ Ⓓ Ⓔ   41 Ⓐ Ⓑ Ⓒ Ⓓ Ⓔ   61 Ⓐ Ⓑ Ⓒ Ⓓ Ⓔ   81 Ⓐ Ⓑ Ⓒ Ⓓ Ⓔ
2 Ⓐ Ⓑ Ⓒ Ⓓ Ⓔ   22 Ⓐ Ⓑ Ⓒ Ⓓ Ⓔ   42 Ⓐ Ⓑ Ⓒ Ⓓ Ⓔ   62 Ⓐ Ⓑ Ⓒ Ⓓ Ⓔ   82 Ⓐ Ⓑ Ⓒ Ⓓ Ⓔ
3 Ⓐ Ⓑ Ⓒ Ⓓ Ⓔ   23 Ⓐ Ⓑ Ⓒ Ⓓ Ⓔ   43 Ⓐ Ⓑ Ⓒ Ⓓ Ⓔ   63 Ⓐ Ⓑ Ⓒ Ⓓ Ⓔ   83 Ⓐ Ⓑ Ⓒ Ⓓ Ⓔ
4 Ⓐ Ⓑ Ⓒ Ⓓ Ⓔ   24 Ⓐ Ⓑ Ⓒ Ⓓ Ⓔ   44 Ⓐ Ⓑ Ⓒ Ⓓ Ⓔ   64 Ⓐ Ⓑ Ⓒ Ⓓ Ⓔ   84 Ⓐ Ⓑ Ⓒ Ⓓ Ⓔ
5 Ⓐ Ⓑ Ⓒ Ⓓ Ⓔ   25 Ⓐ Ⓑ Ⓒ Ⓓ Ⓔ   45 Ⓐ Ⓑ Ⓒ Ⓓ Ⓔ   65 Ⓐ Ⓑ Ⓒ Ⓓ Ⓔ   85 Ⓐ Ⓑ Ⓒ Ⓓ Ⓔ
6 Ⓐ Ⓑ Ⓒ Ⓓ Ⓔ   26 Ⓐ Ⓑ Ⓒ Ⓓ Ⓔ   46 Ⓐ Ⓑ Ⓒ Ⓓ Ⓔ   66 Ⓐ Ⓑ Ⓒ Ⓓ Ⓔ   86 Ⓐ Ⓑ Ⓒ Ⓓ Ⓔ
7 Ⓐ Ⓑ Ⓒ Ⓓ Ⓔ   27 Ⓐ Ⓑ Ⓒ Ⓓ Ⓔ   47 Ⓐ Ⓑ Ⓒ Ⓓ Ⓔ   67 Ⓐ Ⓑ Ⓒ Ⓓ Ⓔ   87 Ⓐ Ⓑ Ⓒ Ⓓ Ⓔ
8 Ⓐ Ⓑ Ⓒ Ⓓ Ⓔ   28 Ⓐ Ⓑ Ⓒ Ⓓ Ⓔ   48 Ⓐ Ⓑ Ⓒ Ⓓ Ⓔ   68 Ⓐ Ⓑ Ⓒ Ⓓ Ⓔ   88 Ⓐ Ⓑ Ⓒ Ⓓ Ⓔ
9 Ⓐ Ⓑ Ⓒ Ⓓ Ⓔ   29 Ⓐ Ⓑ Ⓒ Ⓓ Ⓔ   49 Ⓐ Ⓑ Ⓒ Ⓓ Ⓔ   69 Ⓐ Ⓑ Ⓒ Ⓓ Ⓔ   89 Ⓐ Ⓑ Ⓒ Ⓓ Ⓔ
10 Ⓐ Ⓑ Ⓒ Ⓓ Ⓔ   30 Ⓐ Ⓑ Ⓒ Ⓓ Ⓔ   50 Ⓐ Ⓑ Ⓒ Ⓓ Ⓔ   70 Ⓐ Ⓑ Ⓒ Ⓓ Ⓔ   90 Ⓐ Ⓑ Ⓒ Ⓓ Ⓔ
11 Ⓐ Ⓑ Ⓒ Ⓓ Ⓔ   31 Ⓐ Ⓑ Ⓒ Ⓓ Ⓔ   51 Ⓐ Ⓑ Ⓒ Ⓓ Ⓔ   71 Ⓐ Ⓑ Ⓒ Ⓓ Ⓔ   91 Ⓐ Ⓑ Ⓒ Ⓓ Ⓔ
12 Ⓐ Ⓑ Ⓒ Ⓓ Ⓔ   32 Ⓐ Ⓑ Ⓒ Ⓓ Ⓔ   52 Ⓐ Ⓑ Ⓒ Ⓓ Ⓔ   72 Ⓐ Ⓑ Ⓒ Ⓓ Ⓔ   92 Ⓐ Ⓑ Ⓒ Ⓓ Ⓔ
13 Ⓐ Ⓑ Ⓒ Ⓓ Ⓔ   33 Ⓐ Ⓑ Ⓒ Ⓓ Ⓔ   53 Ⓐ Ⓑ Ⓒ Ⓓ Ⓔ   73 Ⓐ Ⓑ Ⓒ Ⓓ Ⓔ   93 Ⓐ Ⓑ Ⓒ Ⓓ Ⓔ
14 Ⓐ Ⓑ Ⓒ Ⓓ Ⓔ   34 Ⓐ Ⓑ Ⓒ Ⓓ Ⓔ   54 Ⓐ Ⓑ Ⓒ Ⓓ Ⓔ   74 Ⓐ Ⓑ Ⓒ Ⓓ Ⓔ   94 Ⓐ Ⓑ Ⓒ Ⓓ Ⓔ
15 Ⓐ Ⓑ Ⓒ Ⓓ Ⓔ   35 Ⓐ Ⓑ Ⓒ Ⓓ Ⓔ   55 Ⓐ Ⓑ Ⓒ Ⓓ Ⓔ   75 Ⓐ Ⓑ Ⓒ Ⓓ Ⓔ   95 Ⓐ Ⓑ Ⓒ Ⓓ Ⓔ
16 Ⓐ Ⓑ Ⓒ Ⓓ Ⓔ   36 Ⓐ Ⓑ Ⓒ Ⓓ Ⓔ   56 Ⓐ Ⓑ Ⓒ Ⓓ Ⓔ   76 Ⓐ Ⓑ Ⓒ Ⓓ Ⓔ   96 Ⓐ Ⓑ Ⓒ Ⓓ Ⓔ
17 Ⓐ Ⓑ Ⓒ Ⓓ Ⓔ   37 Ⓐ Ⓑ Ⓒ Ⓓ Ⓔ   57 Ⓐ Ⓑ Ⓒ Ⓓ Ⓔ   77 Ⓐ Ⓑ Ⓒ Ⓓ Ⓔ   97 Ⓐ Ⓑ Ⓒ Ⓓ Ⓔ
18 Ⓐ Ⓑ Ⓒ Ⓓ Ⓔ   38 Ⓐ Ⓑ Ⓒ Ⓓ Ⓔ   58 Ⓐ Ⓑ Ⓒ Ⓓ Ⓔ   78 Ⓐ Ⓑ Ⓒ Ⓓ Ⓔ   98 Ⓐ Ⓑ Ⓒ Ⓓ Ⓔ
19 Ⓐ Ⓑ Ⓒ Ⓓ Ⓔ   39 Ⓐ Ⓑ Ⓒ Ⓓ Ⓔ   59 Ⓐ Ⓑ Ⓒ Ⓓ Ⓔ   79 Ⓐ Ⓑ Ⓒ Ⓓ Ⓔ   99 Ⓐ Ⓑ Ⓒ Ⓓ Ⓔ
20 Ⓐ Ⓑ Ⓒ Ⓓ Ⓔ   40 Ⓐ Ⓑ Ⓒ Ⓓ Ⓔ   60 Ⓐ Ⓑ Ⓒ Ⓓ Ⓔ   80 Ⓐ Ⓑ Ⓒ Ⓓ Ⓔ   100 Ⓐ Ⓑ Ⓒ Ⓓ Ⓔ